THE
GREAT AMERICAN GAMBLE

How the 1979 Daytona 500
Gave Birth to a NASCAR Nation

JOE MENZER

WILEY

John Wiley & Sons, Inc.

Published by John Wiley & Sons, Inc., Hoboken, New Jersey
Published simultaneously in Canada

All photos by RacingOne/Getty Images

The views, opinions, and statements expressed in this publication are strictly those of the author and do not necessarily reflect, and are not attributable to, the National Association for Stock Car Auto Racing, Inc. (NASCAR), any of its affiliates, and/or any of their respective owners, members, employees, and/or agents.

For general information about our other products and services, please contact our Customer Care Department within the United States at (800) 762-2974, outside the United States at (317) 572-3993 or fax (317) 572-4002.

Wiley also publishes its books in a variety of electronic formats. Some content that appears in print may not be available in electronic books. For more information about Wiley products, visit our web site at www.wiley.com.

Library of Congress Cataloging-in-Publication Data:

Menzer, Joe.
    The great American gamble: how the 1979 Daytona 500 gave birth to a NASCAR nation / Joe Menzer.
        p.   cm.
    Includes index.
    ISBN 978-0-470-22869-2 (cloth)
        1. Daytona 500 (Automobile race)—History.   2. Stock-car racing—United States—History.   I. Title.
    GV1033.5.D39M45   2009
                                                                    796.72'06'875921—dc22

As always, for Sarah and the kids and for my parents
But also for Aunt Mary Ann, who is always there for us

Contents

Photographs follow page 154

Acknowledgments

It is a cliché to say that writing a book is a team effort. It also happens to be true. Much the same way as a NASCAR race team has never been about just the driver, who tends to get all the glory when everything goes right and every ounce of blame when he wrecks in the fifth lap of a 500-mile event, writing a good book takes a coordinated effort among many talented people over a sustained period of time.

This collaboration was no exception. It would never have happened in the first place if not for the vision of Stephen S. Power, my editor at John Wiley & Sons, who saw the 1979 Daytona 500 as not just an epic race but also a truly historic, sport-changing event, one thus deserving of deeper exploration in a book. So to him and all those pulling the strings behind the scenes at Wiley, a huge thanks.

None of my books ever would make it to publication without the tireless efforts of my literary agent, Shari Wenk, who always sees the silver lining and offers words of encouragement no matter what challenges may arise during the course of writing them. Another huge thanks goes out to her as well.

Those who know me the best understand what a trying time it was in the fall of 2006, when my nearly twelve-year run as beat writer of a National Football League team for a newspaper abruptly came to an end. Fortunately for me, within literally hours of being unceremoniously and at least somewhat unexpectedly downsized, I was put in touch with Duane Cross, managing editor of NASCAR.com. We spoke that very afternoon as I drove home from the meeting where the ax fell at the newspaper. It was on a Friday. We talked again the following Tuesday, and shortly thereafter Duane was kind enough to offer me a job.

Little did I realize at that moment that it would be a better job in every way. It is one that I feel truly blessed to have now, going on two years later. I took it only under the tepid stipulation that Duane knew I already had agreed to write this book, and he not only did not let that stand in the way but also openly and actively encouraged me to pursue it. Thus, my worlds collided, and I suddenly was covering full-time the very sport I already had immersed myself in for a previous book and was beginning to do so again for this one. I told everyone that last time, I had parachuted into the NASCAR world for eighteen months and then floated back out; this time, I was coming to stay, hopefully for a whole lot longer. It proved to be a perfect match, and I applaud Duane not only for understanding my pursuit of material for this book from the start but for cheering me along every step of the way. He is without a doubt the best boss I have had in more than twenty-five years in the journalism business.

Others on staff at NASCAR.com, a division of Turner Sports New Media, have been helpful throughout my relatively short tenure there. Among them are Josh Pate, Bill Kimm, and Jarrod Breeze, who take the stories I write for the Web site and make sure they make sense while also dressing them up with all kinds of nifty graphics (these guys also get out of the office in Atlanta to make occasional appearances at racetracks and help produce content); plus my colleagues who regularly help cover events at the tracks on race weekends: Mark Aumann, David Caraviello, Dave Rodman, and Raygan Swan. For as small as our staff is, we cover a whole lot of ground and cover it well, which is why NASCAR

.com is the most popular Web site in the nation when it comes to fans of stock car racing who are looking for honest and straightforward features, opinions, and news, much of which is stuff they simply cannot get anywhere else. There also is the matter of the proactive long-range vision and energy that surges through the entire Turner platform behind the scenes, starting with our boss's boss, Scott Doyne. It truly is an honor to be a part of it as we move forward and on to even greater achievements.

Special thanks has to go out to Aumann, by the way. I happened to be covering a race with him in Phoenix in November 2007 when our conversation turned to the 1979 Daytona 500, and he began enthralling me with tales of attending the race and sitting in the grandstands that magical day with his father, Robert. I had been looking for someone who could provide some first-person perspective from that unique angle, and it turns out he was sitting right next to me all along!

None of this could have transpired, however, without the never-ending assistance of the good folks at Petty Enterprises. Richard Petty not only is a super and tireless ambassador for the sport he once dominated as a driver, but he possesses as little ego for a man of his stature in a sport of any legendary competitor I have ever had the pleasure (and occasional displeasure) of interviewing. And I've interviewed more than a few over the years while covering Super Bowls, NBA playoff and All-Star games, World Series games in baseball, and big-time events at the collegiate level. Richard's humbleness and downright honesty is nothing short of refreshing. He gave many interviews for this book, including one lengthy one in his modest office in Level Cross, North Carolina, where it was just him and me. Thanks also to public relations men Jeff Dennison and David Hovis for helping make that happen, and for making the King accessible to his many racing subjects just about whenever anyone makes a reasonable request of him.

Richard wasn't the only one in the Petty Enterprises family who was unbelievably generous with his time for this project. In fact, it's safe to say that no interview subject was more giving of his time and energy than Richard's second cousin and longtime crew chief, Dale Inman. It took both men quite some time to sort out their memories about how often and exactly when Richard was forced to the hospital to have work done on a stomach contaminated with ulcers; and other times Inman had to serve as the Petty tiebreaker on historical matters when Richard and son Kyle Petty didn't quite agree on the way something went down. But Inman was tireless in his efforts to help me get it right, and for that I am deeply appreciative.

Plus they all agree on one thing. Whenever Richard did get out of the hospital after getting worked on for those troublesome and painful stomach problems, he always had the same request that made the King seem all the more a mere human mortal.

"He always wanted us to take him for ice cream," said Inman, smiling as he so often did when telling one of his great stories.

Thanks to Kyle, too, for he was generous with his time as well. The same goes for so many others who agreed to be interviewed at one time or another, usually in a one-on-one session but sometimes in a group setting prior to the running of a NASCAR race or another event. These included Bobby Allison, Donnie Allison, Cale Yarborough, Junior Johnson, Buddy Baker, Darrell Waltrip, A. J. Foyt, Ned Jarrett, Humpy Wheeler, Ken Squier, Richard Childress, Jim Hunter, Dick Fleck, David Pearson, Doug Rice, Max Muhleman, Ricky Rudd, Geoffrey Bodine, Sterling Marlin, Marvin Panch, Leonard Wood, Eddie Wood, Larry McClure, and Michael Waltrip, among others I'm sure I unintentionally have forgotten to mention here. For that I apologize. My thanks go to anyone and everyone who helped tell this story.

That includes the one and only Benny Parsons, who passed away after a battle with cancer during the very early stages of my researching this book. I relied on previous interviews with Parsons, including one lengthy and rather revealing, intimate one that he granted during my research for a previous book, *The Wildest Ride*. Parsons is missed by all who run in NASCAR circles, and even by many who orbit outside it. He was a great ambassador for his sport, and for life itself.

Bill France Jr. also passed during the early stages of research for the book, but obviously none of this would have happened without him and his father, Big Bill, the founder of NASCAR. As much as anything else, this is the underdog's story of how they combined to convince the powers-that-be in television that theirs was a sport worthy of live television coverage. Their influence in that direction alone set up the dominoes that fell into place in remarkable fashion at Daytona International Speedway in February 1979, which in turn helped their sport soar to heights even those fantastic dreamers might not have envisioned.

Others who offered tips and guidance, sometimes without even knowing as I struggled to find my way in the new sporting universe I inhabited in January 2007, were a number of fine journalists who specialize in making sense of the often confusing, controversial world of stock car racing. Among them: David Newton of ESPN.com; Jenna Fryer of the Associated Press; Nate Ryan and Gary Graves of *USA Today*; Dustin Long of Landmark Newspapers; Brant James of the *St. Petersburg Times*; Mike Hembree, Bob Pockrass, Kenny Bruce, and Jeff Gluck of *NASCAR Scene* magazine; Ed Hardin of the *Greensboro News & Record*; Brett McMillan of Performance Racing Network; Tom Jensen of Speed Channel/SpeedTV.com; Brad Daugherty of ESPN; Viv Bernstein of the *New York Times*; Jill Irwin and Ralph Paulk of the *Richmond Times-Dispatch*; David Poole of the *Charlotte Observer*; Monte Dutton of the *Gaston Gazette*; and Reid Spencer of the *Sporting News*. If I left anyone out who lent an assisting hand at any point, I apologize.

In addition, Newton assisted with a few interviews and some tape transcription. Without his assistance and also that of Steve Reed of the *Gaston Gazette* in the voluminous and at times seemingly overwhelming tape transcription, I probably never would have advanced from that final stage of research to the actual writing of the book.

And from NASCAR's hierarchy itself, I appreciated the overall welcome and generally kind assistance I have received throughout the transition period in my career from the likes of the aforementioned Jim Hunter as well as Ramsey Poston, Kerry Tharp, Herb Branham, Josh Hamilton, Denise Maloof, Jennifer Powell, Ashley Jones, and Michael Payne. I would be remiss if I didn't also mention Mike McCarthy, who no longer is with NASCAR but is getting just the winter weather he deserves after taking a job instead with Getty Images and moving back to Chicago from sunny Daytona Beach, Florida.

There also were a number of books and magazine publications and articles pulled from various sources deemed credible on the Internet (mostly the outstanding archives of NASCAR.com, of course) that proved helpful. Particular thanks goes to author Hembree, whose book *The Definitive History of America's Sport* is exactly what it says it is. But no book was a more reliable reference source than volume 4 of author Greg Fielden's *Forty Years of Stock Car Racing, The Modern Era*, which was purchased on the advice of none other than Dale Inman.

Then there is the DVD of the race itself, available for purchase through the Computer Group, Inc., and the usual wholesale outlets on the Internet such as Amazon.com. Consider this an open advertisement to go out and buy it and watch it from start to finish. You will not be disappointed. This is one race that lives up to all the hype, all the time, and the ability of the announcing team to bring it to life during what by today's standards seem almost primitive working conditions was tremendous, beginning with Squier's penchant for making viewers at home think they were watching a modern-day version of the epic chariot race in the classic film *Ben-Hur.*

Finally, that brings me to the most important bunch of all: my family. I could never write any book without the complete support of wife, Sarah (the best Realtor in all of North Carolina, in my humble opinion), and children, Andrew, Elizabeth, Emma, and Michael. Thanks to all for staying out of my office at least most of the time when I asked, and for listening to me complain about how I was never going to get this book finished when I felt the need to cry on somebody's shoulders. Elizabeth even helped by typing up the bibliography for me at the very end, when I literally had nothing left to give and still more to do. Of course I had to pay her ten bucks to do it, but sometimes you must do whatever it takes to get the job done.

It was a complete team effort. I hope it shows.

Prologue

Every once in a great while comes a sporting event that defies description, if not in great detail, then at least in brief summation. It also contradicts all accepted logic. It is as if all the stars and planets in the sky align perfectly in the sporting world and the event transcends all others around it for that day, that week, that month, and, in the rarest of cases, for the rest of time.

The 1979 Daytona 500, without question, was such an event.

Many factors combined to make this particular race perhaps the most memorable of all in National Association for Stock Car Auto Racing (NASCAR) annals. It had drama upon drama. It had veteran drivers Donnie Allison and Cale Yarborough racing each other for the win, only to wreck each other on the final lap. That opened the door for legendary driver Richard Petty, who hadn't won a race in more than a year and was fighting whispers that he might be washed up, to outduel two other racing icons in Darrell Waltrip and A. J. Foyt for the victory. It even had unexpected post-race entertainment when Allison and his more famous brother, Bobby, squared off in a brief fistfight with the enigmatic and enraged Yarborough in the infield at storied Daytona International Speedway. In truth, it wasn't much of a fight; but it became the most talked-about scuffle in the history of the sport.

Most important of all, the 1979 Daytona 500 had television. It was the first Great American Race broadcast live from start to finish by network television, and yet it almost didn't come off. Skeptics doubted that it could work in the first place. And even after they had been coerced into at least giving it a chance, Mother Nature reared her ugly head and poured rain down on Daytona Beach in buckets, leading up to nearly the beginning of the scheduled start. As if on cue, however, the rain ceased and what of the storm hadn't already moved up the East Coast took flight, the rain turning to sleet and snow just hours up the highway and producing literally a snowball effect that gave millions of television viewers who otherwise wouldn't have given NASCAR a second, let alone a second look, no alternative but to tune in.

What they witnessed was a race for the ages, in which Petty reclaimed lost glory, the Allison brothers and Yarborough launched themselves into one another and into racing infamy, and others such as rookie drivers Dale Earnhardt, Terry Labonte, and Geoffrey Bodine began to make names for themselves in a sport that always has celebrated its heroes, even tainted or tragic ones. It was a race that ended up having a little of everything, and it deserves better than to be encapsulated unfairly as simply the Daytona 500 that ended with a spirited but in the end vastly overpublicized fistfight in the infield. There was so much more to the day.

"There have been events and circumstances that have lifted this sport to a new level—Richard Petty's two hundredth win, or Dale Earnhardt's seventh championship, or ESPN showing all the races live on TV, or the 1979 Daytona 500," said Michael Waltrip, the younger brother of Darrell who watched from the infield as a spectator on February 18, 1979, and later would go on to claim two Daytona 500 victories for himself as a driver. "There are just certain events that have helped define what this sport has become. And as I look back, that day is one of those events. I feel like I'm such a huge historian of the sport, especially in the modern era, so being there that day is something that's special to me."

Michael watched from the infield as his brother sped to the start-finish line with Petty at the race's end. It was special to all who were there—and even to many who weren't and watched on television, falling in love with the sport for the very first time. Some watched from their couches as snow fell softly outside their windows, disappointed at first that the inclement weather had canceled most other sporting events they might have hoped to catch that day on one of the three channels their television sets could pick up in those precable, predigital days. Then there were the fans, well over a hundred thousand of them, who braved the brisk winds and questionable weather to pack the Daytona superspeedway infield and grandstands. It wasn't like attending a race would become decades later.

"In 1979, your experience was completely predicated on what you could see from your seat, and perhaps ascertain from the public-address system during lulls in the action," Mark Aumann wrote years later for NASCAR.com, giving his first-person account of attending the race that day with his father, Robert. "There were no video boards, no race scanners, no live timing and scoring links. There were a few people at the track who wore huge radio headsets—but their success of hearing the race broadcast depended solely on whether you could pick up the local AM station over the din of the race.

"It was almost impossible to get up-to-date information without being there in person. This was before the Internet, cell phone messaging, satellite radio, or twenty-four-hour cable sports channels [ESPN wasn't launched until September of that year]. If you were lucky, the local television sports anchor might give a quick recap of the race in his five-minute segment. If not, perhaps the newspaper might have a short recap and results.

"And yet for the estimated 130,000 fans who did their best to stay warm and dry at Daytona International Speedway that day, most never had any idea of exactly what transpired until they read the paper the next morning."

Finally, of course, it was special to the participants, some of whom had a sense that they were playing out an important act in their sport's history that would be rewound in their minds and that of others for generations to come. For others, it wouldn't dawn on them until much later what it all meant.

"The big deal with the 1979 Daytona 500 is that it was on Sunday afternoon on CBS, and there was the snowstorm," Richard Petty said. "There was nothing but ABC, NBC, and CBS if you were watching TV. I don't know what else was on, but a lot of people ended up tuning into the race and leaving it there. We had seventeen or eighteen inches of snow that day in some parts of North Carolina. That's like twenty foot anywhere else.

"At the time it happened, I didn't even look at the TV as being that big of a deal . . . or the fight . . . or the snowstorm. But when people talk about the history of Daytona today, that's probably the one race that's noted.

"Take [the 2007 Daytona 500], for instance. Kevin Harvick comes out of nowhere to win the race in dramatic fashion because of circumstances. It was a real big deal right then—but then it loses its magic real quick. The 1979 Daytona 500 deal seems to have gained magic over the years. It wasn't that big of a deal to us when it happened, but now when you look back over [more than] fifty years of holding that race, it seems to hold more magic than any of the others."

Richard's son, Kyle, was then eighteen years old and working in the pits for his father during the race. Nearly thirty years later, he smiled as he recalled the day and the enormous impact it would have on the sport he quickly came to love. "We have the vantage point now of being able to look back at days like that, and moments like that," he said. "That one moment, that one day out of 365 days in 1979, changed this sport forever. I think when you look at things like that, and you have the advantage of being able to look back, you can say the sport changed that day. It changed right in front of all those people in the grandstands that day. It changed for all the competitors. They didn't know it at the time, but it changed the sport forever for all of us."

This is the story of that day from various perspectives—not only from those of the participants but from those who watched from the grandstands and from their living rooms, and from those who made watching racing from the couch a reality in spite of many who were so certain that televising a race of that distance and magnitude live from start to finish couldn't possibly work.

One of the other drivers that day was Richard Childress, who would go on to gain his own measure of fame as a car owner and the founder of Richard Childress Racing. "It's history," he said of the race. "The timing was just right. To see it happen on TV sparked the interest of race fans and media. It was in New York and all over the place. It was a big deal for the sport. You go down through the history of the sport, and you could probably point out a handful of things that really changed the sport—and that race was without question one of them."

Close examination shows that the race by itself was outstanding. Though the fight—The Fight, as it became known—in the infield between vanquished competitors Bobby Allison and Cale Yarborough in the aftermath (Donnie Allison also was in the mix but barely) has unquestionably helped secure its place in pop-culture history, the truth is, it wasn't much of a fight and hardly any of it was caught on live television.

But vivid photographs showed the fury and passion with which these men were going at it. The incident demonstrated that they cared deeply about what they were doing, giving the sport an aura it had been lacking in the national subconscious. Suddenly stock car racing was seen as roller derby in cars at two hundred miles per hour, only better—because it was real.

"Anywhere you go, people talk about that. If you watch the telecast of any Daytona 500, you'll see that probably several times.

They've shown it every year since then. It's always part of the pre-race buildup," Bobby Allison said. "A lot of times I'm sitting there watching TV, some midweek thing, and it'll pop up on there. Or you'll go into a store and see a magazine or a newspaper or watch a history clip, and there that thing is again. It was the biggest public-ity thing that ever was done anywhere in our sport that I know of."

Yarborough added, "I can't believe it. It's everywhere I go. People still talk about it. It's the biggest thing that ever happened in NASCAR. Nothing is even a close second."

Yet it was a bonus, the dessert to an entrée that would have been pretty darn filling, if admittedly a whole lot less memora-ble, without it. On a day when everything that could have gone wrong on live television and buried the sport into obscurity for-ever instead all went right—right down to the most popular driver in its history winning in unlikely fashion because of a spectacular wreck at the end, followed by The Fight.

After watching a tape of the race all the way through probably ten or twelve times, and specific parts of it on dozens more occa-sions at various times over the last eighteen months, it seems a lit-tle tragic that what is most remembered about it is The Fight. So much more went on, and that is what this book is mostly about—all the other great stuff that occurred during those five hundred miles that led up to The Fight, with tidbits about the personali-ties involved and stories about their places in racing at the time thrown in for good measure. It should be, like the race itself, a long green-flag run of pure fun for the reader.

Without live television, without The Fight, without the dra-matic finish, it might have been just another Daytona 500. Instead, all elements combined to make it arguably the most memorable Daytona 500 of all time.

"Over the last several years, I've been fortunate enough to go to autograph sessions in Timbuktu or wherever," Bobby Allison said. "And everywhere I go there are some people there that comment about that very thing, or ask me about it. I say, 'Boy, that is really the thing that gave NASCAR that kick. It showed the world that we were sincere.'"

To understand the impact, just know this: it helped fuel phenomenal growth and popularity in the sport. In 1979, some Winston Cup races were attended by fewer than twelve thousand people. Twenty of the thirty-one races on the schedule drew crowds of fifty thousand or less.

In the 1980s, the crowds began exploding and attendance of a hundred thousand or more at many events became the rule rather than the exception. By 1990, an estimated 3.3 million fans were attending NASCAR Winston Cup races. By 2000, that figure had skyrocketed another 97 percent to 6.5 million.

Suddenly the sport that once had to struggle to get on live television landed a six-year, $2.8 billion contract with the Fox, NBC, and TBS television networks to split live coverage of thirty-eight events, plus much, much more. There were prerace shows and postrace shows. There were midweek shows. There even was the birth and phenomenal growth of the cable Speed Channel, which is devoted to all forms of auto racing but is rooted in NASCAR. And in December 2005, another eight-year television deal was signed between NASCAR and ABC/ESPN, Fox, and TNT, with those networks splitting coverage of thirty-seven live events, and the Speed Channel gaining the exclusive rights to one event, the All-Star race at Lowe's Motor Speedway in Charlotte, North Carolina—yet another event that did not exist in 1979.

While attendance and television ratings leveled off and even fell off some after spiking around 2005, the sport obviously has come a long way since the running of the 1979 Daytona 500, a race that almost didn't even come off as scheduled. You may know the race winner and you may think you know all about The Fight.

But this is the complete story, which is bound to include lots you didn't know while providing clues as to how one race jump-started an entire sport.

Hopefully, reading it will provide as much entertainment to you as writing it did for me.

1

"Rain, Rain, Go Away . . ."

Darrell Waltrip stared out from below the visor of his ball cap through the foggy mist and surveyed the landscape at Daytona International Speedway. It was wet, no doubt about that. The rain had slowed to a drizzle, almost stopped, in fact. But Waltrip couldn't help noticing the large rain puddles that had formed throughout the infield. It was cold and a little too windy for his liking as well. Even though it was mid-February, it wasn't the kind of weather he or any other visitor to usually sunny Florida expected this time of the year.

Like many others at the track that morning, Waltrip had other concerns. The scheduled start of the 1979 Daytona 500 was only a couple hours away, and the stakes of dropping the green flag on time were enormous.

"If this event doesn't go off on time, a lot of people are going to lose a lot of money," Waltrip muttered to himself and anyone else within earshot.

Waltrip was slated to start on the outside of Row 2 on the starting grid, having won his 125-mile qualifying race earlier during Speedweeks. Sitting on the pole was Buddy Baker, who had the fastest car in the field and a good chance, like Waltrip, to win his first 500. Others who were sure to be contenders included

Richard Petty, who was trying to shake the worst slump of his storied career; the tough-as-nails three-time defending points champion Cale Yarborough; open-wheel demon A. J. Foyt; the feisty Allison brothers, Bobby and Donnie; and other veteran former 500 winners such as David Pearson and Benny Parsons, who could never be counted out. A strong rookie field included the likes of a little-known kid named Dale Earnhardt, a Yankee driver named Geoffrey Bodine, and others who would go on to make names for themselves in Winston Cup racing, including Harry Gant and Terry Labonte.

At the moment, none were sure the race was going to come off as planned.

Certainly the weather hadn't been anticipated by Big Bill France, who at times in his storied life had seemed to control Mother Nature with the same ease that he appeared to command all else when it came to stock car racing. Not far from where Waltrip stood, Big Bill and his son, Bill Jr., were contemplating their dilemma. Big Bill officially had handed over the reins of the family's fledging NASCAR empire to his eldest son in 1972. But this day was to be the culmination of another of Big Bill's grand visions for the sport he had helped found in 1948, not long after he and thirty-five other men met in a smoke-filled room at the Ebony Bar on the top floor of the Streamline Hotel on Highway A1A in Daytona Beach in December of 1947. With tracks at the time scattered throughout the Southeast, each facility ruled by a different promoter with his own set of rules for races, Big Bill had argued successfully that the sport of stock car racing desperately needed leadership. In the single most impressive move of his long and highly accomplished life, he had generously offered his own. Naturally, he then got everyone else in the room to go along with it.

Thus, the National Association for Stock Car Auto Racing was formed.

In truth, the younger Bill wasn't really a Junior, even though everyone called him that. His father's legal name was William H. G. France, and he was William C. France. A large man at six feet five and over 210 pounds, William H. G. France soon enough became "Big Bill," and the nickname stuck. Like many things in NASCAR, all was not quite as it seemed—neither with the Frances' names nor their relationship in terms of how much influence one had over the other, and everyone else, in the sport by 1979. Technically, Little Bill was running the show as NASCAR president and Big Bill was only a consultant, although he also wielded considerable power and influence not only as a parent and former NASCAR president but as chairman and president of the International Speedway Corporation, which had built the 2.5-mile Daytona International Speedway under his guiding hand in 1959.

Twenty years later, as father and son looked out together at a rain-soaked facility just hours before what was to be the most important race in the thirty-one-year history of NASCAR, they wondered if the event was going to come off as planned. Others noticed their worried, pained expressions. Had they examined Big Bill just a little closer, they might have noticed something else.

He also wore the unmistakable look of sheer determination.

Big Bill still seemed intimidating when he wanted or thought he needed to be, even at age seventy. He didn't fear anything and certainly had no intention of letting a little rain spoil his special Daytona 500 party. After much arm-twisting the previous spring, executives at the CBS television network had agreed to televise this running of the Great American Race live, from wire to wire. It was the first time any television network had agreed to broadcast a major NASCAR race live from start to finish, but there was a caveat to the deal. The TV folks had wanted assurances beforehand that the green flag would drop on time so the telecast could begin precisely as scheduled and end on time. It was that simple.

Big Bill France and his son had guaranteed they would do everything in their power to see that the green flag would be dropped on time.

So as he looked out at the track through the light rain early that morning of February 18, 1979, Big Bill considered his promise. "Yes," he thought, "this race will go off as scheduled." He was sure of that. In fact, he told himself that he personally would make sure of it.

●   ●   ●

Waltrip remembered back to the previous spring, when he had flown to Los Angeles along with popular racing broadcaster Ken Squier to meet with television executives from CBS affiliates about the possibility of their individual stations carrying the Daytona 500 live, from the dropping of the green to the waving of the checkered flag at its conclusion. The meeting hadn't been an immediate success.

"All the people from the affiliates thought we were crazy," Waltrip said. "I'll never forget. I was with John Madden. He was just starting his career as a football analyst. He was there. I sat at the table with him. And people were looking at Ken Squier and I, and we got up and told everybody how great NASCAR was and what a great event this was going to be and how it was going to change the way people thought about racing from that Daytona 500 on.

"We got up, and Ken, in all his eloquence and all the things he could do, he was selling away. He's telling them like only he can do. I get up, and I'm a guy that's kind of the hot guy in the sport at the time. I'm young and I had the silver tongue. I could sell anything. And we're up there doing our dog and pony show, and people were looking at us like we had lost our minds."

If anyone had the ability to sell a race to a roomful of skeptics, it was Waltrip. By the time the running of the '79 Daytona 500 rolled around, he had just turned thirty-two years old but was still well in the prime of his driving career.

Waltrip had burst onto the NASCAR scene seven years earlier, immediately running his mouth, if not his cars at first, wide open. His first victory came in May 1975 in a car that he had built himself, and that started getting him noticed more for his abilities in the garage and as a driver on the track than for his often annoying habit of tireless self-promotion. Until he started racing with the proper financial support, the native of Owensboro, Kentucky, was known more for his fast talking than his fast driving.

By the mid-1970s, however, Waltrip had begun backing up all of his boasts with victories. He began winning regularly in 1977, when he made six trips to Victory Lane, doubling his career total. He even guided one car there that season without getting official credit for it in the record books, driving the final twenty-three laps for Donnie Allison in the Talladega 500 after Allison had to retire because of heat exhaustion.

Waltrip had bowed out of that race after 106 laps when the engine blew in the No. 22 Chevrolet he was driving for DiGard Racing. He was milling about the garage area, thinking of leaving the track early, when he suddenly heard himself being paged on the public-address system.

"I heard my name on the P.A., so I hurried on down to Donnie's pit," Waltrip said. "The heat had gotten to him. So I was glad to help him out."

That was the way it was in NASCAR most days. Fierce competitors on the track, drivers were known to assist one another any way they could after their own chances of winning had been dashed. But only after that and usually not a moment before.

It was one of the few times early in his career when Waltrip actually endeared himself to his fellow competitors. Oftentimes he upset them with his rare combination of skill and self-serving savvy when the television lights came on and someone thrust a microphone in his face for an interview. "I'm gonna make these folks forget all about Richard Petty," he boasted once.

That comment in itself was downright scandalous in a sport that had been dominated for years by the Petty family in general and by Richard in particular. Heading into the 1979 Daytona 500, Richard Petty owned 185 career victories—the most in what was then known as Winston Cup Grand National history, and 170 more than Waltrip could claim at the time.

Despite his far loftier achievements, Petty was a different animal in front of the television cameras than Waltrip. He came across as humble, gracious. His goal seemed to be to promote the sport itself. Waltrip seemed more interested in lauding his own accomplishments, which initially turned off fans and fellow drivers alike.

Yet Waltrip made no apologies for his brashness. When he arrived on the scene, television was just beginning to make what would ultimately be a huge impact on the sport. Whereas many of the old-timers and even many of the newcomers to the garage lacked a grasp of that, or shunned the spotlight because it just wasn't their deal, Waltrip leaped at every chance to take center stage. Others might have joked that every time he saw a camera in the garage area, he saw an opportunity; but to Waltrip, that wasn't a joke. It was fact, and one that he was proud to say he wouldn't deny.

He also became one of the sport's greatest ambassadors, eventually learning that helping popularize it any way he could might ultimately benefit him and the other drivers in future ways they couldn't yet imagine.

"I'd watch some of the other guys get interviewed on TV and I'd say to myself, 'Man, if they would just look at the camera, open their mouths, and talk, maybe people would get to know them better and the sport a little better.' Maybe they'd get their message across," Waltrip said.

"So that's what I decided to do. And man, whenever that red light on the camera went on, I went to work."

In the spring of 1978, Waltrip was being asked to go to work in front of the guys who had to be convinced to give the green light to the live TV broadcast of the following February's Daytona 500.

"It'll be a fantastic event," Waltrip told them. "Lots of excitement."

"These races are packed with great drama. It'll be riveting," Squier offered.

The TV executives sat there stone-faced, completely unconvinced.

"There's no way," one of them replied.

"A three-and-a-half- or four-hour live event on a Sunday afternoon? Nobody's going to watch that," said another.

Waltrip had his own doubts. "They may have been right, except for a couple of things that made this very interesting," he said years later. "The TV people were worried about the time it was going to take to run a five-hundred-mile race at Daytona. Because they knew it could take five hours. Well, you couldn't block off five hours of television on a Sunday afternoon at that time. They were real concerned about it starting on time and having a pretty small window of ending it when they wanted. And so Mr. France guaranteed 'em that the race would start on time, without exception.

"Well, guess what? We get to the racetrack on Sunday morning and it's raining. It had been raining all night, it was raining Sunday morning—and this race had to start on time, or the deal was off."

Actually, the deal would not have been off. But it likely would have been altered in such a way that its impact on the history of the sport was negligible. Certainly many of the higher-ups at CBS would not have ended up being enamored with the sport as a live TV offering, as evidenced by their attitude upon being greeted with heavy rain showers when they arrived at the track the morning of the race.

"We don't have to pay for this if it rains, do we?" one of the high-powered executives asked Neal Pilson, who had helped negotiate the deal for CBS. "Yes, we do," Pilson replied. "And if it gets rained out, we have to run it live tomorrow. That's our commitment."

The CBS bigwig frowned. He did not look pleased at all.

•   •   •

It wasn't the first time NASCAR had stuck its toes in the fickle waters of television. Dating back to the earliest days of the superspeedway at Daytona, Big Bill France had an understanding of what the relatively new medium might do for his sport. It was with this in mind that France began staging a variety of short races at Daytona International Speedway shortly after the facility opened. Among them were a pair of 10-lap "pole position" qualifying races that were run two weeks before the Daytona 500, with the winners of the two 25-mile sprints earning spots on the front row for the Great American Race.

In 1960, the big automobile manufacturers in Detroit also began mass production of "compact" cars such as Ford Falcons, Chevrolet Corvairs, Plymouth Valiants, Pontiac Tempests, Mercury Comets, and others. Never one to miss an opportunity to get in on the ground floor of anything that had the potential to develop into a promotional tool for his sport, Big Bill immediately slipped into the pre-500 program, now called Speedweeks, two races for these types of cars in addition to the two qualifying events. Then he started looking for a television network willing to televise the four short races.

Big Bill knew then that television wasn't anywhere close to being ready to televise a longer race. He needed to start small and build on what he was certain would be the successes of the smaller races, once they caught on with TV viewers.

As would be the case nineteen years later, it was CBS Sports that responded to France's pleas for attention to the sport. In

January of 1960, CBS officials sent a technical crew to Daytona to scout out the territory. They began to set up to televise the four short races on January 31, making history in the process. It was the first live network television coverage in stock car racing history.

Greg Fielden wrote of the significance of this in volume 4 of his series of books, *Forty Years of Stock Car Racing*. "CBS was venturing into uncharted waters," Fielden wrote.

The four events which were run at Daytona on January 31, 1960 seemed to be an ideal set-up. The races were short—the pole position races were both less than 10 minutes in length—and network executives could conveniently slip commercials into the programming without cutting much, if any, of the racing action.

The experiment was termed a success. CBS packed up its gear and headed back to New York—14 days before the running of the second annual Daytona 500. They didn't dare attempt a telecast of a four-hour marathon.

Big Bill France realized at least some of the difficulties of televising long stock car races that needed to be overcome. But he vowed to eventually get the gem of the Winston Cup Grand National race schedule televised live and in its entirety. He continually pushed for other events to be televised as well, at least in part if not entirely, and at least on a tape-delayed basis if not live.

His persistence worked to only a very limited extent on this occasion. Over the next four years, CBS merely dabbled in the sport, usually airing heavily edited versions of Grand National races during the *CBS Sports Spectacular* show.

Next it was ABC's turn to dance more regularly with Big Bill's dream. Beginning with the 1961 Firecracker 250 at Daytona—a summer race that was the circuit's second visit to the new track each season—ABC started showing extended race highlights on the *ABC's Wide World of Sports* program. Such shows as *CBS Sports Spectacular* and *ABC's Wide World of Sports* seemed perfectly suited to auto racing at the time. Although France wanted more, network producers found these shows attractive outlets for racing because they could edit out as little or as much of the race as they wanted, depending on which time slots they had allotted for the footage and which parts of certain races they thought were exciting or boring. Most times, they condensed an entire race into packages of thirty to forty-five minutes of actual footage, with the majority of races being televised a few weeks after the running of the events.

It is important to point out that NASCAR was not alone in craving, but not necessarily receiving, live love from the television folks at the time. It wasn't until the mid-1970s that ABC, by then the undisputed American leader of auto racing telecasts, began televising the open-wheel Indianapolis 500 in prime time on the same day it was run. And even then, ABC delayed its telecast by several hours.

There were occasions when the networks whetted the appetites of France and race fans who yearned to learn more about what was happening during a race on the day it was run. For instance, ABC showed portions of the 1962 Daytona 500 live. Legendary print and broadcast journalist Chris Economaki covered the event from pit road and later related to author Mike Hembree an incident that illustrated the lack of understanding many had of the sport in those days.

"The ABC crews were all union," Economaki told Hembree in *The Definitive History of America's Sport*. "A lot of them were older guys. When there came an assignment in Florida in the middle of winter, they all wanted it. So I had a lot of old guys down there with me, including my cable puller."

Unlike in later years when TV equipment would become more portable, easier to haul around, and eventually altogether wireless, pulling cable and moving cameras and other gear for a roving reporter in those days was heavy-duty hard work. Sitting on the pole for the race was Glenn "Fireball" Roberts, one of the sport's biggest stars at the time (he eventually would win the race as well).

"The race started, and Fireball Roberts came off the corner and into the pits after about ten laps, which, of course, was surprising," Economaki told Hembree.

It also seemed newsworthy to Economaki. But when he started to move toward Roberts's pit area, the guy pulling cable and carrying equipment for him stayed put at first.

"Let's go!" Economaki shouted.

"There's a car coming!" his coworker shouted back.

"I know," Economaki said. "That's why we're going!"

All the while, France kept pushing for one of the networks to televise one of his Winston Cup series races live and in its entirety. He finally found his first taker not in 1979 at Daytona, as so many would later come to believe, but in 1971 when ABC agreed, again with some reluctance, to televise from start to finish the Greenville 200 from the half-mile Greenville-Pickens Speedway in upstate South Carolina. The catch? The race had to be packaged to fit into the ninety-minute window offered via the *Wide World of Sports* format.

How they arrived on running the historic race in Greenville, not one of the Cup circuit's more well-known tracks, is interesting and significant.

"About a month before the race, a guy from ABC in New York called," the late Pete Blackwell, who operated the track for years, told Hembree. "They had talked to [Big] Bill France, and they were looking for a race they could get in on *Wide World of Sports* in an hour and a half. They had gone through results sheets and saw that we had finished a race in about an hour and twenty-five minutes."

The ABC man on the other end of the phone line got right to the point.

"Do you think you could do that again?" he asked.

Blackwell did not hesitate in answering.

"I said, 'Sure,' although there was no way I could be sure."

Eager to make it happen for their own benefit and ABC's, the governing body of NASCAR trimmed the starting field from thirty cars to twenty-six, the idea being that fewer cars on the track should mean fewer wrecks, fewer caution flags, and, as a result, a faster race that would neatly fit into the tight *Wide World* window of opportunity.

"This is great. This could lead to bigger things," Blackwell told Richard Petty before the race.

Petty nodded.

"Please, then, no cautions," Blackwell added.

"You won't have to worry about no cautions," Petty replied. "I'm going to lead all the way. Just tell everybody to follow me."

Petty was confident, and why not? He had won five of the first nine Winston Cup races to that point in the '71 season, including the Daytona 500 for the third time. Making it even sweeter, Buddy Baker had finished second in the 500 while also driving for Petty Enterprises.

But folks were going to be watching live racing at Greenville-Pickens, and Blackwell was hoping to make it special. He directed scaffolding to be erected at various locations around the track for ABC's cameras and worked with the network to have a portable studio hastily constructed near the first turn to serve as a temporary home for announcers Jim McKay and Economaki. Quarters were cramped, as one technician handling the feed from the track back to New York soon discovered when he realized he would be working out of one of the track's small restrooms.

Blackwell told Hembree years later that he was worried the crowd would be smaller than normal. Needlessly, as it turned out. Shortly after opening the gates, he realized that the grandstands were going to be packed to capacity. A crowd of more than fifteen thousand jammed into the venue.

"I felt like everybody might stay at home because it was on TV. But it worked the other way around. Everybody wanted to be here to see it," Blackwell said.

Hembree later described how it unfolded from there:

The field was circling the flat half-mile on the parade lap when *Wide World of Sports* opened. After receiving a signal from a technician that the broadcast had started, flagman Bill Blackwell [Pete's cousin] unfurled the green flag.

Although track, television and NASCAR officials were nervous, the event went well. There was only one caution, and Bobby Issac zoomed under the checkered flag first to finish the race in one hour and sixteen minutes, well within ABC's prescribed time period. The purse, boosted by television money, was twenty thousand dollars, a record for a NASCAR half-miler.

Despite the confidence he professed beforehand, it wasn't Petty's day. He battled mechanical problems all afternoon and ran seventh, four laps off the pace that was set by Issac, who finished two laps ahead of second-place finisher David Pearson.

"They squeezed that one in. That was the important thing," Petty recalled many years later. "That was one of them ABC deals. We all had a chance to go on TV, and we were excited about it. But all I remember is that we ran terrible, and Bobby Issac blew everyone away. We ended up seventh, but we weren't even in the race."

Pete Blackwell fielded a phone call during the race from a fan who said he was watching the event on television from a bar in Kentucky.

"I made a bet with another fella here about who was going to win," the caller said.

There was a pause on the line.

"So tell me," added the caller, "who wins?"

Only then did it dawn on Blackwell what the caller was really thinking. As he later told Hembree, "He wanted to know who was going to win because he was sure the race was recorded."

•   •   •

Hours before the 1979 Daytona 500, Big Bill France and Bill France Jr. were still confident that this first major race to be televised from start to finish would go off as planned. Others weren't so sure.

Meanwhile, the weather was playing a role in the bigger picture far to the north of Daytona Beach. Much of the eastern portion of the United States awoke on the morning of February 19, 1979, to find itself in the icy grip of a massive winter snowstorm. Nearly twenty inches of snow fell in parts of North Carolina, about the same or more came down in parts of South Carolina, four inches closed the Atlanta airport, and four of the five Great Lakes were frozen for the first time in modern history. Prolonged freezing temperatures in the Northeast and Midwest made going out of the house not only nearly impossible but highly dangerous, and in New York City the thermometer plunged to zero degrees Fahrenheit. Other cities along the East Coast not only had to cope with the snow still falling but also with high winds that produced snowdrifts taller than most human beings.

Humpy Wheeler awoke Sunday morning to the pitter-patter of rain in Daytona and had heard the weather was worsening toward the north. As much as he wanted to stay for the race, he had a scheduled speaking engagement for the next day in Charlotte and didn't want to risk missing it. So he decided he would try to drive back to Charlotte, even though it meant leaving Daytona Beach before the 500 started.

"I knew something bad was going to go on [with the weather] and I had that speech the next day in Charlotte. So I took off at eleven o'clock in the morning and hit sleet in St. Augustine," Wheeler said.

St. Augustine is only fifty-five miles north of Daytona.

"Oh, shit," Wheeler thought to himself. He stopped at a pay phone and placed a call to Ken Squier at the track.

"I have some bad news for you. It's sleeting in St. Augustine," Wheeler grimly told him.

Wheeler climbed back into his car and kept driving.

"And it was ice big-time by the time I got to Savannah [Georgia]," he said.

Soon he was driving through heavy snow, which only increased in volume and severity the farther he pushed to the north.

"I got to Columbia [South Carolina] and couldn't go any farther. By the time I got to Columbia it was twenty-three inches of snow and nothing was moving," Wheeler said.

While Wheeler at first thought it was bad news for the running of the Daytona 500 as well as for those caught in the maelstrom such as himself, the fact was that for NASCAR, the perfect storm was brewing. With impassable roads and brutally frigid temperatures forcing millions of people to stay inside from Columbia to Chicago and most points in between, many other sporting events that might have been televised or attended in person that Sunday were canceled. And those millions who were forced to curl up on the couch in front of a fire and their television sets suddenly had only one viable sports option to tune in to that afternoon.

Doug Rice was well aware of that phenomenon. Having grown up in North Carolina, Rice was living in Salisbury, near Charlotte, at the time and had been looking forward to watching the race on television in the mobile home he shared with his wife adjacent to the home of his father-in-law, Ben Mitchell. Rice had somewhat reluctantly become a race fan at the urging of his brothers several years earlier, and by 1979 was really into it.

"There was anticipation about it because there was no [live] racing on television," said Rice, who would go on to work in racing as a play-by-play race announcer and as president and general manager of Performance Racing Network. "I vividly remember after I got into [being a fan of the sport] trying on Sunday when ABC would do updates and they would cut into the *Wide World of Sports* program. It might be the race at Darlington or Talladega, and they would give you ten minutes of the race and literally go to these taped packages of log rolling and figure skating.

"Then maybe forty-five minutes later they would come back and give you ten more minutes of the race. It was simply the most agonizing way to watch a race."

That day, it was going to be different. Rice was sure of that—probably even more so than Big Bill France.

"You wanted to see it because you never got to see it," Rice said of his desire to watch the 500 live. "It was so the opposite of what it would become in later years. There was no racing on television. So even those little snippets you got on *Wide World*, you would plan your day around that.

"There was so much anticipation around this race because we were going to sit down and watch it on television."

Not in his mobile home, however. It was too cold to watch it from there. Shortly after waking up to find themselves pretty much snowbound, he and his wife bundled up and trudged the short distance through the snow to his father-in-law's warmer house.

"Nobody went to church that day because there were like thirteen or fourteen inches of snow on the ground in Salisbury," Rice said. "The storm started the night before. We got up the next day, and it not only snowed a lot, but it was ridiculously cold.

Normally when it snows [in North Carolina], it's twenty or thirty degrees, but it was like ten and it was like blizzard conditions.

"My father-in-law had a pickup truck and he took me to the grocery store because that is what you do in the South when it snows—you go buy bread and milk. It was one of the few Sundays he wasn't in church, and he was real strict about going to church. But he drove me to go pick up some groceries and we talked about the race and getting back to watch it. On the way back it was so cold that he had the heater on in the truck and it was still blowing snow through the vents. It was that bad; the snow was blowing right through the vents."

A man of few words by nature, Ben Mitchell growled disapprovingly.

"This is like Yankee snow," he told his son-in-law.

Rice had heard the expression. But for the first time in his life, now he believed he understood what it meant.

Many miles to the south, it wasn't snowing. Better yet, Big Bill France and his son saw that the rain was beginning to cease. In truth, they had been nervous about this day all along. Despite all of the years of work leading up to the landmark television agreement that was struck after Waltrip and Squier and others had directed their sales pitch for the sport at the CBS executives, there had been much lobbying within NASCAR's own inner circle for having the race deliberately blacked out in a large region covering several southeastern states. The thinking was that many of the sport's most loyal fans would stay at home and watch on television instead of making their usual trek to Daytona to watch the race in person.

It was sort of a be-careful-what-you-wish-for moment for the France family. This was what they had always wanted: the Daytona 500 televised live from start to finish. But they weren't sure what it was going to mean. They were confident it could draw respectable TV ratings, but would live TV damage the live gate revenues? After all, this was all about money—money and increased exposure. The Frances didn't want to win one at the expense of losing the other, or vice versa.

"We were scared to death that it was going to hurt the crowd [attendance]," Bill France Jr. admitted to Hembree years later. "We originally had probably the biggest blackout plan in the history of sports, something like seven southeastern states. But we relaxed the blackout as we got closer to the race. Finally, we left Florida in it for a while, then just dropped the blackout, period."

As he looked out over the rain-soaked track and infield, even as the rain slowed to a drizzle and then stopped altogether, the younger France and his father finally allowed themselves small smiles. Not only would the race go off as scheduled, but lifting the original blackout plan had been brilliant. There were well over a hundred thousand fans in attendance despite the bad weather and legitimate questions about whether the race would go off on time. For the first time since they awakened early that morning to the sounds of raindrops, the Frances who ruled NASCAR were certain—really certain—that it would and that this was going to be a watershed day for their sport.

2

The First 500

Richard Petty did not arrive in Florida for the running of the 1979 Daytona 500 as confident as he had been for the running of the Greenville 200 in front of the national television spotlight eight years earlier. He was coming off a frustrating, difficult season, having failed to win a single race in 1978—the first time since 1959, his second season, that he had been shut out of Victory Lane.

"We had been winning so much that we expected ourselves to win something," Petty said. "But we started that year with the '78 Dodge [Magnum], and it was just a terrible race car. We were at Daytona, leading the race, and we blew a tire. It knocked out me and [David] Pearson and [Darrell] Waltrip. We were the three best cars and it knocked us all out of the race. We were coming up on Bobby Allison to lap him, and he ended up winning the race.

"Those were frustrating times. We never could get that Dodge to run that good, so halfway through the season we switched to the Chevrolet, which was completely new and different to us. So we had to learn all about that."

The man known as the King was learning to deal with the harsh reality that he might be on the downside of his storied career. But while he might be getting closer to surrendering his throne to some younger driver, he still firmly believed that he had many race victories left in him.

And why not? The Petty name was synonymous with success in stock car racing, dating back to the days when Richard was an adolescent and his father, Lee, was winning races before Big Bill France had even helped found NASCAR. A mechanic by trade, Lee Petty spent his spare time drag racing down backcountry roads near the Petty home in Level Cross, North Carolina. He pocketed extra cash by working on cars and winning side bets on racing, always betting on himself to win. The elder Petty entered the NASCAR first "Strictly Stock" race at the old Charlotte Fairgrounds in 1949, driving a 1946 Buick Roadmaster, the family car, to the track and then onto it to compete in the race. When he rolled the car halfway through the race, no one in the Petty family was quite sure how they were going to get back to Level Cross, roughly ninety miles away.

Lee Petty had been running second and challenging for the lead when his car flipped four times before coming to a stop. Afterward, he crawled out of the car and sat on the edge of the track, trying to regain his senses and figure out how he was going to explain the totaled Roadmaster to his wife, Elizabeth.

"He turned it over, tore it all to pieces, so we had to find another way home," Richard said with a smile later. "I rode with Daddy and them [other family members] to the race in that car, and we didn't know at first how we were going to get back. I thought my uncle was there, and we were going to thumb a ride with him. But it turned out we didn't have a way home."

Glenn Dunnaway of nearby Gastonia had shown up at the venue without a ride but full of determination to land one. He roamed the pit area until he ran into a gentleman named Hubert Westmoreland, who was looking for a driver for his 1947 Ford and quickly agreed to put Dunnaway behind the wheel.

Amazingly, Dunnaway beat the rest of the thirty-three-car field to the checkered flag. The amazement quickly wore off during postrace inspection, when Big Bill France discovered that Dunnaway's rear springs had been altered by a wedge—a common practice to add speed in whiskey-running cars at the time. The car had an illegal block inserted to jack up the springs on one side, allowing the machine to turn more efficiently. France, as he had promised beforehand, summarily disqualified Dunnaway and gave the victory instead to Jim Roper, driver of a Lincoln who had traveled all the way from Kansas after reading about the race in *Smilin' Jack*, a popular comic strip of the day drawn by a racing enthusiast named Zack Mosley.

Dunnaway was disheartened. Westmoreland was furious and threatened to sue. The sport was off to a raucous start.

Yet in a display of sportsmanship and generosity that also was to define the sport at least in part for many years to come, Dunnaway's fellow drivers felt sorry for him and passed the hat because they knew he had not known that his car had been altered. He ended up taking away more than he would have received as his cut of the $2,000 first-place check. His fuming car owner, the real guilty party, sulked away with nothing.

Richard Petty, the man who would go on to win more stock car races than anyone else in the history of the sport, eventually thumbed a ride back to Level Cross with another friend of the family who was in attendance. All the while, the man who would be called King couldn't help thinking about what his daddy had done to the family car.

"They came the next day with a flatbed truck and got the race car. That's how bad it was tore up," Richard said.

Yet the experience taught Richard and Lee an important lesson. Do what you can to win a race, but be patient and save the car. All too often in those early days, it was the only one a racer owned.

"You can't win the race if you're not in it at the end," Lee told Richard. It would become the family mantra.

Lee Petty certainly believed in it, and lived it from that day forward. He spent much of the rest of his driving career beating back the opposition with what were considered to be underpowered Plymouths. Many times other cars would be faster, but Lee would outlast them. He would find a way to finish on short dirt tracks that were full of ruts, as others fell to the wayside, victimized by the perils of an unpredictable track and their own impatience to get to the front first. From 1949 through the 1961 season, Lee Petty won a total of fifty-four times in NASCAR's top series, more than any other driver.

Tim Flock, one of the other more successful drivers of the era, once said of him, "Lee understood the car as well as driving. He knew you didn't have to always be the fastest to be first."

Lee Petty wasn't always fastest, but he frequently was first at the end. His first race did not do his reputation justice. Like many in racing in those early days, his humble start in the first Strictly Stock race did not foretell of the impact he and his family would have on the sport for generations to come.

At the heart of it all was Daytona. There was no place else like it for stock car racing.

●   ●   ●

To understand the dynamics of the Daytona 500 and the enormity of the event even in 1979, one has to step back in time to the beginning. Before the 500, there were the beach races at Daytona. But even before those could occur, something else had to happen. Once again, the chain of events that would shape NASCAR's future began with Big Bill France.

During the fall of 1934, France was not yet the visionary of a multibillion-dollar racing empire—or even anything remotely close to it. He was simply an automobile mechanic looking for steadier work, hoping to escape not only the winter cold of Washington, D.C., but the bleak economic fallout of the Great Depression. Years later, during an interview with *Sports Illustrated*, France said of his decision to attempt moving from Washington to Miami, "At least in Florida, I could work on cars out of the cold and the snow and the rain."

He might have lived to work on cars, but he loved to race them as well. His father was a bank teller who had never understood this passion. As a teenager, Big Bill frequently risked his father's wrath by sneaking the family car, an old Model T, out to a spacious, banked speedway in Laurel, Maryland. His father often wondered aloud why the tires on the car kept wearing out so quickly, never realizing that it was the result of his son's folly.

So when France moved south in 1934, it wasn't entirely without hope of finding a way to become even more involved in some form of auto racing. While still in Washington with his wife, Anne, and his firstborn son, William Clifton (or William C. France, who came to be called Bill Jr.), Big Bill saved enough money from operating a small service station near the Potomac to purchase his first real race car. It wasn't much to look at; in fact, it was quite crude. It was an open-wheel, single-seat racer with a modified Model T engine and a body woven of canvas. France used this vehicle to compete in a series of local dirt-track races in the Washington area, where he quickly learned that many race promoters were little more than con artists who thrived by cheating drivers and customers alike. He also learned—as the Petty family would some fifteen or sixteen years later—that the most successful drivers always owned the best equipment and spent a great deal of time and effort to maintain it.

When France departed Washington for what he believed would be sunny Miami, he didn't have much to show for his racing efforts or anything else. But he sensed that it was time to make a move. Life wasn't getting any better by staying where he was, so he withdrew his life savings of seventy-five dollars from a Washington bank account and proceeded directly to a hardware/ auto repair shop before hitting the road. There he purchased fifty dollars worth of tools, which he used to make repairs for stranded motorists along his way to Florida. This is how he fed his family and kept moving toward his chosen destination.

Alas, France never quite made it to Miami. He pulled into Daytona Beach one day, took a job at a local Pontiac-Cadillac auto dealership, and never stopped thinking about what he had learned on the dirt tracks in and around his native Washington.

He thought about it often over the next fifteen years. He organized and promoted races throughout the South under a variety of would-be governing bodies, including the infamous and short-lived SCARS (Stock Car Auto Racing Society). Other rival racing organizations included one run by Bruton Smith, who would later become a major player himself on the NASCAR scene.

France began to get seriously involved in the promotion business after a group of civic leaders in Daytona Beach announced plans to sponsor a race for stock cars in the winter of 1936. France liked the idea of running stock cars—cars that were, at least in theory and until racers started messing with them to gain an advantage, identical to the ones being driven on the road by the average American. Fans could identify with that, he thought. And if they could identify with the idea, they would pay to see it. Furthermore, if a Pontiac or a Cadillac could win and look good doing it, that might just lead to more potential customers coming through the door at the local dealerships where he had worked and forged sponsorship relationships.

The first two races in Daytona were run on a 3.2-mile circuit formed simply by parallel straightaways on the beach and paved Highway A1A that were connected by slightly banked corners made of built-up sand. It was, like France's first race car, rather crude. But it immediately appealed to other race car drivers. Among the drivers in the very first Daytona race was Wild Bill Cummings, winner of the 1934 Indianapolis 500—open-wheel racing's most prestigious event. France entered, too, and ended up running fifth in his Ford coupe.

France frequently raced in the very events he organized and promoted, a practice he found to be tricky two years later in February of 1938. After the city of Daytona had lost $22,000 on the inaugural race in 1936, the race's founders agreed to step aside and let the local Elks Club have a crack at turning a profit in 1937. The Elks fared little better, which led France and Charlie Reese, owner of a local restaurant, to step in the following year.

By then France was operating the Pure Oil gas station on Main Street, and his place of business had become the unofficial headquarters for local racers. The Daytona Beach chamber of commerce had approached him, asking him if he knew anyone who might be interested in putting on the race. France said he was, but he didn't have the money. He did, however, know someone who did—and that was Reese, the man who owned the 1937 Ford coupe France had been racing himself on weekends.

"I can line up the cars and the drivers and help sell tickets. But I don't have the money to put this thing on. Will you back it?" France asked Reese.

"If you do the work, I'll put up the money," Reese replied.

True to what would become his form in later years, France made plans not to scale back but to double the efforts. He and Reese announced that they would hold not one but two races each year on the Daytona Beach circuit. France went to work lining up a number of sponsors who donated all sorts of prizes. He wanted drivers to be rewarded not just for winning the race or finishing well, but also for the number of laps they led. Guaranteed prizes to lap leaders included a box of fancy Hav-a-Tampa cigars, a case of Pennzoil motor oil, a pair of five-dollar sunglasses from Walgreens, two cases of Pabst Blue Ribbon beer, a bottle of choice rum, a two-dollar-and-fifty-cent credit at a local men's clothing store, and a twenty-five-dollar credit on any automobile purchased in dealer Dick Rose's used lot.

The first race drew over five thousand spectators, a large crowd for those days. Driver Smokey Purser took the checkered flag at the finish line—and kept on driving straight up the beach toward the center of town. France, running second, followed him.

Purser maintained his lead long enough to get to Roy Strange's garage in town, where France caught him changing the cylinder heads on his race car. Even then, that was illegal. The car couldn't legitimately be called a stock car if Purser had altered it to give himself an edge.

France wasted no time disqualifying Purser on the spot, but he then immediately faced a unique dilemma. Big Bill had finished second and should, therefore, have been declared the winner. He huddled with Reese.

"There's no way I can knock the first-place man out and declare myself the winner without people thinking there's something fishy going on," France said.

Reese agreed.

So they declared Lloyd Moody, who had actually run third behind Purser and France, the race victor.

Then France and Reese took stock of their take at the gate and declared themselves losers two times over. France had not only passed on the cash that went to the winning driver, he realized that all of his efforts as organizer and promoter of the event had been virtually for naught. He and Reese had agreed to charge fifty cents admission and had sold roughly five thousand tickets. After paying off the winning driver and everyone else, they had only $220 to split in "profit" between them—hardly enough to account for all of the man-hours Big Bill had put in trying to make the race a huge success.

"At least I didn't lose money. But we must be doing something wrong," Reese told France.

"No kidding," France thought. But he also thought it should be easy enough to fix.

He and Reese decided to capitalize on the popularity of the February race by doubling their efforts yet again. This time, they also doubled the cost of admission to get in. Even though the next race was to be held only one month later, they decided to increase the ticket price to one dollar. Then they held their breath and went back to work selling tickets.

Much to their amazement and relief, the tickets sold briskly on the morning of the race. Attendance was almost identical to the first race, telling them two things: folks liked what they were seeing, and they were willing to pay a little more to see it. This time, when it was over, France and Reese had something in the neighborhood of $2,200 left over to split. They donated about $200 to the Bundles for Britain campaign—a nationwide effort to provide nonmilitary aid to the British people during the early days of World War II—and divvied up the rest.

"That taught me some lessons I never forgot," France told writer Brock Yates of *Sports Illustrated* many years later, not long before the running of the 1979 Daytona 500.

By the mid-1950s, France knew the beach and road course in Daytona was operating on borrowed time. Anxious developers were eyeing the property near Ponce Inlet Lighthouse, and some subdivisions already were in the planning stages.

The old course would be missed in many ways, however. Marvin Panch, winner of the 1961 Daytona 500 after the race moved from the beach to the asphalt of Daytona International Speedway, fondly recalled both the challenges and the joys of running oceanside. "You would get sand-blasted, and you couldn't see," Panch said. "We had tear-offs you could pull off, but that only lasted a short while. So some of us cut little round holes in the windshield, so we could reach over and kind of peek out. Either that or use a marker out of your driver's window."

That didn't always work, however, as Panch readily admitted. "[Driver] Johnny Beauchamp had a couple with some children sitting on a dune going into the North Turn one year, and he was using that [as a marker] for his shutoff point," Panch said. "Well, evidently they needed a Coke or something and they moved down the beach a little bit. Next time by, he missed the turn and almost went into downtown Daytona [because he drove deeper into the turn before braking]."

Downtown Daytona, for the record, was about ten miles away.

Dick Fleck competed mostly in the Modified stock car division and ran in the last three races ever staged on the sand. He said racing on the beach is a part of NASCAR lore that never should be dismissed or forgotten. "All I can say, really, is that it was a lot of fun. It was great fun. It was different," Fleck said years later. "It was quite an experience. We had to schedule our races, of course, according to the tide—so we had a little bit of something to race on. We would let it drift out a little bit to run in the ocean a little to cool our tires off, so we could finish the races. Tires weren't engineered like they are today. Very skinny.

"And what I'm wearing now is what I raced in then: a short-sleeved shirt, [thin] white pants with a red stripe. Nothing was fireproofed. Our fireproof was the fire extinguisher we had in our car. Our ambulance was a hearse from the local funeral director—and they only had one. So when someone got hurt, they tried to take care of him right there so they didn't have to take it to the hospital. If they took someone to the hospital, we had to stop the race until they got back.

"They had a first-aid kit with peroxide and Band-Aids. And eye wash, they had a lot of eye wash—because you would get sand in your eyes. It was very tough to see. And once in a while you would pop off a seagull, too. It was a bloody mess when it hit your windshield. There was feathers and blood floating 'round."

As amusing as the old stories were, and as much fun as the guys had driving the old beach course, France knew that something had to be done to make it better or the famed Daytona races were doomed to extinction. He thought he had just the idea not only to avoid that, but to take the entire sport to a new level in the process.

*   *   *

It was sometime in 1952 that France decided to build a "super-speedway" in Daytona Beach, the likes of which the world of stock car racing had never seen. Over the years following his first involvement, the crowds had grown for each race on the beaches in Daytona. But while proud of that, France also noticed that the beach races weren't generating much excitement or attention nationally. Furthermore, it was becoming increasingly more difficult to control the overflowing crowds of people who wanted to watch. In the first few years after France had turned the Daytona Beach races into something fans felt they had to watch, manufacturers from automotive-related industries throughout the country had dispatched countless engineers, mechanics, admen, and public relations spin doctors to determine what it might mean for the future promotion and/or involvement of their companies. By the mid- to late 1950s, even as general admission ticket sales kept climbing, the numbers of these professionals looking to possibly invest in France's fledging sport were dwindling. And that meant less publicity for a sport that desperately wanted it and needed it to grow.

France also was tired of sweating out the unpredictable weather for the beach races. He knew he needed to build a new venue that not only was bigger but also more reliable and less dependent on forces he could not control.

Control was very important to France, and he had gained an increasing amount of it in NASCAR in a very short time. It helped that he had the precedent of a federal court case working in his favor. Hubert Westmoreland, owner of the 1947 Ford driven by Glenn Dunnaway in the first Strictly Stock series race at the old Charlotte Fairgrounds back in 1949, had sued NASCAR over the disqualification of his car after Dunnaway had driven it to apparent victory. Westmoreland claimed in his suit that the governing body had no right to disqualify a car it had accepted for entry. Had Westmoreland won, France's stranglehold on the sport might have been broken before it ever was truly in his grip. But a federal court ruled in favor of France and his new organization, and NASCAR thus firmly established its right to enforce its own rules as it saw fit. More often than not, that meant as Big Bill France saw fit.

It was in 1952 that France was having breakfast with Dan Warren, a Daytona Beach attorney and city councilman at the time. Suddenly, France grabbed a doily, pulled out a pen, and tugged at Warren's arm.

"I want to show you what I'm proposing to build in Daytona Beach," France told the councilman.

Then France sketched out a rough draft of what would become a very famous tri-oval. To make it become reality, however, he needed all kinds of help—from engineers who could bring his dream facility to life, to support of the local government, to hard cash (and lots of it) to fund the massive and highly ambitious project. He estimated it would cost in the neighborhood of $3 million, a staggering sum in those days, and soon showed he was serious about his plan by founding a company called Bill France, Inc. to oversee the efforts.

One of the first to take an interest in helping him was Charles Moneypenny, the Daytona Beach city engineer. "I know of no textbook on the subject of how to build a racetrack," Moneypenny told the *Daytona Beach News-Journal* many years later. "When I began research on this track back in 1953, the first thing I learned was that most tracks are laid out strictly by guesswork."

Moneypenny realized instantly that most of Florida's sandy soil couldn't support the weight of a high-banked superspeedway and accompanying grandstands. But he told France he knew of a location west of town, out by the airport, that just might work. "There was a high grade of marl gravel underneath the subsoil there. Most of the soil here is sand and you can't build on it," he said.

Others in local government tried to help with financing. City attorney Thomas Cobb assisted in coming up with a plan to sell $3 million in bonds to cover the projected cost of the project, but an economic downturn shelved that idea. Cobb did draft legislation in 1953 to create the Daytona Beach Racing and Recreation District at the proposed construction site, and by 1957 the commission agreed to lease the 447-acre parcel to France's corporation for the rather nominal fee of $10,000 per year over a fifty-year period.

Armed now with blueprints and land, France still needed to raise working capital to begin building. Critics in the area were beginning to refer to the entire project as "France's Folly." It took Big Bill nearly five years to patch together enough pledges to secure financing to cover the initial $1.9 million construction budget for his dream track. To do so, he took out a second mortgage on his own home, secured funding from Pepsi-Cola president Donald Kendall and General Motors auto designer Harley Earl, and began selling three hundred thousand shares of stock in his newly founded company to local residents.

Finally, in late 1957, work began to clear the land. Actual construction of the facility began in January 1958.

Almost immediately, Moneypenny, who was overseeing the operation, ran into problems. The plan was to build the track with 50-foot-wide straightaways and a 20-foot apron, with a 3,000-foot-long concrete safety wall on the backstretch and 2,700-foot-long walls in the turns. But how to pour the combination of asphalt and concrete—or as France called it, "asphaltic concrete"—at such a steep angle in the turns? And how to create the footings for the banking?

Moneypenny eventually came up with the answers. In order to create the footings for the banking in the turns, he instructed construction crews to excavate millions of tons of soil from the track's infield, creating a hole that covered forty-four acres. It later was filled with water and called Lake Lloyd in honor of Sam Lloyd, one of the original six members of the speedway authority. When France had first relocated to Daytona Beach years earlier, one of his first jobs came when he found work as a brake specialist in Lloyd's General Motors dealership. If nothing else, Big Bill never forgot a favor—some would say he was slow to forget slights, too—and remained intensely loyal to anyone who had assisted him along the way during his climb to power.

In addition, Moneypenny had twenty-two tons of lime rock trucked in from Ocala, Florida, to use as the track's binding base. And then he tackled pouring the track. No one had ever attempted to pave at thirty-one degrees of incline, and the engineer came up with a unique solution. He connected the paving equipment to bulldozers anchored to the top of the banking. Then he had very fine iron filings mixed with France's "asphaltic concrete" to aid in the track's adhesion.

Even after construction began, France needed to keep hustling to make sure of the track's completion. He looked for opportunities to secure additional funding whenever he could. Once he was attending an air show at Elgin Air Force Base in Florida, and he happened to meet Clint Murchison Jr., the son of a gas and oil magnate from Texas. The young Murchison mentioned that he needed to make a quick trip to Miami, but that he didn't have a way to get there. "Well, Clint, I happen to have a private plane here at my disposal. Would you like to use it?" France asked.

Murchison said indeed he would. France then went on to suggest that perhaps the wealthy Murchison, who had inherited his father's empire, would be interested in investing a little money in his Daytona track project. He could, he said, use a low-interest loan in the neighborhood of $600,000—which in those days was, again, another eye-opening sum. Oh, and since Murchison's family was in the construction business as well as real estate, railroads, and oil, could he possibly provide some construction equipment, too?

Murchison agreed to send someone out from his family's construction and real estate businesses to look into the matter. Shortly thereafter, France had his loan secured and was one step closer to completion of his latest dream, which he planned to call Daytona International Speedway.

By December 1958, France had sold all of the shares of his company to the public and began selling tickets to future events. He then used the advance ticket money to complete the final construction phase of the facility so it could actually open in time to host the races he already had been marketing aggressively.

The track was finished early in 1959 and hosted its first series of races in February of that year. True to his form, France had events set up for virtually the entire month, weaning fans off the beach races by staging some events at the old venue, but having them lead up to the grand finale: a 500-mile race for the biggest purse in stock car racing history: $60,160. France initially called it the "500 Mile NASCAR International Sweepstakes." The general admission fee was eight dollars.

The Daytona 500, as it would come to be known rather quickly, was thus born. On the eve of the historic first race, France told *Sports Illustrated* that he was wildly optimistic about his new track's future—and presumably the Daytona 500 race itself. "Over on the beach, the good Lord always looked after us," he told *Sports Illustrated* reporter Kenneth Rudeen. "When things looked bad and we needed an east wind to send those big waves to smooth out the sand, we always got one just in time. If we keep getting the breaks, this track will have to be equal to any."

Others weren't nearly so sure of that. Among the dissenters were many of the drivers, including the popular Glenn "Fireball" Roberts.

•   •   •

By 1958, Roberts was developing into what many believed was the sport's first great superstar. It seemed he was born to race. He certainly was born in the right place to fulfill that calling, having entered the world in 1929 in Tavares, Florida, near Daytona Beach—shortly before Big Bill France made the long drive down from Washington, D.C., and began to realize his calling as builder of all things NASCAR. As young Glenn Roberts moved into adulthood, the sport was literally growing up with and all around him. As a boy, he loved watching the races on the sands of Daytona Beach, promoted from 1938 on by France. He earned his nickname, however, not because of any early driving heroics but because he was an outstanding fast-pitch softball pitcher, playing for the Zellwood Mud Hens American Legion team near Tavares.

By the time he reached the age of eighteen, in 1947, Fireball Roberts was ready to make his nickname work for him on racetracks throughout the Southeast. He entered his first race on August 5, 1947, at North Wilkesboro Speedway in North Carolina and soon was racing modified cars whenever he could, which meant he often ran seven days a week. His first NASCAR-sanctioned race came, appropriately enough, at Daytona Beach in a modified race in 1948. It was a wreck-filled, 150-lap event in which only twelve cars were able to finish, and Roberts was not behind the wheel of any of them. On the ninth lap on the 2.2-mile track made of sand and asphalt, Roberts missed the south turn and ended up in the surf of the Atlantic Ocean, his day finished.

It was undoubtedly that day that Roberts decided he liked driving on asphalt better than sand. But at the time, the handsome and personable Roberts enjoyed driving whenever he could, wherever he could, and in whatever ride he could find. His first NASCAR win came in August 1950 at Hillsborough, North Carolina, in only his third start at the sport's highest level of competition, then called Grand National. Three weeks later he nearly won again—finishing second at the prestigious and high-paying Southern 500 at Darlington Raceway in South Carolina. The media was falling in love with him, and he with them. His wife, Doris, later admitted that Roberts put a great emphasis on qualifying well because if he was successful in doing so, his name would be mentioned more prominently in newspapers.

"I always thought he was one of the first real superstars the sport had—and he did get a lot of attention," said Ned Jarrett, also a driver at the time and later one of the sport's pioneers in television broadcasting. "He was a neat dresser, a clean-cut individual, very dedicated and focused on what he was doing. And he was a tremendous athlete. He might have been the first one who showed that race car drivers are athletes.

"He was a tremendous race car driver and he didn't shy away from the attention. I don't recall him going out and beating the drums to try and get it, but I don't think he shied away from it. I think it was somewhat of a driving force for him. The more attention he got, the more he wanted to succeed to try to live up to what was expected of him."

By the time the first running of the Daytona 500 in 1959 rolled around, that was plenty. After winning a total of $199 and $140, respectively, in the Grand National division in 1953 and 1955, Roberts led 1,107 of the 6,891 laps he completed while winning five times in 1956. His total race winnings jumped up to $14,742, a respectable sum for the day. He followed that up by winning eight more races and $19,829 in 1957, and then really put the hammer down in 1958 when he teamed with Atlanta business-man Frank Strickland as his car owner and the respected and talented Paul McDuffie as his crew chief. Together they won six Grand National races, including the Southern 500 at Darlington, and pulled in a total of $32,219. He also dominated the beloved if short-lived Convertible division.

Racing was beginning to get recognized on a national level, and Fireball's ascension to stardom came at a perfect time. He was poised and willing to capitalize on it, and the sport was eager to capitalize on him. Following the 1958 season, he became the first race car driver ever voted Professional Athlete of the year by the Florida Sportswriters Association.

"He was just what the sport needed at the time," said Jarrett, who became fast friends with Roberts.

So it was in 1959 that France did not need or want Roberts and other drivers publicly voicing their concerns over his new Daytona International Speedway. Another who had become fast friends with Roberts in racing, however, was the outgoing Max Muhleman, a young sportswriter for the *Charlotte News*. Their friendship began one day at Darlington after Roberts had once again qualified for a race on the pole. At first Muhleman was in a group of reporters talking with Roberts under a pagoda that stood in the infield. One by one, though, the other reporters began to drift away, leaving only Muhleman with the driver.

"We had known each other a little bit, and we started kidding each other," Muhleman said. "Somehow it got around to the fact that I had run a good bit of track in high school."

"Is that right?" Roberts had asked.

"Yep. You don't run the track like a real man. You ought to try running it on foot," Muhleman joked.

"Oh, yeah? I bet I could get around it in ten minutes, maybe twelve. Just how fast do you think you could run it?" Roberts asked.

Darlington measured 1.366 miles around. Muhleman thought about it for a minute.

"I bet I could beat you," the reporter finally replied.

"Let's bet a steak dinner on it," Roberts said.

Muhleman started to climb down from the pagoda. "You're on. Let's go," he said.

Roberts laughed heartily. "Wait a minute, wait a minute. Anybody who would actually try that deserves a steak dinner."

So Roberts took Muhleman out to dinner and the two talked long into the night. They seemed to have much in common and cemented a friendship that would last many years.

On the eve of the first Daytona 500, Roberts had Muhleman's ear. And Muhleman was taking notes. He produced for the *Charlotte News* an opinion piece that contended Big Bill was ruling NASCAR with too much of an iron hand. It was beginning to infuriate many of the top drivers, Fireball included. Furthermore, Muhleman wrote, the drivers had legitimate concerns about running at high speeds on the new Daytona track. Was France selling speed at a price that might cost them their lives? They weren't sure yet.

"I wrote that now there were two dictators in Daytona Beach—Fulgencio Batista and Bill France," Muhleman said. "Batista had just left Cuba, where he had been a dictator before Fidel Castro came along. That was a time when a lot of drivers were beginning to grumble. Fireball was sort of the inspiration for that column. He was always complaining to me that it was hard for the drivers . . . about the way the rules were dictatorially levied, and some of the drivers were disagreeing with it. I was taking the drivers' point of view on it and wrote about it."

France was not amused.

"While I admired the heck out of Bill France, it was one of those good lines that comes to you and you decide it's too good to pass up," Muhleman said years later of the comparison he made between Big Bill and Batista. "It did rankle him to the point that he flew up from Daytona Beach and met with my editor,

I presume, to get him to fire me or to threaten a lawsuit or whatever. But I had a crusty old editor named Brady Griffith who was a classic newspaper guy—and he explained the rights of newspapers and of a columnist who could voice his opinion."

It left Muhleman with mixed feelings about what he had written. Over time, he would patch up his relationship with Big Bill France. He also came to think that what he had written about France, while perhaps not stated in the proper context, was pretty much true. France was a dictator in his sport—but the fact of the matter was that it probably was exactly what the sport needed at that time.

"That became clear later on," Muhleman said. "There really was no one I admired more than Big Bill. And we became friends over time. But I was a real young, dumb kid at the time, or at least I was real inexperienced. I didn't appreciate what he was doing until much later on."

In retrospect, Muhleman also came to believe that his controversial column might have been beneficial for France to see.

"If nothing else, there were so few people writing about NASCAR at the time that it probably did some good to let Bill know that if you grow a sport in the public eye, at some point you have a media accountability, too," he said. "The media wasn't always right and I certainly wasn't always right. But still, that was probably a helpful thing. It said to him, 'Be careful what you do, because what you do may be called into question—right or wrong.'"

•   •   •

Right or wrong, Big Bill France's motives for building Daytona International Speedway were being questioned as it prepared to open in 1959. Muhleman experienced more mixed feelings the very first time he visited the place.

"These guys will never survive this track" was his first thought.

He wasn't alone in this dark thinking. Roberts continued to privately confess his concern, as did several other drivers. It was a spectacular-looking facility, there was no question about that. There was parking outside for 35,000 cars. Grandstands were in place to seat 18,800, with portable bleachers available to accommodate 6,500 more. The enormous infield could handle up to 75,000 spectators, should the event take off or perhaps even exceed France's lofty expectations.

The track itself was two and a half miles around. It was no coincidence that the lap distance was precisely the same as the one run by Indy cars at the Indianapolis Motor Speedway for the famed Indianapolis 500, which France hoped his event would someday rival in popularity. Again, his many critics thought this was a ridiculous pipe dream.

The shape of the Daytona course, though, differed from Indy or anyplace else. It was a tri-oval, conceived by France to allow an unobstructed view of the track from the grandstands. The track was banked at a stunning thirty-one degrees in its top big turns, and at eighteen degrees in the apex of the swift dogleg that would run past the grandstands. Asked why the degree of the bank was set at thirty-one degrees, France replied simply, "Because they couldn't lay the asphalt [or 'asphaltic concrete'] any steeper." There truly was no place else like it in the entire world of racing.

It also hadn't been as easy as France made it sound to create. Moneypenny, the Daytona Beach city engineer, and Warren, the city councilman, had consulted with engineers from the Ford Motor Company to determine how to construct the high-banked turns. They had gone to the Ford proving ground track, which had banked corners, to study it.

"The banking at Ford wasn't as high, but they had the transition from the flat parts onto the banking," Warren said. "They shared their engineering reports so we could do it, too."

For a sport born in the southeastern mountains when bootleggers had begun squaring off in cow pastures to determine which among the moonshiners could run the fastest in their tricked-out automobiles, this was progress. But many didn't like the looks of it.

"I lamented the loss of the beach course at Daytona. A lot of people did," Muhleman said. "But at the same time, it was clear that there were so few amenities at the beach. It was just basic high school football bleacher stands—where there were any. And it was very hard to police. It was amazing that there were no spectator injuries in the years they ran there. How they secured the course was an unbelievable feat, just to keep people from wandering in wherever they wanted to."

The new track certainly wasn't anything like the old course.

"Once you saw a car go around the new track at Daytona, the impact was something," Muhleman said.

Muhleman and others like him had of course been to Darlington, which previously had been the crown jewel of the stock car racing industry. It was paved and had high banks, which made it a legitimate superspeedway in its own right. But it was an egg-shaped oval, measuring only the 1.366 miles where Fireball Roberts had once dared Muhleman to race him on foot. The thought of anyone staging a footrace at Daytona was laughable. It was nearly twice the size of Darlington.

"I remember going inside [Daytona] the first time and trying to find the backstretch," Muhleman said. "My eyes didn't know where to look. You couldn't see the far end of the straightaway. You had never seen a bank that high before. Darlington had banked turns, but nothing like that. It was an awesome thing. When you saw a car go on it, it was incredible."

It also was frightening, to competitors and spectators alike. It even spooked someone like Fireball Roberts, who was used to running hard and fast.

"That was still in the era when guys would blow tires," Muhleman said. "That was a strange part of racing there then. Everyone would be going along and then you would just hear this *boom*! And you knew immediately what it was. Somebody had blown the side out of a tire. And they would make these cannonlike reports. You would hear one of those and everybody's head would whirl around to see who it was, because you knew somebody was headed into the fence. And the harder they ran, the harder they hit. Fireball was a very hard runner and blew quite a few out. It was always happening.

"The tire technology got better and better as they went along, but in those early Daytona superspeedway days, going fast at the risk of blowing tires took a special kind of courage. It took some real guts."

Driver Jimmy Thompson was more succinct when asked for his assessment of the new facility just prior to its opening. "There have been other tracks that separated the men from the boys," Thompson said. "This is the track that will separate the brave from the weak after the boys are gone."

The first Daytona 500 was run on the afternoon of February 22, 1959. True to NASCAR form, it was embroiled in controversy from the start of the race until nearly three days after its completion. The field included all of the top drivers of the day: Roberts, Junior Johnson, Curtis Turner, Joe Weatherly, Lee Petty, and the rest. Richard Petty was entered in the field as well, driving a convertible in what would be the final race of mixed company between convertibles and hardtops (even France, who originally thought it was a novel idea, quickly realized that open convertibles simply could not match the aerodynamic speeds of the enclosed hardtops). No matter what they were driving, all of them were concerned because none of them had ever exceeded 140 miles per hour during a race. They joked among themselves that perhaps Turner or Weatherly had achieved those kinds of speeds while racing against each other in rental cars, but none had actually done so on a track of any type. In this one, they all knew they would have to. And it wouldn't be long before they figured out how to go even faster thanks to the wonders of aerodynamic drafting, something they knew nothing about in 1959.

Some of the drivers embraced the new style of high-speed racing on the big-banked track much more enthusiastically than others.

"It was absolutely just awesome," said Johnson, who would go on to win the second Daytona 500 a year later. "You couldn't imagine what it felt like going around that racetrack at the speeds we were running and the capabilities of what the cars could do. The racetrack was a big advancement for anybody that had ever raced prior to that, because there was nothing even comparable to it."

What came to be known as drafting was mysterious and new, and didn't even have a name that day.

"I learned in the first race that I could get back and get a running start and pass somebody," said Richard Petty, who struggled to keep up otherwise in his convertible. "I had no idea whether I had more horsepower than they had. I didn't even think about the wind part, as far as the aero deal. That came a little at a time. I learned a little something, somebody else learned a little something, he learned something, and then we all got to talking about it. I think when we first started, they called it 'sucking up.' Then they thought, 'This don't sound good, we need to get another word for it.' So they came up with 'drafting.'"

Johnson added, "I was on the racetrack running wide open and Cotton Owens came by in a Pontiac. He was fast enough to just go right on by me. When he went by, I ducked in behind him. About a half-mile from there, I was running all over him and I wasn't even at half throttle."

Already one of the sport's great thinkers, Johnson started talking to himself as he drove the car. "Hey, I don't understand this.

My car can't keep up with him, but I can run all over him when I'm behind him," Johnson mused. "I kept thinking about it and kept trying to figure out what was going on. I finally figured out that I was running in his dead air space, so it didn't take as much for me to run as fast as he did."

Thus one of the great secrets of running at the new Daytona track was discovered. Others would soon realize it held the key to running well there. Still others just tried to hang on.

"It was more like flying an airplane than it was like driving a race car," said Panch, who, like the younger Petty, had accepted a $1,000 bonus to turn his hardtop race car into a convertible for the race.

It was one of the few miscalculations France made. He thought it would make for a more entertaining race to have the ragtops mix it up with the hardtops, even though the aerodynamics ensured that there was no way the convertibles would be able to keep up. They ended up getting lapped about every ten laps during the race by the hardtops.

"But hey, a thousand dollars was a lot of money back then," said Panch, who finished seventeenth. The top fifteen finishers all drove hardtops.

Richard Petty wasn't so fortunate in his ragtop. He lasted only eight laps before a bad fuel pump ended his day, relegating him to a fifty-seventh-place finish.

"We needed the money, too," said Richard, then only twenty-one years old. "All we did was just cut the top off one of Daddy's cars and make it into a convertible. Of course, then he ran in a hardtop. He wasn't no fool."

It made quite a difference. With fifteen laps remaining in the race, it came down to a bumper-to-bumper duel between Lee Petty and Johnny Beauchamp. They exchanged the lead five times over the next fourteen laps before Petty moved in front just before taking the white flag that signified one lap to go.

As they came around the track a final time, they encountered the ornery Weatherly, who would not get out of their way even though he was two laps down and had no chance of winning the race. The three cars tore around Turn 4 and charged into the track's unique tri-oval with Weatherly's No. 48 Chevrolet slightly in front of Petty's No. 42 Oldsmobile and Beauchamp's No. 73 Thunderbird.

They barreled toward the finish. Beauchamp slipped to the inside and attempted what would later come to be known as a classic slingshot pass. The three cars crossed the finish line almost simultaneously—and confusion reigned immediately after the checkered flag was thrown at Daytona International Speedway for the first time.

Johnny Bruner, the official starter, declared Beauchamp the winner. Big Bill France agreed with him. But in a poll of twelve newsmen who had been watching, Petty was the unanimous choice as the victor.

As Beauchamp made his way to Victory Lane, Petty became increasingly angry that he had not been awarded the win. A smiling Beauchamp was photographed with one arm thrown around a three-foot-high trophy and the other around a Daytona beauty queen, unaware that Lee Petty already was campaigning furiously to have France change his mind and rule him the winner instead.

It was reminiscent of the first Daytona beach race France had promoted, when he had followed apparent victor Smokey Purser into town and caught him tinkering with his car in a local garage, which led to Purser's disqualification. Or of the very first Strictly Stock series race at the old Charlotte Fairgrounds in North Carolina, when France had disqualified the Glenn Dunnaway car that at first had been declared the winner and given the victory to Jim Roper instead, infuriating Hubert Westmoreland, the owner of Dunnaway's machine.

Only this time, France did not immediately change his mind. Petty stuck around Daytona Beach for three days after the race, pleading his case to anyone who would listen. France finally did. He called Petty on the phone sixty-one hours after completion of the race and declared him the winner. His average speed for the race was amazing for the era: 135.521 miles per hour.

But that wasn't the figure that interested Lee Petty the most. He wanted the first-place money. "His biggest story about '59 was getting the check—not about anything else," said grandson Kyle Petty many years later, long after Kyle had become a driver himself on the NASCAR circuit. "They just wanted the money. It wasn't about the trophy or anything else. They protested and stayed in town, just to get the check. I think Beauchamp already had left town with the trophy.

"That was one of his quotes through all the years, whenever anyone asked about it. He was like, 'Yeah, just get me the trophy sometime, whenever you can. But just cut me the check and let me go back to North Carolina.'"

Pete DePaolo, the car owner who earlier had registered a number of Grand National victories with Fireball Roberts as his driver, was a former Indianapolis 500 winner who hinted that France had wanted controversy all along. DePaolo insisted that France had milked the situation for every ounce of publicity he could get for the race at his new track.

"Let's face it," DePaolo told reporters. "Hollywood would have rejected a race script like this as too unbelievable."

Suddenly it was Petty's turn to be ecstatic, and Beauchamp's turn to be furious. But Lee Petty was shaken by the experience, and when talking about the new facility sometime thereafter he made a startling confession that he had been frightened running at the higher speeds.

"There wasn't a man there who wasn't scared to death of it," Petty said.

Two years later, Petty spun out at Daytona and sailed right on out of the new venue in his car—soaring 150 feet into the air over the guardrail on Turn 4 before landing with a terrifying crash in the parking lot beyond. The man who had long ago learned to drive safely and save his equipment for the end suffered a crushed chest cavity, a broken collarbone, and a broken leg. He would race only six more times after that horrible accident and never won again, telling son Richard at one point, "I feel like I'm working now. It's not fun anymore."

It was Daytona International Speedway that had taken the fun out of it for Lee Petty. His son, famous by 1979, had found joy there many times but was beginning to wonder if he, too, would soon find driving to be more work than he could stomach.

3

Getting Started

It wasn't until the month of June following the very first Daytona 500 that Kyle Petty even entered this earth, having been born on June 2, 1960. By February 1979, however, Kyle was full of vigor and anxious to follow in the family tradition of strapping himself into a race car and zipping around tracks at a high rate of speed. Unlike how it would come to be in later years in Cup racing, there was no apprenticeship served in the cockpit of a fast car as a youth. Richard actually refused Kyle permission to race until well after Kyle's eighteenth birthday—and chose Daytona International Speedway as the venue at which his son would be allowed to make his debut.

As there had been since the first day Big Bill France opened the place, a number of preliminary events led up to the running of the Great American Race. One was the ARCA 200, to be held one week prior to the bigger, more famous extravaganza. Still, it was a big deal to the Petty family. For years Kyle had experimented with other sports and hobbies before always coming back around to the idea of going into the family business. His mother had encouraged him to pursue a nice, safe career as a pharmacist, but no one ever really thought that was going to happen.

Kyle was charismatic, outgoing, and fun. He was quite the athlete as well, starring as a quarterback at Randleman High School in North Carolina and playing center on the basketball team and taking up baseball there as well. He was good enough to be offered college scholarships in football, while other schools talked to him about possibly playing baseball. In later years, he would dabble in a side career as a member of a country music band that opened for high-dollar acts such as Randy Travis, Janie Fricke, and the Oak Ridge Boys.

But deep down, even as he tried his hand in those many other areas, Kyle Petty knew he had been born to race. It was in his blood, part of his DNA. And so as he headed to Daytona Beach in February 1979, one week after getting married and at the tail end of the brief honeymoon he shared with his wife, Pattie, he was embarking on a new and old life at the same time, as he had been part of racing literally since before he could crawl.

Kyle remembered going to tracks such as the one in Martinsville, Virginia, as a child. Martinsville was the closest NASCAR-sanctioned track to Randleman and Level Cross, and the Petty family always had enjoyed great success at the storied short track. "Martinsville has always been a special place for us," Kyle said.

Kyle remembered watching his daddy race and win there, or at least trying to watch Richard compete before he often got off into other things even as the race of the day unfolded. He especially remembered the old scoreboard, which had to be manipulated manually. It was done so at a far more leisurely pace than the sport would later be willing to tolerate.

"You physically had to change the scoreboard. There was a man who sat on a stool, and every ten laps he would walk down and change the numbers. Then he would go back and sit down," Petty said. "Ten laps later, he would go back to the end of the scoreboard and change it again."

The scoreboard had room for the top five leaders in the race. And that was about it. When the race was over, Petty and some of the other offspring of the famous drivers whose car numbers had just graced the scoreboard would stage a race of their own—on foot. Usually it was with the sons of drivers David Pearson and Bobby Allison, or car owners Glen and Leonard Wood.

"We would run across the racetrack when the race was over, and we would put [number] 43 on everything. We would climb up the steps and put 43 straight across the board. The scoreboard wasn't but five feet off the ground," Petty said. "You'd stand around for a little while and then Larry and Ricky [Pearson] would put 21 on everything for the Wood brothers [whom Pearson drove for at the time]. Or Davey [Allison] and those guys would run across and put 12 up for Bobby when he was driving the Coca-Cola Chevy in the early '70s, when we were ten or twelve years old.

"It's cool because those are my memories of these places. Playing football in the infield, hanging out in the infield. Watching the race, but at the same time taking in just all the little things like the grandfather clock [that went to the winner of the Martinsville race] and just having a blast as a kid."

Looking back on it years later, Kyle said that he always knew he eventually would follow in his father's footsteps. "When I grew up, I wanted to be a race car driver," he said. "I dreamed about driving a race car. That's all I dreamed about—driving a race car and getting a trophy."

He knew that there would be some drawbacks about going into the business with his famous last name, just as there would be other major advantages. "There are some negatives," he once told columnist George Vecsey of the *New York Times*. "You'll always be compared to your father. But a lot of us went with our families to the tracks and we got to know the business."

Kyle had been bugging his father to let him drive competitively on some level since he was sixteen. Richard kept pointing out that his own famous racing father, Lee, had made him wait until he was twenty-one. "You'll have to wait until you're twenty-one, too," he repeatedly told Kyle.

But in the spring of 1978, Kyle began working at the Petty Enterprises shop in Level Cross, with Richard's encouragement. Father saw it as an important first step if the son really wanted to learn how to drive. "He needs to work on the car," Richard said at the time. "He's got to understand everything about the car before he ever gets in and starts driving it. He goes to school a half day and then works in the shop. He tells me he definitely wants to try driving a car. Where he goes is anybody's guess."

It was then that Kyle also began working as a member of the pit crew, at least once school was out. His initial assignment was as the crew's designated tire carrier.

Richard was impressed with Kyle's dedication to the job. He had switched manufacturers from Dodge to Chevrolet in the middle of the previous Winston Cup season when he became dissatisfied with the handling of the Dodge Magnum. Several of the ill-handling cars were now sitting in a corner of the Petty shop collecting dust. Richard finally decided that maybe Kyle could drive one in the season-opening ARCA race at Daytona—a full three years ahead of the schedule the King had previously showed no signs of budging on.

The elder Petty said he had his reasons. "The trend today," he said at the time, "is toward the superspeedways. If [Kyle] did well on the short tracks, he'd have to unlearn everything he learned when he finally came to a big track. And if he can't cut it here, there's no sense in messing around on the short tracks."

So it was in late 1978 and early 1979 that Kyle, finally with Richard's blessing, received his first opportunity to climb into a race car and drive it on a real racetrack. He quickly discovered that nothing could compare with the rush one received while pushing an automobile to its limits. Upon going to Daytona

International Speedway with Dale Inman—Richard's second cousin, crew chief, and close family confidant—Kyle also discovered a few other things about driving a fast car that gave him the distinct feeling that he had much left to learn about the family business.

"We went down there and tested, and I was trying to help him," Inman said with a chuckle many years later. "And he was like a lot of kids that age—heck, he's still like that—he thinks he knows everything."

Richard talked at length with his son about drafting and about what line to take in the corners at Daytona. But in the end, he admitted that it would all be up to Kyle. "I can talk to him about things till I'm blue in the face," the King said. "But when it comes right down to it, he's going to have to go on instinct."

Kyle was just happy to be in Daytona, about to get behind the wheel of a fast race car. But he was still just an impressionable eighteen-year-old kid.

"The testing wasn't like it [would become in later years]. You'd call up the speedway and they would let you test or they wouldn't let you test," Petty recalled. "We only had a couple of days to test, and Goodyear had the racetrack, testing motorcycle tires with Kenny Roberts—who was road-race champion at the time.

"So we were down there, and I would go out and run two laps. And then Kenny Roberts would go out and run through the infield and run around the racetrack on that motorcycle. That was the coolest thing in the world, man—watching him run around that track on that motorcycle. I remember more about that than when I actually ran in the race."

Inman's job was to try to get Petty focused and to give him some valuable and much-needed seat time on the track where he would run his first race. But he could see Kyle was more consumed at the moment with a thousand other things in his life, including Pattie and his latest infatuation with the high-flying

motorcyclist who had caught his attention upon their arrival at
Daytona International Speedway. Inman tried to rein the kid in,
offering him some sound advice.

"Kyle, you're going to go out there and you'll be runnin' 190
mile an hour," he said as patiently as possible, as Kyle stared at
him with a bored, faraway look in his eyes. "And after you run it
a while, the sensation of speed goes away and you'll come down
pit road—and you'll think you're runnin' slow enough to stop
and bring the car into the pits. But it's going to be hard for you to
judge if you're really getting down slow enough to stop."

Inman was speaking from experience. He had seen driving leg-
ends such as A. J. Foyt, Mario Andretti, and Johnny Rutherford—
all winners of the Indianapolis 500—come to Daytona to try their
hand at stock car racing and have trouble stopping the heavier
stock cars, which weighed thirty-four hundred pounds, on pit road.

"I had seen Foyt, Andretti, and all of 'em come down there—
Johnny Rutherford and all of 'em—and the little Indy cars would
stop. But these cars were heavy and didn't all have good brakes
on 'em and all that. You had to know how to slow 'em down to get
'em to stop where you wanted," Inman said.

When he was done with his little talk, Kyle just looked at him
and said nothing. "He looks at me like, 'What the hell do you
know, old man?'"

Inman tried to remain patient. As they continued to test, he
told Kyle that they needed to practice stopping in the pits. "We'll
practice it one time. Go out there and run five laps. I'll bring you
in on the fifth lap. I'll hold the blackboard up for you so you know
where to stop," Inman said.

So Kyle went out and attempted to do as he was told. As he
came barreling into the pits at an obviously high rate of speed,
Inman was waving the blackboard and trying to count down to
where his pit stall was, as was the usual practice for Richard and
all other more experienced drivers.

"We had radios. So I was like, 'Pit five . . . pit four . . . pit three . . . pit two . . . pit one . . . pit!' So he comes down on the fifth lap and I'm standing there holding up the sign. He goes by me doing at least a hundred mile an hour," Inman said.

"So help me God, Kyle must have gone two hundred yards past me. He stopped right in the middle of pit road and got out of the car, and said, 'You moved.' It wasn't his fault. He said I moved, which I didn't."

Kyle laughed when remembering the moment many years later—except he recalled speeding past Inman even faster and traveling even farther before he could get the car to stop. "You didn't have a pit-road speed. You just come right down pit road. It's hard to run 190 and learn to decelerate and just stop. We went down there and tested and we practiced it. After a few times, you get used to it.

"But, yeah, that first time he was standing out there counting me down: 'Five . . . four . . . three . . . two . . . one.' And then I came by him runnin' about 200 miles an hour. I went all the way to the end of pit road.

"I finally stopped and got out of the car and looked all the way back to him. I was busting on him. I told him, 'You shouldn't have moved. I would have stopped where you were if you hadn't moved.'"

Inman's face, already red from the Florida sun, grew even redder.

In truth, Kyle appreciated Inman's expertise and knew he was sitting pretty as he prepared to delve deeper into the sport. His father even got on the track with him for several test runs, and continued to talk to him about what he needed to do to succeed. He knew he would have some of the best equipment the sport had to offer at the time, and that he should be faster than most of the other ARCA cars he would eventually race against. And he said his initial difficulties on pit road were more or less to be expected.

"Hell, I didn't drive a race car, period. That was the first place I ever raced, so it wasn't like I had ever come down pit road at Concord or Caraway or any place like that," said Petty, mentioning short tracks in North Carolina near where he had grown up. "I had never come down pit road anywhere. Daytona was the first pit road I ever came down. So I think when you look at it like that, I did okay."

The rest, in fact, turned out to look remarkably easy. Kyle went out and ran a qualifying lap of 189.243 mph, second-fastest on the grid behind only the 191.416-mph lap laid down by pole winner John Rezek.

The morning of the race, he claimed he didn't feel any pressure to win. "If it's there, I don't feel it," he said. "I'm not the favorite. I know I probably won't win the race."

Yet when the race began and Kyle took off in his blue-and-white Dodge sponsored by Valvoline, he went right to the front. He led most of the way in the 80-lap, 200-mile race, even though he still encountered some trouble slowing down to get into his pit stall for pit stops, and then getting out quickly again without stalling the engine. He ended up holding off Rezek by two car lengths for the victory, far exceeding the expectations of himself, Inman, and even the King.

"I went down there and I was eighteen years old. They give you a car that'll run 195 miles an hour," Kyle said. "You got guys that work on your car that know what they're doing. You got Richard Petty talking to you. You got Dale Inman working with you. What's your responsibility? I got no responsibility. I just had to sit in the car and turn the thing—so that's what I did.

"It's funny, when I try to remember the race I really don't remember a lot about it. Because I was just having fun."

Inman said he eventually had to tell Kyle to slow down a little, because he was getting too far ahead of the rest of the field at times during the race. Most of the other cars weren't nearly as well funded or maintained, and no one had a better pit crew because Kyle was using the same Cup crew—minus himself—that his father planned to use in the ensuing Daytona 500.

"We knew that particular [Dodge] Magnum drove good [compared to most of the other cars entered in the ARCA event]. But we were surprised Kyle ran that good," Inman said. "The problem was Kyle was running 190, and some of the other cars were running 140 and 150. That's the way ARCA was then. . . . They told him they would have a caution and tighten the field up if anyone got too far ahead."

Kyle came in to pit one time—actually stopped right where he was supposed to on this occasion—and then got out of the pits so quickly and so far ahead of the rest of the competitors that Inman was shaking his head. He knew what was coming next.

"We put about half a lap on 'em because they used Richard's pit crew and they got out so fast. So then they threw a caution," Inman said.

Eventually, Kyle slowed down enough to take the checkered flag. Just before it flew, driver Buddy Arrington, who would borrow one of Petty's old Dodge Magnums to drive in a Cup race at Talladega later the same year, told Richard, "A lot of people are going to be shaking their heads over this day for a long time."

Daddy was thrilled. "That was a big weekend for us. He got married the week before. Then he went down there on his honeymoon and he comes out and wins the very first race he's ever been on," Richard said. "See, he had never run Busch races or Saturday night races or go-kart races or motorcycle races. He had never been on a racetrack until we took him down to Daytona. We took him down there [beforehand] and tested a little bit, and then we took him back for the race.

"Poor Kyle. We just throwed him to the dogs to begin with."

Poor Kyle was feeling pretty rich and proud after winning the race, however. So was Richard and everyone else associated with the Petty Enterprises operation.

"It had to be special. In my mind, if he could just go out and run the whole race and have all four wheels rolling when it was over with, I would have been more than satisfied with that," Richard said. "But then we look up and he wins the race. That was beyond anybody's expectations."

It also was televised, or at least was going to be. As part of the agreement finally hammered out and shook on by Bill France Jr. and CBS executives earlier at France's favorite restaurant, Steak 'n Shake, at the corner of Nova Road and Highway 92 in Daytona Beach, the ARCA event was one of four that was taped by the network for later broadcasts. They also taped the inaugural Busch Clash, a 50-mile invitational event for pole winners from the previous season; and the two 125-mile qualifiers, which were shown the day before the 500.

All in all, it was quite a day for the younger Petty. Suddenly he was living the dream.

And then, just as suddenly, it was time to get back to reality.

"I was on my father's pit crew the next week. But that was my job: working on the pit crew and working on the car," he said. "My job back then wasn't driving a race car."

It was good for him, then, that his famous father knew a little more about when and where and how to stop it after getting it up to speeds approaching two hundred miles per hour.

•   •   •

As the rain slowed to a drizzle and then finally stopped on the morning of February 19, 1979, Mark Aumann was making his way to his grandstand seats at Daytona International Speedway. The son of an engineer who was a graduate of the General Motors Institute in Flint, Michigan, and had taken a job with Pontiac before Mark was born, Aumann was a student at the University of Florida in Gainesville. He was excited about meeting his father and watching the Daytona 500 live with him. It was to be Mark's second 500 in a row, having gone the previous year for the first time and greatly enjoying the experience.

"Dad was always interested in racing and took us to tracks. . . . But I had not seen a stock car race. Anyway, he had been to the 1961 Daytona 500 and he talked about how cool it was. So when I moved back to Florida to go to school I thought I would go to the race. I was only a couple of hours away," Aumann said.

"So I got a ticket to the '78 Daytona 500 three weeks before the race and it was the most I had ever spent on a ticket for anything. It was like $15. . . . The next year I talked to my dad and told him to come up from Broward County, where he was living then, and meet me and we'll go to the race. So I bought the tickets. I ended up with tickets at just about the entrance at pit road, coming toward the tri-oval. The year before I was down toward Turn 1. This time I was between 4 and the tri-oval."

The crowd and traffic had not been much of an issue the previous year, when Aumann had watched Bobby Allison win to break a sixty-seven-race winless streak while driving for legendary car owner Bud Moore. So he took his time after rising in Gainesville to find the weather disagreeable: cold, windy, and wet. Naturally, this time, the crowd and traffic did prove to be a problem as some roads leading into the track that he previously had used were shut down so traffic could flow from the other direction.

"It took two and a half or three hours to go eight miles. Dad had the same problems coming the other way. He ended up being up north and doubled back," Aumann said.

When they met up, Aumann noticed right away that his father had broken out some heavy-duty weather gear. "It was cold enough that he had a heavy woolen coat that he only wore when he was up in Detroit. It was cool enough to where it felt damp and chilly," Aumann said. "I don't think the TV ever showed that to its true effect. It was a good steady rain all morning and we looked at each other and thought, 'Well, we just wasted a whole day because of the weather.'

"But the race was scheduled to start at twelve-thirty, and by eleven-thirty the rain had tapered off. They put out the trucks and it was the wreckers going around. I don't remember the track being completely dry. There were some dark patches down on the apron below the yellow line. It was pretty dry to the top."

There also were some huge puddles just off the track in the infield areas. That could cause some trouble for drivers who might get knocked a little off the beaten path for some reason or another, Aumann and his father thought.

But at least now it appeared a certainty that the race would be run. That was good news for everyone.

Aumann remembered back to the 1978 race. One of the reasons he decided to come to that race was because he was a huge fan of A. J. Foyt, the open-wheel legend from Houston. Foyt liked to run the 500 every year and was, in truth, a big fan himself of the drivers who ran the NASCAR circuit regularly. Foyt had won the race in 1972 and figured to stand a good chance of doing it again in '78, having run the third-fastest qualifying lap behind pole sitter Cale Yarborough (187.536 mph) and Foyt's own Buick teammate, Ron Hutcherson.

"A. J. had always been my hero. After I lived in Florida [as a kid], my dad took a job in Houston," Aumann said. "So growing up, here was this guy from Houston and I liked open-wheel cars. I was a fan of the Indy 500. He won it twice before I got interested—and then when he won it again in '67 that cemented him as my favorite."

When Aumann first settled into his seat for the '78 race, he wasn't quite sure what to expect. What he discovered caught him off guard, but thrilled him nonetheless. "I had never been to a track that big. I had been to half-mile tracks. I don't think I had even been to a mile [track]," he recalled. "When you are at a grandstand at a half-mile, you can view the entire track without turning your head more than twenty-five or thirty degrees— basically sort of twist back and forth.

"I went to Daytona and they came out and made that first parade lap and you look at the entire field and they were moving around at a pretty leisurely pace. The second time they came by, they were going pretty fast. And then when they let the green flag go I was amazed because I had not gotten used to how to view cars going that quickly. If you look straight ahead, all you see is just a flash of colors go by. And you can't pick out any car at all."

Aumann kept searching for Foyt. "It took several laps before I got used to looking way down beyond the starting line and picking out a car and then swiveling quickly to Turn 1 so you could keep your eyes focused. It's natural now, but it felt very unusual for me back in '78," said Aumann, who would go on to cover many races for radio stations, newspapers, and, many years later, for the popular Web site NASCAR.com. "These guys were doing 190 miles per hour, and I think most of the places if they got over 90 miles per hour back then it was a huge surprise. Some of the biggest tracks I had been to were road courses so you never got that sensation of speed. It was really different."

There were no television replay screens should a fan miss something, nor were very many fans equipped with the scanners that monitored team radio traffic and would become so popular in later years. Basically, the fan was on his or her own. If you didn't catch what you were looking for with your own eyes, tough luck. And good luck next time the cars came flying around.

After a while, though, Aumann settled into the rhythm of watching the race. He picked out Foyt and mostly kept his eyes on him, tracking his favorite driver's progress.

On Lap 70 of the race, however, Benny Parsons blew a tire and it sent him spinning into the infield. Running directly behind Parsons, Foyt hit his brakes immediately but was drop-kicked from behind by Lennie Pond, who wasn't able to slow down quickly enough. Foyt's Buick careened off the track and began a wild series of flips. When it finally came to rest, Foyt was unconscious. He eventually regained consciousness but was rushed to the track infirmary and then to a local hospital, where he had to be kept overnight for observation.

Much to Aumann's horror, the accident unfolded right in front of him. "They were rolling right in front of me," he said. "When [Foyt] got tapped by Lennie Pond, he went barrel-rolling and probably flipped over about three or four times. Again, I wasn't used to the sensation of speed; the first thing I could think of was, 'Oh no, they've killed my hero right in front of me!'

"But he survived it. He was beat up, but he ended up being okay. That was a scary incident."

It was yet another reminder of how dangerous the sport could be. The day before the running of the 1979 Daytona 500, another such reminder occurred when Don Williams was involved in a fiery crash during the Sportsman race and had to be rushed to Halifax Hospital, where he remained in a coma the following day. Worse yet, Williams would linger in a semicoma, unable to speak or move, for the next ten years before finally passing away from injuries caused when a loose driveshaft careered through his windshield and struck him in the head during the accident.

"You make a choice in life," driver Buddy Baker said. "A test pilot or a race driver or a football player or a boxer, there are certain things in our sport you know can happen. You try to believe it won't happen, but you understand being at the wrong place at the wrong time just anything can happen."

•   •   •

As the rain ceased, the drivers prepared to climb into their cockpits for the running of the race. But as Aumann had duly noted from his seat in the grandstands, the track was far from dry just yet.

It was time, however, for the television broadcast to commence. Joining Ken Squier in the booth was David Hobbs, a veteran of many disciplines of auto racing but relatively unknown in NASCAR circles. Also on the broadcast team were former driving champion Ned Jarrett and respected auto racing writer Brock Yates of *Sports Illustrated*. They would work the pits during the event.

Race coverage opened with Squier and Hobbs talking about how fast pole sitter Buddy Baker had been all week. Jarrett did a quick interview from the pits with Herb Nab, Baker's crew chief. Nab did not look nervous. In fact, he was so calm that he was smoking a cigarette as Jarrett interviewed him and the cars began to roll onto the track behind them.

Then the announcers revealed another innovation that would be tested this day: the in-car camera mounted in Benny Parsons's machine. Secretly CBS executives were hoping Parsons would run well to give viewers more chances to understand stock car racing from the driver's perspective. Others weren't so sure it was going to work. And most of the other drivers didn't care whether it worked or not; they simply were glad it wasn't in their car because it weighed nearly thirty pounds, and none of them wanted to carry the extra weight in their cockpit.

Inside his No. 88 Oldsmobile sponsored by Gatorade, Darrell Waltrip sensed that it was still raining a bit. "We started the race in the rain, under caution. We rode around for I think what was about fifty miles, trying to dry the track. We didn't have the jet blowers back then. We just had the cars going around, trying to dry the track. We were trying to get the track dry so we can go green," Waltrip said.

"We ran fifteen or twenty laps or whatever it was. The track was starting to come in. The rain had ceased, and it looked like it was about time to go. They called me on the radio and asked me would I check the track. I was sitting on the outside of the second row because I had won my qualifying race."

They called it "being the rabbit," and it was not uncommon at the time. With no jet-engine dryers attached to the back of pickup trucks like what would be used in later years to quick-dry a track, in those days NASCAR officials relied mostly on the collective heat from the undercarriages of the cars to dry off the surface enough that it would at least be marginally safe to run on. Then the NASCAR control tower would radio down to one of the cars running near the front and ask to send a driver out to make a few fast laps to see if, well, it could be done.

It was risky business. If the track was slick, which it usually was at least in some places under such circumstances, what if the driver "being the rabbit" lost control and damaged his car or others during a fast lap?

Hobbs was curious about the practice, musing on-air, "What do they do if Darrell Waltrip blows up? Who sues who?"

Inside his car, Waltrip wasn't worrying about that. He had deeper concerns. "So I take off to be the rabbit—and my car is skipping. It's going around the racetrack and it's just skipping. Something had happened to the engine," Waltrip said. "I thought maybe we had filed down a spark plug, from all the slow driving we had been doing around the track while waiting for it to dry."

So Waltrip frantically started calling his crew chief on his radio. "Hey, there's something wrong with the engine," he said almost immediately after taking off to be the rabbit.

Much to Waltrip's surprise, the team members on the other end of radio sounded almost pleased. "Well then, this is great. You're going to get a chance to blow it out. Get it cleared out before they go green," they told him.

Waltrip wasn't convinced that was going to be the case. In fact, he thought he was screwed. "So I make the run around the track and something's still wrong with the engine. It won't go. I got a dead miss in it. That's my side of the story," Waltrip said. "They're finally ready to start the race, and I'm sitting there wondering what in the heck is going on with my engine."

Up in the grandstands, Aumann was unaware of Waltrip's troubles. In fact, he thought Waltrip looked pretty good during his stint as the rabbit. "It was interesting when they sent Darrell Waltrip out by himself. They sent him, and he ran three pretty fast laps and apparently he thought it was okay," Aumann said. "They announced they were going to run the first twenty laps under caution, but it wasn't your 55-mile-per-hour laps. They were probably going 110 or 120. They were trying to heat the track up with the engines and the tires at that point. Dry it out. They came by the first twenty laps, and we were all just waiting for that green flag to drop."

Bill France Jr. and Big Bill France were waiting tensely, too. So were all of the drivers and crew chiefs and even the fans watching on television, like Doug Rice, who remained snowed in but tuned in at his father-in-law's house in Salisbury, North Carolina. His father-in-law had met Cale Yarborough through dealings in the car business and had been a fan of the hottest driver in NASCAR ever since. Rice and his wife, on the other hand, were die-hard Richard Petty fans and, in particular, couldn't stand Waltrip.

But they were pumped. Here it was, right in front of them. Live and on television, with the promise that it would be televised from wire to wire. As Rice stared at the TV screen, he couldn't help grinning.

"Watching that thing unfold in the first half hour, we were thrilled because it was on television. We didn't care about the snow or anything else. We were about to watch the Daytona 500 live, from start to finish, and we had never been able to do that before," Rice said. "We just knew it was going to be great."

Neither they, nor the participants, nor the rest of America had any idea how truly great it would be.

4

The Gray Ghost

Sitting on the pole for the 500 was Buddy Baker, who had been having quite a week in Daytona. Baker wasn't like most other drivers, at least not in physical appearance. Many of the other drivers—with the tall, lanky Richard Petty being one of the notable exceptions—were on the short side in stature. That was considered an asset, especially when it came to climbing in and out of the cockpit of a race car, and never more so than when you needed to do it in a hurry to escape a wreck or a fire. But Baker looked more like an ex–college football player. He had to seemingly fold himself into the car when he drove. He had indeed been a fine football player in high school in Charlotte, North Carolina, going about six foot five, well over two hundred pounds, and with a raw-boned, ruggedly handsome look that as the years wore on projected an almost movie-star quality as he would stroll through the garage area.

Baker was on a roll during Speedweeks in 1979. After winning the Busch Clash, which later would become the Bud Shootout and included all of the pole winners from the 1978 races, he had backed that up by also winning his 125-mile qualifying race. He was so fast it was scary.

This, he was sure, was to be the year he won the Daytona 500. No one could run as fast as he could leading up to the race, so why should the race be any different? After trying to win the darn thing since 1961, when he finished fortieth in the fifty-nine-car field in the race won by Marvin Panch, this was to be his year. He felt certain of that.

In fact, things had gone so well for him all week he later said he "was beginning to feel like a rock star."

As with many drivers throughout NASCAR history, Baker grew up around racing. His father, Buck, was a two-time points champion and greatly influenced his career. Buck raced pretty much full-time from 1949 through 1967, then dabbled in Cup racing part-time off and on until retiring for good after making eight starts in 1976. In 636 starts in NASCAR's top division, he won forty-four poles and forty-six races.

"How many people have the chance to grow up in a house with a two-time national champion? If your dad is a banker and you're brought up in banking, naturally you'd probably end up being a banker," Baker said.

There were no bankers in the Baker household. Buck Baker was a hard-core, no-nonsense stock car driver, through and through. A former U.S. Navy man, he came up during the era when notorious party animals like Curtis Turner and Joe Weatherly drove like they lived—fast and loose and always with an eye on fun, often at the expense of others. This sometimes rankled ol' Buck, such as one time at the old Charlotte Fairgrounds when Turner was assigned the mundane task of driving the pace car for a Grand National event he wasn't slated to appear in because he was running mostly in NASCAR's old Convertible division at the time.

Max Muhleman, the local sports columnist for the *Charlotte News*, was standing nearby when Turner—dressed smartly in a gray-silver suit with a white shirt and tie—took his cue to jump in the pace car and fire it up.

"Hop in, Pop. Get in the backseat and you can see real good," Turner told Muhleman.

Muhleman hesitated. He knew firsthand of Turner's wild reputation, having hung out with him on the road many times. Eventually, though, he climbed in. Heck, Turner wasn't even in the race. He was just going to take his 1956 Ford convertible around the track a few times, setting the pace for the drivers who were racing and then getting out of their way by heading into the relative safety of the pit area.

"Being young and foolish enough, I agreed," Muhleman said later of his decision to climb in.

Shortly after clambering into the convertible, Muhleman noticed a familiar look in Turner's mischievous eyes. Right away, it unnerved the journalist, who knew that anything could happen when Turner gave in to his worst impulses.

"Curtis had had a few shooters, as he liked to call them, of Canadian Club—as was his form," Muhleman said. "He was just having fun."

He was about to have some fun with Buck Baker, who wasn't in the mood. At first everything went fine. Baker was sitting on the pole for the race, and was on the front row with Speedy Thompson. They were both driving Chryslers for eccentric car owner Carl Kiekhaefer.

"We started going around, and the pace car speed on a dirt track is pretty slow, which is what I had envisioned," Muhleman said.

It was what he wanted, too. As he turned in the backseat and looked at Baker and Thompson, Muhleman smiled to himself and thought, "Curtis was right. This is a pretty neat view."

Then they came around on the lap where they dropped the green flag after negotiating Turn 4. "And on a half-mile dirt track, that's very close quarters," Muhleman said.

About that time Turner turned in his seat, looked at Muhleman, and grinned. "Hey, Pop, you want to make a lap?" he asked, using racer's lingo for taking the car to its top speed.

"Nope, nope. God no, I don't want to make a lap," Muhleman replied. "Let's get the hell off the track like we're supposed to."

"Aw, no. We're going to make a lap," said Turner, laughing.

With that Turner punched it and took the pace car into Turn 1 sideways. There were no seat belts in the car, and Muhleman almost went flying out. Riding along behind, Buck Baker was not amused.

"[Turner] just laughed and went on," Muhleman said. "And of course it's not real smooth. There were a lot of bumps in there. I was desperately trying to find anything I could hold on to. I was trying to grab on to the bottom of the seat and hang on."

The race cars behind, including the one being piloted by Baker, were having trouble keeping up at first. Once they figured out what was going on, they became enraged that Turner was going so fast and wouldn't get off the track so the real race could start. Along with Thompson, Baker pulled up as close as possible and started yelling obscenities, flipping Turner the bird.

By that point, Muhleman was almost as scared of Baker as he was of Turner's reckless driving. "I thought I was going to go flying out of the car and get run over by Kiekhaefer's Chryslers," he said. "I was hanging on for dear life. I could see Buck. He was shaking his fist and all pissed off. He was running up like he was going to hit Curtis. Whenever I had time to squeeze in a look behind me, it never looked good.

"And in the front, here's Curtis laughing and driving like he's in a race. And I don't know if the wheels are going to fold up and fly off or what, or if we're going to get knocked through the fence by Buck, or if I'm going to go flying out of the car and get run over by the rest of the field. It was harrowing but memorable."

Later, that same description might have been used by Buck's son, Buddy, as he embarked on his own driving career in his father's footsteps. "From the time I was twelve or thirteen years old, I pretty much knew what I wanted to be. I just had to hope I had the talent to make it," Buddy Baker said.

His own father wasn't so sure he did. He hired Buddy to drive for him, but didn't give him a very long leash. Buddy had watched his daddy drive for years, and finally got his own chance at Columbia Speedway in South Carolina on April 4, 1959. He started eighteenth and finished fourteenth after suffering a broken shock absorber—unremarkable overall, but still five spots in front of his father.

His father obviously was not impressed. Buddy didn't last much longer driving for him. "I was lucky enough that my dad got me started, but two months later he fired me," Baker said.

To Buck Baker, it seemed the logical thing to do. "I promised you a start. I didn't promise you a career," he told Buddy. Then he added, "You will never appreciate anything if you have everything given to you."

In other words, Buck Baker was still ready to help. But he wasn't offering charity. His son had to earn his stripes as a NASCAR driver.

Buddy was bitter at first. He couldn't believe what he was hearing. "Dad, have you lost your mind?" he asked.

But Buck Baker's mind was set. And the old man could be stubborn. His son would have to find his way at first like aspiring drivers who didn't own the last name of Baker. He would have to do it the hard way.

Buddy Baker had always found it difficult to be patient, on the racetrack and in life. When he was born in Florence, South Carolina, he arrived so quickly that his parents never had time to get to the local hospital. Christened Elzie Wylie Baker, he was born at home.

"I was born in the house. I was in too big of a hurry to go to the hospital," Buddy said.

He had to learn patience working his way to the top in stock car racing. He drove more than a hundred races without a victory before finally landing a ride with the respected Ray Fox Sr. in 1966.

"I went out and started driving for other people, like Jess Potter out of Johnson City, Tennessee. You name 'em, I probably drove for 'em," Baker said. "I drove for just about everybody at one time in my life.

"When I had the opportunity to race for Ray Fox, that was my springboard. That's when I won my first major race [at Charlotte Motor Speedway in October 1967]. It led into me driving for some of the best car owners in the business. I drove for the Wood brothers and won for them. I drove for the Pettys and I won for them. I drove for Ray Fox—that got me all started—and won with him. Bud Moore and I won three straight Talladega races together."

He may have enjoyed driving for the legendary, straight-talking Moore the most, perhaps followed by the equally legendary Wood brothers, Glen and Leonard.

"Oh, he's the best," Baker said of Moore. "The nice part about Bud was when you walked through the front door he sat you down in that office in there, and when he got through with that little talk he did with you, you had a clear-cut version of who's the boss.

"We had like a twenty-second lead in Ontario [Motor Speedway, in California] one time—and he told me to slow down. Of course, when I slowed down the car started rolling better through the corner and it actually picked up speed. Our lap times went down."

Moore was furious. "Apparently you're not going to listen to me!" he shouted into his headphones, just before violently yanking them off and throwing them out into the infield.

Moore had his reasons for telling Baker to slow down, as Baker had gained a reputation for running his cars so hard that they often broke down late in races. Baker came more from the Junior Johnson school of thought on driving—push the car as hard and as fast as it would go until it wouldn't go any longer. If that got you into Victory Lane, fantastic; if not, at least you would know you gave it all you, and the vehicle, had.

●   ●   ●

In 1979, Baker was driving an Oldsmobile for Harry Ranier. And he liked how the team looked, right from the start.

"This was the super team," Baker said. "This was the best of the best. The best engine builder, the best machinist—all the way around. The owner was the perfect guy. I knew right away we were going to win some races together."

It certainly looked like he was going to be right during the early part of the season. As was the custom at the time, although few could understand why, the season actually opened more than a month before the Daytona 500 with the Winston Western 500 at Riverside International Raceway in Riverside, California. That race was run on January 14, 1979, with Baker finishing a respectable seventh. Darrell Waltrip won the race and the first-place prize money of $21,150, with David Pearson running second, Cale Yarborough third, and Donnie Allison fifth.

Baker backed up the Riverside run by getting on a serious roll during the pre-500 events in Daytona. "I won the first of what they call the Bud Shootout now," he said some thirty years later. "It was the Busch Clash then. I won it, won my qualifying race, and won the pole with a record time. I turned into a rock star almost. I won everything up to the race."

His No. 28 car was so dominant, it earned the nickname "the Gray Ghost."

"They called it the Gray Ghost for a lot of reasons," Baker said. "It was black and silver, and it was so much quicker than the other cars in the Busch Clash. Darrell pulled out once [to try and pass] and I pulled out five car lengths from him, so he dropped in and settled for second. That same car sat on the pole in the summer race there [nearly five months later]. It was like four or five miles per hour better than the next car.

"I helped in the building of it. When I got the opportunity to drive the 28 car in '79, if somebody told me the night before the race I wasn't going to win I would have punched them."

Baker had come close to winning the 500 previously, but had not yet been able to pull it off. He had an eighteen-second lead one year when a flat tire did him in. In 1971, he was driving for Petty Enterprises and running second to the King late in the race. After running Richard down from behind and getting on his tail, all of a sudden Dale Inman's voice came over his radio.

"We're not telling you not to race Richard, but if we're running first and second that's just about as good as we can do with two cars. Let's make sure you guys don't wreck each other," Inman told Baker.

Baker eased off. He ended up finishing second as Richard won his third Daytona 500.

"It wasn't team orders," Baker later added of the incident. "They never told me not to race him for the win. They just said don't wreck him. Let me tell you, second to Richard Petty isn't anything to be ashamed of.

"I'm not sure I could have beat him anyhow—but when I caught him, I ran him down from a good ways back. When I caught him with a few laps to go, I thought, 'As a team member, we'll finish first and second. I'm proud of that.'"

Still, as one season faded into the next and his own Daytona 500 victory remained elusive, Baker hungered to win the crown jewel event of the NASCAR circuit.

"I had a race locked up one other time and the timing chain broke. I was beginning to think, 'Well, I could run a Schwinn bicycle at Talladega and win. But the Daytona 500, maybe I won't,'" Baker said.

These feelings of uncertainty had faded by the time Speed-weeks were over in 1979 and Baker was rolling around Daytona International Speedway in front of everyone else. In fact, he felt almost invincible in the car as the race finally was about to go green.

"No way we're not going to win this thing," he said to himself confidently.

Sitting behind him on the starting grid, Richard Petty thought to himself, "Buddy's fast, to be sure. But the fastest car don't always win."

•　　•　　•

By the mid-1970s, ABC had become the undisputed leader of auto racing telecasts. In addition to beginning to televise the Indianapolis 500 in prime time on the same day the race was run—although tape-delayed by several hours—the network also was stepping up its coverage of NASCAR events. As early as 1970, the network had begun televising the final ninety minutes of a number of NASCAR events live, and of course there was the experiment in 1971 when it televised the entire 100-mile Winston Cup Grand National race live from the tiny track in Greenville, South Carolina. From 1974 through 1978, ABC had aired the final portion of the Daytona 500 live—usually televising the final two hundred miles or so.

But Big Bill France, still working behind the scenes even as Bill France Jr. was technically the France in charge of NASCAR, wanted more. It was during Speedweeks of 1978—even as ABC-TV was preparing to do its fifth consecutive Daytona 500 telecast—that negotiations began in earnest with CBS to have the 500 aired live in its entirety. Barry Frank, senior vice president of CBS Sports, was doing the negotiating on the television side along with Neal Pilson and some others. And to no one's surprise,

Big Bill was actively involved in the talks along with Bill Jr. from the NASCAR side. The deal, in fact, was technically between the track where Big Bill was still president and the network, more so than between NASCAR and the network.

Reporters got wind of the proceedings and pressed the elder France about it around the close of Speedweeks in 1978. He put them off, but did admit that he had held some talks with CBS. The two sides continued talking even after Darrell Waltrip and Ken Squier made their "dog and pony show" pitch to a group of CBS affiliates in the spring. When the parties finally came to an agreement, the younger France splurged and took CBS executive Pilson to lunch at one of his favorite restaurants: the Steak 'n Shake in Daytona Beach.

The official announcement of their history-making agreement came on May 15, 1978, in New York City. Frank and executive producer Bernie Hoffman revealed that CBS had signed a five-year contract with Daytona International Speedway to televise the Daytona 500 from start to finish, beginning in 1979. The network would set aside four hours to air the entire 500-mile race.

"These are the finest stock car drivers in the world," Frank said. "It assures CBS of a strong viewing audience. It is the gemstone of our major auto racing package."

One of the next tasks for the network was to figure out who would be part of the telecast. Ken Squier was tabbed, naturally, to be the play-by-play announcer. To the surprise of some, David Hobbs was signed to be his color man in the booth; he would be counted on to provide expert insight into a sport he had only dabbled in himself, with most of his previous experience as a driver and commentator coming in other forms of auto racing.

The two pit reporters made more sense. One would be Brock Yates, the respected writer from *Sports Illustrated*. He also would work on some feature stories before the race that would be sprinkled in throughout the telecast to provide some behind-the-scenes insights into the world of stock car racing. The other would be Ned Jarrett, the former driving champion who had been making a name for himself in the broadcasting world since his retirement as a driver in 1966. Squier had worked with Jarrett and thought highly of him as a person and a broadcaster, and Squier made the recommendation that Jarrett be brought on board as part of the broadcast team.

While the selection of Jarrett to fill a prominent role made sense in 1978, it might not have seemed logical to anyone had it been predicted while he was driving to a points championship years earlier in 1961. The son of a farmer and sawmill operator, Jarrett was quiet and shy, sometimes painfully so. He did not normally enjoy the spotlight in any way, shape, or form.

Upon winning the championship, however, Jarrett pledged to change all of that. "The thing that got me into broadcasting— originally in radio—was that after I won the championship in 1961 I had foresight to take a Dale Carnegie [self-improvement] course," he said. "I grew up in the country working on the farm and in the sawmill, and I didn't have many opportunities to talk, other than to close family and friends. I was somewhat of a shy type of an individual."

He also was a smart individual and realized what he needed to do to prepare himself for a better future after his driving career.

"After I won the championship, I didn't know how to handle the situation of being a national champion. I didn't feel like I could represent my sport or my family the way I wanted to," Jarrett said. "So I took the course and that got a good bit of attention because it was the first time anyone had heard of a someone [in racing] trying to improve themselves in that manner—as opposed to just always trying to get better at driving race cars.

"As a result, what few media people were covering the sport at the time sought me out—because once you go through the Dale Carnegie course you want to tell the world what you know. So it changed me completely from a guy who walked around with his head down to one who was looking people in the face. That fourteen weeks taught me there is a better way. And so [the media] sought me out for interviews, and that opened the door to go into broadcasting when I decided to quit driving in 1966."

The cost of the Dale Carnegie course: $150.

The value of it over the next four decades to Ned Jarrett: priceless.

"It was the best $150 I ever spent," he said.

Hank Schoolfield, who operated the Bowman Gray track in Winston-Salem, North Carolina, also ran a radio racing network. He got wind of Jarrett's new air of self-confidence and decided to hire him shortly after Jarrett retired as a driver.

"Hank had a universal racing network, and that was the dominant racing network of the time," Jarrett said. "That was before MRN [Motor Racing Network] was getting started. So anyway they asked me to work with them on the radio broadcasts. And if I had not taken that Dale Carnegie course, I'm sure I would have not have been asked to do that."

That soon led to other opportunities, but none as great as the one that he was presented with when Squier told him he wanted him to be part of the first announcing team to bring an entire Daytona 500 to the nation on live television. Jarrett knew right away that he was being asked to be part of something that should be very special.

"This was definitely a groundbreaking situation," Jarrett said. "I had worked with Bob Montgomery and Schoolfield on a deal where the Daytona 500 was televised live to theaters across the country in 1967 and 1968. I'm not sure if it was done any more than that.

"But I worked in the booth on both of those races with Bob Montgomery. It was not a network telecast, but we did them from start to finish and they were pumped into theaters around the country. I did a tour starting on January 1, 1967, and we visited twenty-one major cities during the month of January to try and promote this thing. We went to the towns where it was being shown, and that was quite an experience."

Asked years later how successful those theater efforts were, Jarrett was succinct and right to the point with his answer. "I guess it was successful, but it couldn't have been real successful or they would have continued on with it," he said.

So when the announcing team for the CBS telecast was rounded out in the spring and summer of 1978, Jarrett was ecstatic to be part of it. He sensed also that the live, wire-to-wire telecast could be a watershed moment for NASCAR.

"I was thrilled to death because I knew it was going to be good for NASCAR and for the sport of auto racing," Jarrett said. "For me to be a part of that was beyond my comprehension."

It shouldn't have been. He was perhaps the most experienced broadcaster with a background as a successful former driver available to the network.

"I had been doing a number of things for the racing network that they packaged and syndicated. I worked with Mike Joy and Ken Squier on some of those," Jarrett said. "I would fly up to Syracuse, New York. I guess that was the only television station they could use. They had to do it after the eleven o'clock news when the equipment was down. It wouldn't be used [by the station] until the next morning.

"We would go in and do voice-overs until four o'clock in the morning. I say that to make the point. I had experience at it. It was not live other than those teleprompt events but I continued to do radio during that time, too—so I would have been a natural choice because I had more experience than anyone else. But it was still mind-boggling to think that I was going to be on the national network live. That was a thrill."

So was working with Squier, who more or less had handpicked the rest of the broadcast team he would be working with. Jarrett had always admired Squier. "He was a great leader and had a great voice and he knew the sport. He was great to work with because he would allow you to use your strengths and allow you to build upon those strengths to help the telecasts."

For Jarrett, that meant adding his expert commentary to whatever insight might be offered by those he interviewed in and around the pits. "I had enough experience at radio that it came sort of natural," he said. "And I tried to let the focus be on them, not myself. I don't know how it turned out on TV. But it wasn't that I wanted to be on camera that much. Sometimes you needed to be. But I wanted the focus to be on them. I put it out of my mind that 'Hey, we're on national television and we're live.' And we just tried to do the job like I had been doing radio for a number of years."

The rest of the broadcast team tabbed by Squier and approved by CBS included color commentator Hobbs, who worked with Squier in the booth; and the journalist Yates, who would work one-half of pit lane while Jarrett worked the other.

Hobbs was born in Royal Leamington Spa, England, just months before the outbreak of World War II. He had driven race cars for decades in various disciplines, including making two Winston Cup starts in 1976, when he actually led the Daytona 500 for two laps. He had raced touring cars, Indy cars, and Formula One cars. In other words, he knew his stuff when it came to racing—despite those NASCAR purists who might have been put off initially by his English accent. Some also looked at him as the CBS version of Jackie Stewart, the more famous former driver and color commentator who had worked the previous five Daytona 500 telecasts for ABC, four of them with legendary play-by-play man Keith Jackson.

"I didn't know much about him before then," Jarrett said. "I didn't know David that well, but he was a blast to work with. He was a friendly guy and very knowledgeable of the sport, and he had a unique way of putting things. I think it added a lot to the telecast."

Not everyone agreed. Sitting in his father-in-law's home in snowbound Salisbury, North Carolina, as the race got under way, Doug Rice wondered what the Englishman was doing in the booth.

"I still to this day wonder why David Hobbs was on the broadcast because he just didn't seem to fit," said Rice, who later would go on to become a respected and well-known race announcer himself with Performance Racing Network. "He was knowledgeable, but maybe this is tainted from watching it again [later on videotape]. Clinically he knew racing, but to me there was a disconnect between his intimacy and NASCAR's type of racing.

"At one point during the race, he said, 'They raised the bonnet on the car.' That was first time I ever heard that as opposed to 'the hood is up on the car.'"

Rice didn't have that problem with Jarrett.

"I remember Ned Jarrett and I was familiar with him," Rice said. "I remember him being the pit reporter and his style was so much more conversational. You couldn't ask him to be an announcer. He was Ned Jarrett. He always had a catchphrase. Like he would say they were 'unbuckling their safety paraphernalia.' I think that might have been the first time I heard that word. He was very authoritative."

So was Yates. "Brock Yates at the time was considered one of the top writers in motor sports," Jarrett said. "He was knowledgeable—not so much the technical side but on the overall sport, and he had a different perspective there."

Yates was to provide quick-hitting news bites from the pits during the race. All of these things would come to be the norm in race telecasts in future years, but were considered groundbreaking at the time.

Neal Pilson of CBS later would tell writer Jerry Bonkowski of Yahoo! Sports in 2008, "We figured that for three and a half hours, we had to give the public more than just roundy-rounds. We had to get inside the race itself, talk about driver personalities, interview the drivers and crew chiefs, talk about the cars."

Jarrett didn't know much about "roundy-rounds" or "raising the bonnet," but he had some ideas of his own to enhance the telecast.

"My goal was to watch from the technical side [of television] as well as helping to keep up with what was going on in the race itself," he said. "Even though I was working in the pits, God gave me some ability to keep up with the race—which is not an easy thing to do. It's easier now with all of the computers and the [electronic loop] scoring, but we didn't have all of that stuff then. I was just gifted in that sense that I could keep up with what was going on, even though I was working in the pits. That was one of my strengths."

Yates worked the pits with Jarrett, but each knew his territory. They really didn't have any choice; there was no way they could cross over into the other's.

"We didn't have remote type equipment," Jarrett said. "We had cables that you had to drag and we were limited as far as how far you could go. Yates was set up on one end of the pits and I was on the other end. We had enough cable where we could go only so far, to the middle, where we could meet each other.

"We had people that dragged those cables, and that was a chore running up and down the pits with the people in there—especially when you needed to get somewhere in a hurry. That's one thing that I came to appreciate once you got the equipment where you could go anywhere you wanted to and didn't have anything attached to you. You didn't realize how hard it was until we got something better [years later]."

●   ●   ●

Baker led the first fifteen laps of the race, which were run under caution. But his confidence faded rapidly almost as soon as the green flag dropped on Lap 16. Donnie Allison quickly surged into the lead in his No. 1 Oldsmobile owned by Hoss Ellington as Baker's car faltered.

Having brought the same camera crew to the race that had done the Super Bowl only a few weeks earlier, CBS tried to give the viewers at home as many different viewing angles of the race as possible. They had a total of nineteen cameras in place— impressive for the day, but far short of the seventy-seven that would be in put in place by Fox Sports for the fiftieth running of the Great American Race in 2008.

One of the favorite camera angles was an overhead view, but this time the opening overhead shot didn't come from the Goodyear blimp. It came from a helicopter, and even the heli- copter initially wasn't permitted to fly because of the lingering poor visibility that resulted from the rainstorm that had raged through the area prior to the race. When the weather did clear enough, the helicopter could fly for only relatively short periods of time before having to land and refuel. The famous blimp finally made its appearance and took over providing the popular over- head shots when the cloud cover lifted altogether.

As Donnie Allison surged to the lead, the helicopter provided a glimpse of what was taking place. Cale Yarborough settled into second, Benny Parsons (who was carrying the first in-car camera in NASCAR history) was in third, Bobby Allison fourth, and Darrell Waltrip fifth.

Soon, though, they started battling back and forth in a seven- car draft, even as Baker began fading quickly. Yarborough passed Donnie Allison for the lead going into Turn 4, but soon Parsons executed the famed Daytona "slingshot" pass on Yarborough and took the lead as Bobby Allison passed his brother and moved into third, shuffling Donnie back into fourth.

Baker, meanwhile, was fuming inside his "Gray Ghost."

"We took off when the green flag started and right away had engine trouble," Baker said. "It was skipping and popping. When it just started skipping, it went from a 205-mile-per-hour car to 180."

Right away, Baker had a thought. "If we just don't panic and we can figure out what's wrong and get it fixed, we can still win this Daytona 500," he told his crew.

He couldn't have known, but it was a relatively simple problem with ignition wires that was causing the problem. His crew chief, Waddell Wilson, would not discover this until a day later upon getting a closer look at the car in their Charlotte shop.

Baker said, "I tried to diagnose what was wrong. The first thing I said was I think we broke a timing chain, which got everybody looking at everything other than the electrical."

Meanwhile, Baker faded not only from the lead but soon was out of the race after a total of only thirty-eight laps. He pitted to try to fix the problem and the car went dead. It wouldn't restart.

Baker said, "What was disappointing was everybody got into just a madhouse about the car. When I said something's happened to it, it won't run. One guy fixed it by plugging in the secondary ignition. Another guy got excited and jumped in and unplugged it and put the bad one back in. So we got home and Waddell Wilson, who built the motor, said, 'I can't believe you had motor trouble.' So he got in there and unplugged it and plugged it in the second ignition, fired it up, and it ran better than it did when we left home. We took that same car there the next year and sat on the pole and won the race. I feel fairly certain that if we had not panicked, we would have won two Daytona 500s in a row."

Baker could not believe how simple the problem that put him out of the race would have been to fix. "You want to talk about a sick pup. It would have been nothing to do," he said. "The reason it happened the way it did, they welded on the car that morning and didn't take all the connectors loose from the ignition. The secondary [ignition] was all right. We got home and Waddell Wilson said I can't believe that's all it was. If I knew that then, we could have gotten back out. I could have made up four or five laps, as good as that car was over everybody else."

Instead, his day was done. His dream of winning the Daytona 500 would have to wait another year.

5

Peaches and Black-Eyed Peas

As Baker faded from the front of the pack, the lead changed hands twice more before Lap 31 was complete. First Bobby Allison passed Benny Parsons to move to the front, and then Darrell Waltrip, even though he was experiencing some engine troubles of his own, surged to the lead as the elder Allison fell behind his brother Donnie and a couple of others. Most of the cars were still running together in a pack, with a mere three seconds separating first place from thirteenth.

Running so close at high speeds, it seemed only a matter of time until there was trouble—and the drivers found it on Lap 32. It started with the Allison brothers, as Bobby appeared to get into the left rear fender of Donnie in Turn 2 on what Hobbs called "the spookiest place on the track." As Donnie came off the turn and drifted low, Bobby—perhaps with a little aerodynamic assist from behind from Cale Yarborough—drifted just a tad high and clipped Donnie, sending Donnie spinning and almost airborne before he pinwheeled off into the sopping wet infield. Bobby went spinning off the track and into the infield as well, eventually coming to rest against an earth berm that was the only thing standing between him and a trip to the depths of Lake Lloyd. Yarborough drove straight through the middle of the mayhem from behind but soon found himself flying at high speed through several huge puddles of water in the infield, water spraying out from underneath both sides of his Junior Johnson–owned Oldsmobile bearing the familiar No. 11.

"Bobby Allison just taps his little brother and that's all there is to it," Hobbs said.

Squier added excitedly, "Bumper tag at 195 miles per hour—and you see the results!"

The biggest problem all three drivers faced immediately was getting their cars out of the mud and back onto the track, where they could coax their damaged machines onto pit road for repairs. Crew members from each team ran to the scene and began pushing the vehicles out of the mud as best they could. Despite considerable damage, including a gaping hole in one side of his machine and damage to a tie rod that affected his steering before being repaired, Donnie Allison's engine was fine and he roared out of the pits after a couple of quick stops under caution. He was back onto the track after losing only one lap. Yarborough's biggest dilemma after getting extracted from the mud was drying his engine out. He, too, got back on the track eventually, but not before falling three laps behind the leaders. Bobby Allison emerged from the melee two laps down.

As Donnie Allison left pit road, Brock Yates noted the damage to his car, and offered this opinion: "The car doesn't sound very strong. We wonder how long he can last."

About the same time, Ned Jarrett interviewed Baker as he sat in his car on pit road, crew members frantically working on the Gray Ghost.

"What went wrong out there, Buddy?" Jarrett asked.

"I don't know, Ned. Something is fouled up with the engine and it won't run," Baker replied.

Shortly thereafter, Baker was back in the pits again and being interviewed for the last time on the day by Jarrett. The pole sitter was ready to call it a day, his face lined with creases of deep disappointment.

"I can't believe this. . . . I guess we'll have to come back next year and try again," Baker stammered.

He wouldn't know the truth until he, and the car, returned to Charlotte and Waddell Wilson could get a closer look at it. Then the disappointment would hit him even harder, as he realized the ignition problem could have been easily fixed.

Meanwhile, back on the track, the Allison boys and Yarborough were being left to cope with the hand that had been dealt them. Or rather the one they had been left with after Bobby got into the back of Donnie.

"There is still plenty of time left to get back in this race," Donnie told himself.

Initially running three laps off the pace, Yarborough was thinking the same thing. So was his car owner and crew chief, Junior Johnson.

"We're fast. Just keep digging and we'll get back up there," Johnson told his driver.

Back in the broadcast booth, Squier was filled with excitement that seemed to spill over to viewers all across America. "Talk about an event-filled race. This is it!" he said.

No one could argue with him.

•   •   •

Naturally, the headstrong Bobby did not think the accident on Lap 32 was his fault. He blamed Yarborough. But then Bobby usually did blame someone else, and with good reason. It usually was someone else who messed up.

Bobby Allison knew he was stubborn and oftentimes a little impatient with other human beings. He knew he could have a temper.

He liked to tell the story about how, at age fourteen, he was working under the hood of an old Model T Ford that belonged to the headmaster of the Catholic school he was attending. Even at that early age, he already had gained a reputation as someone who could tune up engines.

Noticing young Bobby's feet sticking out from underneath his car, the headmaster stopped and asked, "Mr. Allison, have you found the problem?"

"No, not yet," he replied quietly.

The headmaster did not hear him. "I say, Mr. Allison, have you found the problem?"

Allison thought he had just answered the question. Frustrated that he hadn't yet figured out what was wrong with the car and irritated with the questioner for interrupting, the novice mechanic now answered plenty loud enough for the headmaster to hear.

"Hell, no! I haven't found the problem yet, okay?"

Then Bobby realized to whom he was speaking. He popped his head out from under the car and began to apologize profusely to the headmaster, whose scowl spoke volumes. At age fourteen, Bobby Allison already was building a reputation as someone who spoke his mind and often got himself in trouble for it.

In his early and formative years, the elder Allison worked weekends at his father's hydraulic car lift business and gave little or no thought to driving a race car for a living. But after an uncle took him to a modified stock car race at the fairgrounds dirt track near what would become his adopted hometown of Hueytown, Alabama, Allison was hooked on the sport. From that moment on, he seemed to spend every spare moment studying the race cars and their drivers. He found himself harboring an overwhelming urge to race.

He worked to buy his first race car, which doubled as a means to get him to school during the week. After a while, once race officials realized how young he was, they required a parental permission slip to let him run in events. His mother, who had no idea he had been running in races on previous Saturday nights, balked at the idea. Night after night, Bobby begged her to sign the permission slip. She finally relented, thinking it was a one-time deal. Bobby thought otherwise; he took it as a sign of perpetual parental permission, and was off to the races.

He never asked for permission again. When he wanted to enter a subsequent race, he borrowed the driver's license of a friend and raced under the assumed name of "Bob Sunderman." That worked for a while, until Bobby's father saw his son's photo in the local newspaper. Imagine his surprise when he saw his grinning son, identified not as Bobby Allison but as Bob Sunderman, celebrating yet another victory at the local dirt track.

"If you're going to race, you might as well use your own name," he told his son.

His mother took longer to win over, but eventually she, too, gave in to Bobby's new obsession.

Humpy Wheeler remembered one time when young Bobby Allison was racing at Bowman Gray Stadium in Winston-Salem, North Carolina. Curtis Turner was one of the big stars of NASCAR's Grand National circuit at the time, while no one had any idea who in the heck Bobby Allison was. At first Allison made them remember for all the wrong reasons.

"Bobby showed up on the circuit in a little Chevelle, and this was when the rest of the guys were running big cars. We had big Fords, big Plymouths, and big Dodges," Wheeler said. "And here comes this little maroon-and-white Chevelle. It was sort of almost a joke at the time.

"He was a rookie driver, almost by himself. He had his brother Eddie with him and that was it. But, boy, was he competitive."

That much quickly became clear as the race progressed and Allison's little Chevelle kept pressing Turner's big ol' Ford for the lead.

"No one knew who Bobby was at the time," Wheeler said. "He was a guy who won a prolific amount of short-track races, but so what? So did most of the people running that race.

"They were at Bowman Gray, the flat quarter-mile track, which was hard to pass on. But Bobby kept trying. Turner was driving a Ford, and the track wasn't but thirtysomething feet wide. Turner could block a racetrack better than anybody I've ever known."

Eventually, though, Allison wore Turner down and briefly took the lead—much to the surprise of everyone but Bobby. It didn't last long, though, as Turner ran him down and simply—literally—ran him off the racetrack. A star of Turner's magnitude wasn't about to let a rookie driver in a weak car get the best of him.

"So Curtis got by the last few laps. That was like an elephant versus an ant with the little old car Bobby had," Wheeler said. "And so Curtis won the race after he knocked Bobby out.

"They didn't have a winner's circle there. They just had the start-finish line, and that's where they had the victory celebration. Curtis's car was sitting there."

All of a sudden, Bobby Allison's Chevelle came rushing back into the picture before Turner could properly set off his latest victory celebration.

"Here comes Bobby driving his car backward, wide open," Wheeler said. "You knew exactly what was going to happen because you'd seen it a hundred times on some little quarter-mile dirt track. He slammed right into Curtis's car."

Bobby jumped out of his car and wanted to fight, but Turner backed off. He thought this newcomer was crazy, just crazy enough to be dangerous. He also made a mental note that Bobby had just driven the heck out of an underpowered race car—and almost beat him.

"Curtis Turner was a lover, not a fighter," said Wheeler, laughing at the memory many years later. "He would do anything to get away from that, so he kindly let some folks step in and break it up."

Wheeler and the others who witnessed the Bowman Gray incident found Bobby Allison very hard to forget. "He loved to race more than any human being I've ever known," Wheeler said. "He would race seven days a week. Sometimes he did if he could, wherever it took him. And he had an abandon on a racetrack that was pretty extraordinary, particularly later when he got to running on the superspeedways."

But it was on the short tracks such as Bowman Gray where Bobby Allison, and his younger brother Donnie, made names for themselves.

"We ran a lot of short tracks, kept busy all the time," Bobby said. "We ran three or four nights a week during the heavy part of the season a lot of times, and sometimes even more than that. And we worked on our own equipment. It was important to have that conditioning—but we got our conditioning from all the work we were doing."

Well, that was only partly true. Bobby supplemented the work he was doing by driving around the Alabama countryside during the steamy summer months with his car windows rolled up tight and the heat blasting. He said it was to further condition himself for the rigors of running long, hot NASCAR races.

"What was the most funny about riding around in the car with the heater on in the summertime was the guys [around town] who were over there sweating with their tongues hanging out," he said. "Really, it was more about having fun to see that than it was for the conditioning. But I did do that, yes."

Bobby fielded his own cars in 1965, battling better-financed Winston Cup teams on a shoestring budget. It was in 1966, when he won three times and finished tenth in NASCAR's points standings, that he attracted the interest of the Ford Motor Company and the legendary John Holman and Ralph Moody of Holman-Moody Racing.

He and Holman had nothing in common and feuded almost from the start. It was like fixing the headmaster's car all over again every time, as Bobby drove for—and almost always eventually feuded with—owners such as Junior Johnson, Bud Moore, Harry Ranier, Mario Rossi, Richard Howard, Bill and Jim Gardner, and Bill and Mickey Stavola.

Allison started winning regularly at the Grand National/Winston Cup level about the same time Yarborough did. They soon developed an intense rivalry, as Bobby also did with the great Richard Petty.

Off the track, Allison could be engaging and even friendly with most of his competitors. It was an act that didn't match up with how he was on the track.

"I like to shake hands and smile with people off the track," he once said. "But don't let that fool you."

Wheeler added, "Bobby was combative. He was a tremendous, tremendous competitor."

And fellow driver Neil Bonnett once said of him, "If there is anybody tougher or more determined than Bobby, I've never met them."

His resolve to win at all costs soon became legendary, and he did not deny it. "I believe if I'm even on the lead lap going into the last lap, I'll win," Bobby said at one point around the running the 1979 Daytona 500, when he was driving the No. 15 Ford for Bud Moore. "I will find a way or I'll crash."

He didn't crash at Daytona in 1978, when he finally won his first 500 after years of trying and falling short. In the process, he had displayed his tenacity and persistence by coming from farther back in the field than any previous winner of the race—having started thirty-third. He thus came into the '79 race with naturally high expectations, and remained determined even after the Lap 32 fracas with his little brother and Yarborough.

•   •   •

Two years younger than Bobby, Donnie Allison followed his older brother into stock car racing determined to make a name for himself, partly because Bobby once told him he'd never make it as a driver. Like Bobby, and sometimes more so than Bobby, Donnie had his opinions and could state them loudly and with little concern for anyone who might disagree with him.

The brothers grew up together on 19th Street on the north side of Miami, Florida, with Donnie being the sixth of thirteen Allison children. Perhaps that is why the two brothers weren't afraid to speak up and have their voices heard, and to back it up with their fists if need be; in a house of thirteen kids, you had to let your presence be known or you might just go hungry, or worse. Donnie grew up with what he felt was a clear sense of what was right and what was wrong. He believed in treating those around him fairly, and never straying from his beliefs, even if the rest of the world seemed against him.

The pair learned how to budget their money the way most people do: out of necessity. There was a time early in their driving careers when they were racing modified coupes up and down the East Coast, pulling their own cars. They would pool their money and buy bushels of peaches, which they would then consume for breakfast, lunch, and dinner. If there ever was a decision to be made between buying parts for their cars and eating something more— or even anything at all—they had a mutual understanding that the race cars came first.

Although they grew up in Florida, they would gain racing fame together as members of the "Alabama Gang," along with Bonnett and another Florida transplant who had earlier ended up settling in Hueytown, prolific short-track driver Red Farmer. Through his conversations with Farmer and other drivers making the rounds at the short tracks then, Bobby learned that tracks in Alabama paid more money across the board than anyplace else in the Southeast. So he talked Donnie into moving there with him. Part of the move was financed when Donnie sold a shotgun their father had given him for thirty-five dollars; anything else Donnie had left over went to buy more parts for his race car.

Donnie operated in Bobby's shadow from the start. Bobby was offered a ride in the Daytona 500 in 1961 by his brother-in-law Ralph Stark, starting thirty-sixth and finishing thirty-first in the fifty-eight-car field. That marked the beginning of a long career that eventually would include 716 starts and eighty-five victories, including three Daytona 500 victories, even though it wasn't until 1966 that Bobby ran a full-time schedule.

Donnie, meanwhile, didn't make his first Grand National start until 1966 and didn't win until two years after that, when he beat Bobby to the finish line by two laps to win at Rockingham, North Carolina. Through the years, Rockingham—and almost every track on the Winston Cup circuit—became a special place for the extended Allison families.

"We'd show up at Rockingham and we had a grass area out there where all the families, all the wives and kids, would get together," Donnie said.

Even Bill France Jr. and his wife, Betty Jane, would come out and join the crowd, which always included the Petty family and the two Allison families. "It was one big family," Donnie said. "We all watched them raise their kids, and they all watched us raise ours. Really, that's the way it was and that's what this sport was built on.

"Big Bill France had the dream, but the France family built this organization. And I mean it's the whole family. Anybody who knows me knows that I can get hacked off at the Frances, too. I have been against their side several times. But by the same token, when it comes down to the nitty-gritty and you look at the way the sport was built, and what makes it thrive, it's that it's still the only family sport we've got going.

"For me, it's perfect family entertainment. . . . The women and children, the moms and the sisters, can all be involved to some degree with the effort that's going on in the race. It's a great sport, it's great entertainment, and it can involve the whole family."

Rockingham was where Donnie earned his first NASCAR Grand National win, but Talladega was where Donnie and Bobby loved to race after it opened in 1969. Not everyone did, of course, but as charter members of the Alabama Gang and as two of the better superspeedway drivers then operating, they loved the place.

"It was just an amazing place to go around," Bobby said.

Bobby remembered going to Talladega to run some of the first test laps at the new track, for Chrysler. He wasn't yet the big star he was to become a short while later. "For the Chrysler car test at Talladega, I was in awe. But it took me a while to get in a car," he said. "The Chrysler deal was at the track all week and they never got me in a car until Saturday afternoon. And I went out and went around and went the fastest of any of the Chrysler guys by a pretty good margin."

The Chrysler engineers and officials huddled after that, studying their charts and speed figures. Then, according to Bobby, they emerged from their meeting and said something to the effect of, "Well, we're going to study the tapes, and see how this dummy from Alabama can beat all our hot-dog racers."

Buddy Baker and Charlie Glotzbach were their top drivers at the time. Several other drivers were on hand for the test. None posted a faster time than the 199.90 mph that Allison registered.

"We're going to keep Allison and Baker and Glotzbach and run again tomorrow afternoon," the Chrysler officials said.

At the time, breaking the 200-mph barrier was considered a pretty big deal in NASCAR. It hadn't been done before, not even at Daytona. Bobby Allison, always the competitor, wanted to be on record as the first to do it.

"So we came back the next day, and they realized that I held the steering wheel straighter than the other competitors," Bobby said. "And when you'd wiggle the wheel, the car would wiggle and aerodynamically it would scrub off speed. They let the other guys run and run, and they got going pretty good. They finally let me back in the car late Sunday afternoon."

He turned two laps. Then the engine blew up.

The Chrysler guys almost didn't even care. They checked and rechecked their stopwatches: Allison's two lap times were 200.001 mph and 200.009 mph. They called everyone at the test together, including Bobby.

"Okay, we don't want Ford to know we went 200 miles per hour, so anyone who lets the word out is fired. So go on home," they told Bobby and the rest, with one exception, as Bobby later found out.

"They kept Buddy Baker around and changed the engine, and so he did the first official 200-mile-per-hour lap," Bobby recalled nearly four decades later. It still rankled him that he hadn't been given credit for the first 200-mph lap at Talladega.

Donnie and Bobby liked to race together at the superspeedways like Talladega and Daytona. They understood the art of drafting, and the importance of working together to get the most out of it. They entered the 1979 Daytona 500 prepared to hook up in the draft yet again, and had done so early in the race prior to the wreck on Lap 32.

"I know Bobby and myself hooked up many times in the draft together," Donnie recalled in the spring of 2007. "When you race at a place like Talladega, you're in a different world. You can sit out there and you want to get the car slowed down to your speed. And what I mean by that is when you go out there and you're racing, you don't feel like you're going 185 miles per hour or 190 miles per hour or whatever it is. You don't actually feel that inside the car.

"It's no different now than it was then. You go down the back straightaway and you're running into each other; not meaning to, but with the wind making you. . . . It's an altogether different feeling. We've been racing side by side at Talladega ever since it was built; Daytona the same way. And it's fun. These guys can tell you they don't like it. But once you get inside that car and get going, it's fun. It's not fun when the big wreck happens—but it's fun."

Donnie knew what it was like to wreck on a superspeedway. So did Bobby. When it happened, it usually wasn't pretty, especially back in the days before restrictor plates were mandated by NASCAR at the superspeedways in an effort to slow the cars down and make sure none of them went flying off the track.

"The speed is one thing, but we cannot stand the action that might happen," Donnie admitted. "These race cars, running at 200 miles an hour, will fly. When they get turned around backward—and we've all been there—you've got no control. It's between you and the guy upstairs, and you'd better hope you said something nice to Him that morning before you left for the track, because it's not going to be a nice ride."

•   •   •

Cale Yarborough knew all about going fast and sometimes getting the feeling that a little divine intervention was needed to keep disaster from striking. But mostly, Yarborough relied on his instincts to keep him out of that kind of predicament on the racetrack. He was at the top of his game as a driver in 1979, having become the first—and through 2007, the only—driver to win three consecutive points championships by doing so in 1976, 1977, and 1978.

With the unprecedented back-to-back-to-back titles came glory and fame and a good bit of money. Cash was something Cale always appreciated, having spent many of his earlier years in severe shortage of it.

Yarborough grew up the son of a tobacco farmer in the small town of Sardis, South Carolina, just a gear shift away from stock car racing's first superspeedway in Darlington. He had to milk a cow each morning before leaving for school. He excelled at football long before racing, but got his taste of the latter sport because his father, Julian, loved to see cars go fast and frequently brought young Cale to the dirt tracks that dotted the area. Cale would long remember going to the races with his father and hanging on the fence, trying to catch as much of the action as he could.

By the time Yarborough was ten years old, he had circled every inch of the perimeter of the 1.366-mile Darlington track in search of a break in the fence that would allow him to sneak into the place and watch the bigger, faster cars run there. He eventually found what he was looking for, and at the age of eleven was able to witness his first Southern 500. At age twelve, he competed in his first race: not a stock car race, much to his disappointment, but a soapbox derby. His "car" and the race weren't nearly enough to satisfy his growing appetite to drive things that went fast.

"There's no motor in it. Those soapbox cars just don't go fast enough," he complained to his mother, Annie Ray Yarborough.

Shortly thereafter, young Cale's life changed forever when his father was killed in the crash of a small airplane. While he was heartbroken, the terrible tragedy did nothing to quell Cale's need for speed. As a member of the local 4-H Club, he roped a calf, raised it, and then sold it—all to raise money for an old car he just had to buy. Then he built a shed where he could work on the car, and spent long hours rebuilding it so he could race it at dirt tracks in nearby towns like Sumter and Hartsville. Along the way, he wrecked and rebuilt that old jalopy and wrecked and then rebuilt countless others like it in that makeshift shed, where a single bare light bulb hung at the end of a long cord and burned long into the night on many occasions. He often had to beg his mother to give him money to fuel his increasingly expensive racing habit.

By the time he was eighteen, Yarborough had found his way into the big superspeedway at Darlington many times. He often hung around the garage area near his close friend, older driver Bobby Weatherly, only to get shooed away eventually by track personnel. One time in 1957, when NASCAR officials were preoccupied with other prerace duties, Yarborough slipped behind the wheel of Weatherly's Pontiac and actually drove in a Grand National event. It was a dubious beginning to his career: he started forty-fourth, and finished forty-second after experiencing mechanical trouble, earning himself a whopping $100.

It wasn't predetermined that he would become a legendary race car driver, or any kind of driver at all. He loved it, but after getting married he felt compelled to find more steady work to put food on the table for his family. He tried his hand in the poultry business and also played semipro football for a while before finally deciding that if he was going to give racing a go, it deserved his full attention.

"I just decided one day that I had to either go one way or the other, that I had to lay all that other stuff down and go racing, and that's what I decided to do," Yarborough said. "But it was tough. There were a lot of lean years, I can tell you."

As the years passed, Yarborough did many wild and crazy things, only some of which involved driving a race car. He developed a friendship with fellow driver Tiny Lund, who was anything but tiny (like most men with that nickname), and the two of them were constantly playing practical jokes on each other. They would be driving along on public roads away from the track, and inevitably the conversation would drift into an area where Yarborough, who was tough as nails but stood no more than five foot six in boots, was spouting off about something he used to do as a kid back in South Carolina.

He often bragged about wrestling alligators, and one time Lund abruptly pulled off the road and demanded that he prove it.

"Okay, I will," said Yarborough, and then he was off to dive into a swamp, where he took on and subsequently pinned an unsuspecting alligator.

Other times he would boast about grappling with other wild animals, or he would fish water moccasins out of their homes, just to prove a point. He later developed a fondness for skydiving, and eventually made more than two hundred jumps from airplanes. Another time, Yarborough wrestled a pet bear given to him by one of his pit crews. He almost failed to win that match.

Yarborough gave the general impression that he could have gone into battle in a bloody war, led a suicide charge up a hill against overwhelming odds, and still somehow emerge without a scratch. He once made an emergency landing of an airplane in a field, even though he had no prior experience as a pilot. Another time he survived a rattlesnake bite. And as a topper to his résumé as a guy who lived on the edge all the time, on and off the track, he also lived through getting struck by lightning—not once but twice.

It wasn't until Yarborough moved to Charlotte, just north of the South Carolina border, that he finally began to make a name for himself as a stock car driver. He first found work at Holman-Moody, where Ford Motor Company was having its race cars built at the time. It wasn't glamorous: Yarborough swept floors, turned wrenches, and did whatever menial work was assigned to him.

Then again, he was getting paid $1.25 an hour. One time he and his wife, Betty Jo, were at the grocery store, loading up their cart with the cheapest and most filling foods they could find. They thought they were stretching their dollar pretty well until they headed for the checkout line and discovered a display offering cans of black-eyed peas for ten cents apiece.

"I grabbed Betty Jo by the hand and said, 'You come with me.' We went back around to all the counters and put everything back that we had in the cart, and went back and bought every can of those black-eyed peas that they had," Yarborough said. "I'm telling you, we had black-eyed peas for breakfast, we had black-eyed peas for lunch, and we had black-eyed peas for supper. It was amazing, but I still liked black-eyed peas even after that."

All the while he was shoveling black-eyed peas down his throat and sweeping the floors at Holman-Moody, he kept reminding anyone who would listen that he was a darn good race car driver and all he needed was a chance. He was working as a member of a pit crew when he finally got that chance, and he turned in an impressive showing.

Soon he was running races fairly regularly on the Grand National tour. He won his first race in 1965 and firmly established himself as an up-and-coming star by winning six of twenty-one events, including the Daytona 500, in 1968. It was the first of four times he would win the prestigious event, and he would go on to win the Southern 500 at his home track of Darlington five times.

But it wasn't until the 1970s that he really began to hit his stride, finishing second in the points championship standings in both 1973 and 1974, when he won four and ten races, respectively, while winning the hard-earned respect of everyone he competed against, including the Allison brothers, Petty, and Baker.

"He was a fierce competitor. Whether he was ten laps down or ten laps ahead, he would run just as hard as he could cotton-pickin' go. He had one speed, and that was wide open," Petty said. "He probably put more into driving than any other driver I ever drove against. He drove more down the straightaway than I did in the corners, as far as turning the wheels. I mean, he was up on the wheel all the time."

Bobby Allison once added, "Cale jumped in the car and pushed the throttle to the floor before he switched it on. When the green fell, he locked the throttle on 'kill,' gritted his teeth, and held on."

Baker was most impressed by Yarborough's dogged determination, no matter what the situation or how the odds might seem stacked against him. "I don't know if there's ever been an athlete who had that outlook on the last ten laps that Cale Yarborough had. He didn't give up until the last inch of the race was over," Baker said.

In other words, no one was surprised when he started to charge back through the field in the 1979 Daytona 500—even though he was three laps down at one point. Making him even more formidable that day was his car owner and crew chief, the indomitable Junior Johnson. It was Johnson who had one time leaned over to his driver with final instructions before a race, telling Yarborough to drive the wheels off the car.

"Just bring me back the steering wheel," Johnson had said.

In the three years immediately leading up to the 1979 Daytona 500, Yarborough did more than that. He brought back three straight Winston Cup championships for Johnson.

•   •   •

As the caution flag flew when the Allison brothers and Yarborough tangled on Lap 32 of the '79 race, the other competitors headed to the pits. When they came back out on the track, none other than Neil Bonnett, another member of the Alabama Gang, was listed in first. A. J. Foyt, the self-proclaimed "outsider" from open-wheel fame, was in second, followed by Richard Petty, Darrell Waltrip, and Dave Marcis.

It was at this point in the CBS telecast that the network cued up a feature detailing Bobby Allison's passion for flying airplanes. No one said it, but viewers were left with the impression that perhaps it was aired because Bobby's chances of winning the race, which might possibly have made it a better story to run later on, were over.

Speaking to Squier during the feature piece, which had been filmed as Bobby flew his two-engine airplane over Daytona International Speedway to land at the nearby airport, Allison talked about how he hoped to repeat as Daytona 500 champion. He also talked about the dangers of competing in any race at the venue.

"It's a place where disaster can strike in a split second, and you've got to be aware of that," he told Squier.

While Bobby was two laps off the pace by the time he got back on the track, Donnie was only one lap down and still had a very fast car. Yarborough, likewise, had not suffered significant damage that affected the handling or speed of his machine.

At this point, Hobbs mentioned that perhaps Yarborough did have something to do with the accident involving the three cars. Hobbs also lamented the tough day endured—again—by the snakebitten Baker. "People say he's a car-breaker, that he pushes his cars too hard," Hobbs told the television audience. "Well, they can't say that about him today. It all went wrong for him while he was riding around under yellow."

As Lap 39 rolled off the board, Junior Johnson, Yarborough's car owner and de facto crew chief, was interviewed on pit road by Jarrett. If there was any panic in him, it didn't come across in his voice or his calm mannerisms.

"I think we're in pretty good shape, except maybe when he spun out he got in the water and it might have wet the air cleaner down and it caused [the engine] to miss for a little bit. But we're going to run it a little bit to see if it'll clear on up. We're just going to leave it alone," Johnson said.

Jarrett added, "Since the dirt-track days of NASCAR, I can't remember anyone having to change an air cleaner on a car. But he went through a lot of water over there when he made that spin."

The top rookie running in the race at that moment was Geoff Bodine, a northerner from Bellingham, Massachusetts, who endured jeers of "Yankee, go home!" almost everywhere he went on the NASCAR circuit then and later. It kept happening even years later when he actually drove for Johnson—the furthest entity from a Yankee ever to step near a southern track.

Leaving a track at North Wilkesboro around that time, Bodine saw signs with the familiar taunt. He rolled the window down in his passenger car and of course then heard them, too. "Why are you still calling me that and telling me to go home? I'm driving for the Man now, the living legend!" he yelled at his tormentors.

"That don't matter! You're still a Yankee! Go home!" they yelled back.

As A. J. Foyt passed Bonnett for the lead in the 1979 Daytona 500 and Bodine battled for position back in the field, another rookie stuck the nose of his car into the mix. Driving the No. 2 Oldsmobile for car owner Rod Osterlund was Dale Earnhardt.

Squier and Hobbs scrambled to determine if this kid, running in his first 500, was actually moving to the front or just trying to make up for lost time by pulling up behind to draft off of the speedy cars of Foyt and Bonnett, who kept trading the lead. "I think Dale Earnhardt might be a lap down in that blue-and-yellow car," Hobbs offered.

The announcers and all of America continued to watch what suddenly was developing into a pretty good duel between Foyt and Bonnett and the upstart Earnhardt, with Bobby Allison, still two laps down, also involved along with another rookie who was surging to the front, Tighe Scott.

"Dale's had a fantastic week here. He really has. But as I said, I think he's a lap down at the moment," Hobbs stated again.

"We're checking now to see if Earnhardt is that lap down," Squier told the TV audience. "First we were told he was a lap down. Now we are told they are rechecking. . . . I tell you what, he sure runs like a champ today."

Then they all watched in amazement as Bobby Allison, who was two laps down but appeared to still be running strong, pushed Earnhardt past Foyt and Bonnett, who had temporarily regained the lead. About the same time, NASCAR sent word to the broadcast booth that Earnhardt was indeed on the lead lap—and now he was at the front of it all.

"Earnhardt blazes to the front of this group again! He is now reported as the leader," Squier said.

6

The Emergence of Earnhardt

The fact that the CBS announcers were encountering difficulty in determining if Dale Earnhardt was, in fact, in the lead of the Daytona 500—or if he wasn't even on the lead lap—actually was not that surprising. Scorekeeping in the late 1970s was still done by hand, and it was unusual but not entirely uncommon for mistakes to occur during the heat of a race.

In the finale of the Winston Cup season only a year earlier, a scoring error led to Donnie Allison belatedly picking up the check and trophy for a win in Atlanta. It had been a long, hard, dry season for Richard Petty, so he was pleased to get to Victory Lane earlier in the day following the afternoon race. It would have been his first and only victory of the trying 1978 season, breaking a forty-three-race winless streak. Scorecards, then kept by hand, were checked and rechecked before the King was declared the winner.

Donnie Allison headed home to Alabama, thinking he had finished third behind Petty and Dave Marcis. Even Allison's own two scorers had been consulted and concurred that he had finished third. Finally, however, it was determined by track officials that a mistake had been made. Allison had passed both Petty and Marcis and was the rightful owner of the race victory, instead of finishing third a lap down as the scorers had initially thought and reported. It wasn't until he was reached at his home in Alabama much later that evening that the younger Allison learned he had just registered his tenth career victory.

Petty and his crew, including Dale Inman, were left wondering about the train wreck that was the winless 1978 season. "That was the first time in sixteen or seventeen years we hadn't won," Inman said. "We were in Atlanta and it come down toward the end of the race, and it was Donnie, Richard, and Marcis racing at the end, and there were a bunch of cautions."

There also was confusion as NASCAR officials obviously miscounted Donnie's laps. Years later, Inman wasn't so sure about that, and he also said that Richard would have raced Allison differently at the end had he known Donnie was on the lead lap.

"Well, they said they had made a mistake," Inman said. "But they kept telling me [Donnie] was laps down. We knew he would make some of 'em up on restarts. But they kept telling me, and the scoreboard kept saying, that Richard was still leading. So Marcis and Richard, on the last restart, they kind of let Donnie go. They were racing each other, and we beat Marcis. He was in [owner] Rod Osterlund's car.

"About midnight down there, after they went through all the rigmarole, they said, 'No, Donnie won it.' There was nothing we could do. That broke our streak of winning [at least] a race per season [which actually had lasted for eighteen years]."

Inman and his second cousin and the rest of the Petty crew didn't like it. But they realized that they had no choice but to accept it. "Well, what can you do? Yeah, you were upset. But they've got the upper hand," Inman said.

Years later, Kyle Petty was talking about how his grandfather, Lee, had to wait around nearly three full days before finally being declared winner of the first Daytona 500 in 1959. Although he made the statement in reference to that, it could be carried over to the Atlanta race in 1978 as well. Considering how little of a fight Petty Enterprises put up over the declaration of Donnie Allison as winner of that race, it seems likely that they knew, deep down, that Allison was the rightful victor.

"You know, it's funny, but this is what I've always said: especially in that time, most drivers know where they're at," Kyle Petty said in 2008. "They don't have to be told they're runnin' fifth or they're runnin' sixth. They know who they're racin'. . . . The King is that way. You can talk to the King about races that were run twenty years ago, and he can tell you what happened lap after lap after lap, like he's just got a recorder in his head. He can remember where he was, or what was going on."

What was going on for the King as 1978 faded into 1979 was depressing. Meanwhile, Earnhardt was about to start making a name for himself in owner Osterlund's machine, and it was during the 1979 Daytona 500 that he began to get himself noticed in a big way.

* * *

It was against the backdrop of Richard Petty's 1978 struggles that Earnhardt first appeared on the Winston Cup scene. Struggling to come to grips with the balky Dodge Magnum, Petty failed to finish four of the first five races in 1978 and was on the lead lap at the finish only once in the first ten events. It perplexed the King.

"When I'm running super good, there's only a couple of cars I have to worry about. But the way I'm runnin' now, I've got bunches of competition," he told reporters at the time.

Petty refused to blame his demise on diminishing skills. At forty years of age—he would turn forty-one the following July—he admitted he might not be the same driver he was twenty years earlier. But he still considered himself the man to beat. "I might not be as good as ever," he said, "but in two years, I can't go from being as good as I ever was to as bad as I am now."

Petty wasn't the only one struggling to get the Dodge Magnum to be competitive. Legendary crew chief Harry Hyde, then with the Jim Stacy Dodge team, gave up on the car in early May and put driver Neil Bonnett in an Oldsmobile.

"We've been running out of a junkyard for three years," Hyde complained. "Trying to run these [Dodge] engine blocks we get from the junkyard is like taking a mule to the Kentucky Derby."

Earnhardt would have ridden a mule if that was the only ride offered him at the Winston Cup level. As the World 600 at Charlotte Motor Speedway approached in May 1978, though, some strange circumstances unfolded that put him in a more competitive mode of transportation and set in motion the series of events that would land him the Osterlund ride for the 1979 season—his first full-time ride at the Cup level.

Many of the headlines leading up to the 600 involved Petty, who was continuing to complain about the deficiencies of the Dodge Magnum and was told by NASCAR one day before the opening round of qualifying that he needed to return to Level Cross to replace the car he had intended to run. Petty was so furious about the edict that he later said he "gave serious thought to not returning at all."

But the biggest headlines were reserved for one Willy T. Ribbs. A twenty-three-year-old road racer out of San Jose, California, Ribbs had become America's most celebrated black driver, and Humpy Wheeler, who once had brought Janet Guthrie to the World 600, wanted Ribbs to participate in his race. Wheeler, the general manager of Charlotte Motor Speedway, had arranged for Ribbs to drive a Ford owned by Will Cronkrite. It wasn't a piece of junk, either. The car had been purchased from legendary owner Bud Moore and had twice been to Victory Lane at Talladega.

Wheeler was thrilled. This was going to be a groundbreaking event. It might put more people in the seats and have long-ranging, positive implications for NASCAR. The veteran race promoter arranged to have his facility available to Ribbs and Cronkrite for two days of private practice sessions, so Ribbs could begin to familiarize himself with the bigger Winston Cup Grand National car.

As the dates for the practice sessions approached, Wheeler began trying to phone Ribbs. But Ribbs, inexplicably, was nowhere to be found. Wheeler couldn't locate him, and messages went unreturned. Worse yet, Wheeler had arranged for a local car dealer to give Ribbs a vehicle to drive around town. Wheeler knew Ribbs was somewhere in Charlotte because the aspiring Cup driver had picked up the car.

Ribbs finally surfaced, but not in the way anyone envisioned he would. On the second day he was supposed to be at the track for his private test, he was arrested by a Charlotte police officer for going the wrong way on a one-way street while driving the loaner from the car dealer.

Wheeler felt he had no choice but to refuse Ribbs's entry into the race. Cronkrite was left fuming, but quickly thought of another young driver who would be able to pilot his Ford in the race. His name was Dale Earnhardt. After learning of Earnhardt's impressive record in local Sportsman races, Cronkrite was sold on the idea. He tapped Earnhardt to fill the vacancy left unexpectedly by Ribbs's folly.

"Dale is an extremely competitive driver," Cronkrite said. "He has the capability of putting a car up front and making it go as fast as it can."

Earnhardt had for years been attempting to do that in whatever he could find to drive. Then twenty-six years old, he was no longer as young as he once was, and he worried at times that his driving career might be passing him by before he could get it up to the speed he wanted.

•   •   •

Wheeler and others, including Cale Yarborough, had known Dale for a long time. They had seen him grow up around tracks because they were familiar with his father, Ralph. Wheeler struck up a relationship with the elder Earnhardt shortly after graduating with a degree in journalism from the University of South Carolina in 1961 and taking a job at what he would call "this fabulous little speedway in Gastonia called the Robinwood Speedway."

Fans there were demanding and tough. One time a fan didn't like what the public-address announcer had to say. So he attacked him, hitting him in the head with a wrench. Another time a disgruntled driver pointed a gun at Wheeler after a disagreement on a ruling at a race. The driver not only pointed the weapon but also fired it—and missed. Wheeler was never sure if he missed on purpose.

"The man is dead now and I always wanted to ask him that question," Wheeler said years later. "But these places were rough. Number one, most of these drivers came from small southern towns. They were in the lower middle class. They were just above poverty. They were tough people to start off with."

That description fit Ralph Earnhardt. He was considered tough, hardheaded, and extremely aggressive. When Dale was born on April 29, 1951, Ralph already had made a name for himself as a successful driver on short tracks throughout the Southeast. He eventually tried his hand at NASCAR's top level of racing, then known as Grand National, making fifty-one starts from 1956 through 1964, but he didn't like all of the attention the series generated. It made him uncomfortable, so he returned to his roots and continued racing at short tracks in Monroe, Concord, Hickory, and at Greenville-Pickens Speedway in Greenville, South Carolina.

By the time he was done driving, Ralph Earnhardt was credited with more than 250 wins on the short tracks and was considered the king of NASCAR's Modified Sportsman division. He also earned a reputation as a meticulous mechanic, whose car always was ready to roll when he hit the track. He would know, too. He usually worked alone.

Dale was born right about the time Ralph started getting serious about racing. So times were tight. Ralph's Modified stock cars cost him roughly $800 and were built with various pieces and parts Earnhardt would find at local junkyards. Unlike Harry Hyde many years later, the elder Earnhardt found a way to make a competitive car out of the mule and take it to the derby.

One day, Earnhardt called Wheeler over at a track and began to explain to the younger man his philosophy about building and maintaining race cars. And, of course, he wasn't bound to the limitations of the likes of Hyde when he put one of his Modified machines together.

"See this '39 Ford?" Earnhardt asked. "It's got a teardrop hood on it. You put a Lincoln radiator in it and the hood will fit right over it. Then you put something between the radiator and the hood like asbestos and then you hold this by the front end with something like rope."

In other words, it wasn't anything fancy. But it ran. And it was fast. It was reliable during the rigors of a short-track race. There was another plus, too.

"If you wreck one, you don't have to think much about it," Earnhardt told Wheeler. "You buy the body for another one for fifty dollars down at the junkyard. And you can find the rest of what you need at the junkyard, too."

Ralph worked mostly out of his garage behind the family home in Kannapolis, North Carolina. Oftentimes, especially during his teenage years, Dale would be right by his father's side as the expert mechanic worked long into the night to prepare his race car for another event. Those times became more frequent as Dale got older.

"I learned more in that garage than anywhere else," Dale later would say.

Wheeler was still learning the business, too. Although he loved running Robinwood Speedway, he soon discovered a downside to it. He rapidly grew weary of dealing with all of the hassles of running a small track and working as a promoter for races at other small speedways throughout the Southeast.

"I made a fair amount of money promoting races, but I didn't get to keep any of it," Wheeler said. "Lawsuits are what brought me down. I was always getting sued for something. I thought I was smarter than I was, I guess. But the fact of the matter was after working awful hard for several years after getting out of college, I didn't have any money. I felt like I was twenty-five going on sixty and sixteen at the same time."

So when the opportunity came for him to take a job with Firestone Rubber and Tire Company as director of racing, he jumped at it. While at the new job, Wheeler had certain drivers test tires for him. He got to know others by driving to races with them. They often would take Wheeler's car and insist that he drive, but then would constantly harass him about going too slow. Usually he was driving at speeds of around a hundred miles per hour on public interstate highways, which made their complaints difficult to digest.

"We'd drive down to Daytona and we'd drive at night," Wheeler said. "We made some pretty fantastic trips down to Daytona. I think the record run [from Charlotte] was five hours and ten minutes. It was pretty fast.

"We would go as fast as the car would run. You could run 130 or 140 miles per hour through some stretches of Georgia. We always had access to some pretty powerful cars. We made sure the tires were good on it, and we usually kept it to 100 miles per hour. But driving with race drivers was a pain in the butt because they're the worst backseat drivers. They would always see things, little details, that you wouldn't even notice."

Ralph Earnhardt was the king of noticing small details when it came to preparing his race car, or finding a way to make it go faster when he was driving it on the track. He was one of the drivers Wheeler enlisted to test tires for Firestone, and one time the two men got to talking about how they had both gotten involved in racing. Ralph began relating how his wife, Martha, had been very concerned that he was merely throwing away the family's meager life savings.

"She really didn't want that going down the drain," Ralph Earnhardt told Wheeler. "I promised her that I would never do that. I promised her that she would never be wanting for anything we needed."

Wheeler thought about that statement for a long time after the two men went their separate ways. "That was a hell of a thing to say back then. Those are the days when they paid one hundred fifty or two hundred dollars to be the winner at the dirt tracks. Those were the kinds of races he ran in," he said.

In other words, the pressure to fulfill the promise was there every time Ralph Earnhardt sat behind the wheel of his race car. Wheeler found himself drawn to this man, who seemed to possess more commonsense racing ability than most others he had encountered during his years in racing. Earnhardt had an Everyman appeal about him that other working-class folks seemed to identify with, much as his son Dale would exhibit as his popularity soared many years later.

Unlike Dale, who would go on to earn unthinkable fame and fortune at stock car racing's highest level, Ralph simply didn't enjoy the big time of NASCAR's Grand National circuit when he ran it part-time from 1956 through 1964. Ralph never won at what would later be called the Winston Cup level (and subsequently Nextel Cup and Sprint Cup). But he did finish second twice—including in his very first race, for which he also won the pole in qualifying.

Over time he simply gravitated back to the short tracks where he was most comfortable and most successful. He pretty much kept to himself. If he didn't know you, he surely didn't trust you. Behind the wheel, though, Ralph was a tenacious competitor.

"If people think Dale is tough," said Ned Jarrett many years later, "they should have raced against his daddy."

Jarrett did, so he knew what he was talking about. "Ralph was one tough racer," he said. "He was one of the best drivers who ever sat behind the wheel."

He also was smart—and patient when he felt he had to be.

"Ralph was taciturn," Wheeler said. "He didn't have much facial expression and he did not talk to anybody much. And when he showed up to race, his typical deal was that he would show up at the track and he might be the only person with his car. I saw him many a Thursday night in Columbia, South Carolina, where he would show up in that No. 8 and he never got a wrench out on that car. He was always maximumly prepared with his cars."

He always had a plan for how to run them during a race, too, according to Wheeler. Time and time again, Wheeler watched in amazement as Ralph Earnhardt pulled off his race plans with precision, ensuring there would be food on the table for Dale and the rest of his family.

"If it was a hundred-lap race and he won it, he usually did it in the following manner: he would run second or third half the race, then he'd run up to second the last half of the race—and then with three or four laps to go, he'd pass the guy running in front and win the race," Wheeler recalled.

"He didn't jump out there in front and stay there. He knew how the game was played, and he knew not to run away with things—because that was when the heat comes down."

That was when track promoters would get suspicious and accuse drivers of cheating. Back in those days, perception often was everything. Run away with a race—or with one too many—and you may just find yourself disqualified whether there was or wasn't something illegal going on with your car.

It was while he was employed by Firestone that Wheeler got to know Ralph Earnhardt as well as just about anybody could, which isn't to say they often engaged in long conversations. But Wheeler appointed Earnhardt to be his "chief dirt-track, southern, weekly test driver" for Firestone racing tires, which meant they did have to communicate at least a limited amount on a regular basis.

"I used to call Ralph up and say, 'How'd the tires do?' And if they were really great he'd say, 'Not bad.' If they were awful, he would try to be polite and might say something like, 'You might want to look into that a little bit more,'" Wheeler said.

"You had to speak his language or you couldn't figure out what he was talking about. He was very quiet. He loved his family and kept them up as best he could."

● ● ●

Dale Earnhardt idolized his father and wanted to be just like him. In many ways, he was. Among those who knew him and watched him develop as a driver with great interest was Cale Yarborough.

"I knew Dale almost from since when he was born and watched him grow up and get started," Yarborough once told Rich Wolfe, author of the book *Remembering Dale Earnhardt*. "I knew if he had any of his dad's genes in him, which he did, he would be a tremendous race car driver. His dad was a fierce competitor.

When he showed up at a racetrack, you knew that if you were going to win, you had your work cut out for you—that he was the man you'd have to beat.

"Dale was just a regular little kid. He was around the racetracks a lot and worked on his dad's car. He was just a regular little pit brat."

Like his father, Dale was a simple country boy from Kannapolis. In his early days of racing, he often borrowed money from friends on Thursday night so he could race on the weekends at the local dirt tracks, with the small matter of whether they would be paid back on Monday morning hinging on whether he won enough to settle up. Often he did; sometimes he didn't. And Earnhardt's goal wasn't just to pay them back. By then he had started a family of his own, and like his father before him, he always wanted to earn a little extra so he could use it to put groceries on the dinner table.

It wasn't an easy life. No one knew Earnhardt as they would come to know him later. He was Ralph's boy, to be sure, and word got around about that. But he was hardly the Intimidator, as he would come to be known, right at the drop of the green flag to his driving career.

Pete Wright, who over many years worked as a shop man and pit crew member for Junior Johnson, Donnie Allison, Darrell Waltrip, Ken Schrader, and others, remembered one night in the mid-1970s when he was at the Martinsville track for a Modified race.

"I'll never forget this," Wright said. "There was this car owner, Charles W. Reed, who had a pretty good Modified car but hadn't done as good as us in the race. After the race, his driver come in and parked right beside us. They had run like a dog; they were terrible. And this car usually wasn't this bad; it usually would be somewhere closer to the front."

Wright watched as Reed walked over to his car.

"Get out of my car! You'll never sit in this car again!" Reed shouted.

The driver in the car looked down dejectedly and did not reply. "You'll never be a race car driver! Get out of the car!" Reed repeated. "You're wasting my time and my money!"

The driver, one Dale Earnhardt, climbed out of the car and left the scene, speaking nary a word. Wright watched the whole incident unfold.

"At that time," said Wright much later, "he was struggling like a lot of guys. He was doing what he could do. And he obviously wasn't the driver Charles wanted at the time, but he didn't quit."

His father did not raise him to be a quitter, at least not when it came to racing. Quitting was simply not part of his DNA. Of course, he was so single-mindedly devoted to it that other areas of his early life suffered.

Dale had been trying to make it in racing off and on since dropping out of school in the ninth grade, ostensibly to devote more time to his passion. The decision to quit school did not sit well with Ralph. But in the long run, it drew father and son closer. They had been distant earlier in life as Ralph always was off either racing somewhere or working on his cars in the garage behind the house. Now the older Dale studied at his side whenever he could, without the interference of going off to school every day.

In the early 1970s, Ralph built engines for his son and Dale did the chassis work. Driving in Modified races at short tracks mostly in North Carolina, Dale won twenty-six events during their first year of working together and even more the following year. Suddenly, the father-son bond that had been missing for so many years began to cement. Ralph Earnhardt was a man of few words, but he did give Dale one piece of advice that the younger Earnhardt would never forget.

"Establish your territory," Ralph told Dale in a brief dissertation on how to survive, and thrive, on a racetrack.

Dale listened and tried to soak it all up. Even then, he realized the man dishing him this advice was more than the guy he saw at the breakfast table every morning. He knew Ralph Earnhardt was a local racing legend.

Earnhardt was beginning to establish his territory on one dirt track after another when his father died suddenly. Ralph Earnhardt, the victim of a massive heart attack, was only forty-five. Dale was grief-stricken. Why now? Why after the two had finally had the opportunity to grow so much closer through Dale's racing?

"He was my hero. Always has been, always will be," Dale said of his father.

Still only in his early twenties, Dale struggled to understand. He seemed lost. He later described the following year, 1974, to friends and family as the worst of his life. He had a wife and two children, although the marriage would not last. They moved from run-down mobile homes to cheap, cockroach-infested apartments, wondering at times how they would feed the kids. He wanted to devote more time to racing but couldn't afford it and no longer had his father around to push him or help out. So he worked installing insulation, rebuilding car engines, and doing anything he could that would fill the bare cupboard shelves.

None of the work was steady, and after moving from one temporary job to another, he found work one winter as a subcontractor with the boilermakers' union in the North Carolina coastal town of New Bern. That December, he worked long hours right through the holidays, including Christmas Day, helping to make welding repairs to machinery in a paper mill. The job was hot and the paper mill stunk, as paper mills do. Earnhardt hated every second of it and longed to get back behind the wheel of a race car.

He continued to race occasionally, and shortly after the welding job, he quit the conventional workforce forever to attempt to build a career as a full-time race car driver. He lost his first wife to divorce, married and divorced again, and continued to struggle until catching the eye of Rod Osterlund and Roland Wlodyka, Osterlund's general manager of Winston Cup racing operations.

By then the president at Charlotte Motor Speedway, Wheeler also kept tabs on young Dale's budding career. Dale would stop in Wheeler's office to chat and pick Wheeler's brain. He would tell Wheeler where he was going to be racing, and Wheeler often went and watched Dale run on dirt. Wheeler later took to calling Earnhardt "the last red-dirt racer."

"He learned to drive a loose race car on those dirt tracks," Wheeler said. "I watched him race on dirt many, many times. . . . Dirt racing is more driver than car. On asphalt, you can't say that. But on dirt, he could take an average car and look great."

One night Dale was racing on dirt against some Cup drivers at Metrolina Speedway in Charlotte. Cale Yarborough was one of the other drivers, getting in a little extra racing action on the side even as he continued to be the hottest thing going on the Winston Cup circuit.

Another driver entered was Richard Childress, an independent operator out of the Winston-Salem area who was to later play a much larger role in Earnhardt's life, as owner of the cars Earnhardt would drive to six of his seven Cup points championships. That night in Charlotte, however, they were just two drivers in a race that had been an invitational for those who had won races on short tracks in the area.

"Cale and I wrecked on the last lap and I won the race. I don't think Cale was able to finish. Dale came by and finished second," Childress said. "I never will forget him coming by. He was just a rough-cut kid, just like I was."

As he drove by on the cool-down lap, Earnhardt leaned out his window and got the attention of Childress, calling out to him.

"Next time I race you, I'm going to beat your ass!" he yelled.

He no longer was the timid driver who had once been chased out of the car by Charles W. Reed. Childress wondered exactly who he was, but he liked the guy's tenacity. They actually became fast friends after that, joining a hunting club together and beginning a relationship that would serve both well.

"Who ever knew where history would carry us both," Childress said.

Another race in particular appeared to catch Osterlund's eye. It also was at Metrolina Speedway, this time on Labor Day weekend in 1978, and Dale was driving for his former father-in-law, Robert Gee (the grandfather of Dale Jr., who would go on to gain his own driving fame). Metrolina was a challenging little dirt track with extremely narrow corners that often caused problems even for experienced drivers.

"He just blasted his way up to the front and won the race with a few laps to go, beating all these really good dirt-track drivers," Wheeler said.

Wheeler was there in the crowd. So was Osterlund, a wealthy Californian who decided on the spot to give Earnhardt a seat in one of his powerful Chevrolets for the upcoming Late Model Sportsman race, the World Service Life 300. It turned out to be the career break Earnhardt had been waiting on for years, setting in motion a series of events.

That was back in the day when Winston Cup cars could run in the Saturday race preceding the Sunday main event. With a crowd of 42,500 clearly pulling for what one journalist later described as "the local short-track artist," Earnhardt led in the closing stages of the event before none other than Bobby Allison finally caught him and passed him with four laps remaining. Allison barely held Earnhardt off over the final laps, however, beating him by a single car length.

In Victory Lane, Allison commented that Earnhardt was an up-and-coming driver to watch. "I want to congratulate Dale Earnhardt," he said. "He gave me all I could handle. He's fast becoming a very, very good race car driver."

The next day, Earnhardt drove for Cronkrite again in the NAPA National 500, finishing seventeenth with relief help from another short-track veteran who would become a Cup rookie the following year, Harry Gant. Osterlund already was thinking about giving Earnhardt a full-time Cup ride, based on what he had seen at the dirt track and in the Late Model Sportsman event (which later would evolve into the Busch Series and then the Nationwide Series).

Yarborough later claimed that it was on his recommendation that Osterlund chose Earnhardt, although there appeared to be other contributing circumstances as well. For one, Dave Marcis, who had been Osterlund's driver, did not like all of the talk of possibly going to a two-car team, worrying that it would affect his ability to get the best of everything for his machine. When he learned of the possibility, he decided to leave the team, clearing the way for Earnhardt to take over as Osterlund's top driver.

But according to Yarborough, Osterlund first came to him for advice. "Cale, I'm going to make a change in my race team, and I'm going to put a new driver in there. That new driver is going to be whoever you tell me put in there. It's that simple. Just tell me who you recommend."

Yarborough said he did not hesitate in his answer. "Dale Earnhardt," he said with conviction.

*   *   *

When Earnhardt decided to try racing full-time in 1975 as a way to make ends meet, he was about to turn twenty-four years old. He was twenty-seven by the time he drove in his first Daytona 500 in 1979. Although fame and fortune awaited him in the not too distant future, no one could have foreseen it at the time.

But there were some clues that were beginning to pile up, beginning with how Earnhardt ran in his 125-mile qualifying race at Daytona that year. In a race dominated by Darrell Waltrip, who led thirty-four of the fifty laps en route to victory, Earnhardt finished fourth behind Waltrip, A. J. Foyt, and Dick Brooks.

"I just remember seeing him run the 125-miler. I remember he drove the shit out of the car," said Childress, who finished twenty-sixth in the other 125-mile qualifier. "He bounced off the wall and still kept going, didn't even slow down. I said to myself, 'Damn, if this kid don't hurt himself, he's going to be good.' And he was. He lived up to everything everybody thought he would be."

He was beginning to do that as he took the lead at the 1979 Daytona 500 on Lap 44. Neil Bonnett took it back from him on the next lap, but then Earnhardt grabbed it again and held it from Laps 46 through 49. Driving for Osterlund a yellow-and-blue No. 2 Oldsmobile that had no sponsor on the hood, Earnhardt was displaying a desire for running up front that surprised only those who hadn't yet gotten to know him and his relentless driving style.

"He was definitely a factor," Childress said. "When he got into that car, he knew it was his chance to shine, and he took advantage of it. That kind of thing is what turned Dale Earnhardt into what he would later become."

Talking on-air, Squier added, "A second-generation driver, his father was one of the most famous short-track drivers in American racing history—the well-known Ralph Earnhardt. His kid looks good today."

Down on pit road, Ned Jarrett was keeping an eye on Ralph's kid, too. This appeared to be Earnhardt's personal Cup coming-out party. "I knew him and I raced against his dad for years in Sportsman type of competition," Jarrett said. "So I had seen him grow up. He was sort of between my two sons age-wise. They were about six years apart and Dale was right in between. So I watched his career and I knew he had a tremendous amount of talent. I was not surprised to see him run up near the front because that was his style. It was obvious. If he could have a car that would allow him to do that, I thought he would. He wouldn't hold back."

As pole sitter Buddy Baker prepared to get as far away from the disappointment of the track as he possibly could after his own car and crew failed him, even he took notice of Earnhardt. "On that particular day, I think Earnhardt let everybody know he was something to deal with in a few years. Lo and behold, the next year he won the championship," Baker said. "Nobody had actually paid that much attention to Earnhardt prior to that. Then he fired off and led quite a bit of the race, and suddenly he had everyone's attention."

He had their attention, but no one was going to let him have anything without fighting for it. As Lap 50 rolled around, Benny Parsons passed Earnhardt for the lead, and millions sat on the edges of their seats at the track and at home. Those watching from the comfort of their homes saw exactly how he did it from Parsons's in-car camera.

7

Benny's World

As Benny Parsons took the lead and the television audience watched via his special in-car camera, he was trailed by Dale Earnhardt and another relative Winston Cup newcomer who was making himself a frequent visitor near the front. Driving the No. 30 Buick for car owner Walter Ballard, Tighe Scott (first name pronounced "Tie") was a driver who had excelled in Modifieds on dirt tracks throughout Pennsylvania, New York, and New Jersey. No one knew much about him in NASCAR circles.

But the popular Parsons was another story, and it was Parsons who was front and center—not only in the race itself but on the TV screen at home. He was giving television viewers their first ride-along with an in-car camera. Network executives were privately thrilled that he was running up front. He was their one-trick pony that February day in 1979 when it came to carrying the in-car camera. Other drivers who had been approached about the idea were dead set against it.

"They weighed twenty-five or thirty pounds, and no one wanted the extra weight in the car," Richard Petty said.

Ken Squier said, "It weighed too much and it was too high. It screwed up the roll center. But Benny thought it was important for the sport, and that's the way he was. Benny went back and talked to [car owner] M. C. Anderson about it and they put it in anyway."

In truth, Parsons's in-car camera was like one of Big Bill France's or Ralph Earnhardt's earliest race cars. It was crude and didn't always work that well. "The thing was spasmodic," Squier said. "The thing that worked didn't really come along until a couple years later."

Squier would have a hand in acquiring that technology from the land down under. He and the future governor of California, Arnold Schwarzenegger, traveled to Sydney, Australia, to do the announcing for the television broadcast of the Mr. Universe show.

"The idea came from ocean-racing sailboats," Squier said. "It came from the Sydney-to-Hobart sailboat race in Australia. That's one of their big events. They cross the Bass Strait, and run down to Hobart and Tasmania. It's a helluva race. They usually lose five or six people every year.

"Anyway, I was there with Arnold Schwarzenegger, and we were doing Mr. Universe at Sydney Opera House. The Bathurst 1000 [automobile race] was the next week, and I had never seen it. They gave it eight hours of television in Australia. It was almost as big as the Melbourne Cup [sailboat race], and that's a national holiday. The guy who was the [local television] producer [of it] said, 'Would you like to stay with us and go see the race?' I said, 'Oh, God, yes.' So I stayed the extra week."

Squier learned that the television producers had taken the camera that had first proved its sturdiness and capabilities during the sailboat races from Sydney to Hobart, and now were applying it to the Bathurst 1000 auto race. He had to think and act fast because there was American competition from ABC there as well "and we both had the same revelation."

The revelation was that what Parsons started during the 1979 Daytona 500 could now be taken to an entirely new and exciting level. Squier called his bosses at CBS back in the United States immediately and told them they needed to acquire the camera technology for their own auto racing telecasts, which they promptly did.

"This camera for the first time really gave you a sense that they weren't just driving around, that these things were like oceangoing sailboats: the only difference was they were going two hundred miles an hour and not twenty knots," Squier said. "And you could see all of that. Bathurst was a four- or five-mile course like a Christmas tree; it went up a mountain and down the other side. And they could do the 180 [degree spin] and look out the side and all of that. And they had the capability to talk to the driver.

"It was the business of turning a reality sport, which we all do, like swimming and trying to play golf, into a fantasy sport. The fantasy sports are the football and the boxing, where you can sit on the couch and you don't have to get knocked over by people swinging at you or tackling you. And the fantasy is you can try to outthink what they're doing, but deep down you know that they're doing something most of us couldn't really do.

"And car racing in the big cities at the time was considered more of a reality sport. Everyone thought they could do it. It was like, 'What's the big deal? They drive around and have a wreck once in a while.' Well, that camera was the one that said to America: these guys are really talented. You see them getting out of control and bringing it back all the way around the track."

The newer camera was much different than the crude model Parsons was packing in 1979. "It weighed almost nothing. That was the big secret. And it had that capability of revolving," Squier said. "Benny's camera weighed thirty pounds. It gave you some perspective. But the fact that the later camera could turn, so you could see forward and backward and those kinds of angles, or look out the side and see that they were running door handle to door handle, made the big difference. Suddenly saying they were running side by side was not a cliché; it was a reality."

•   •   •

Parsons was the one who set television down the path that eventually would lead through Australia, agreeing to add the unwieldy version of the camera on board his car during the 1979 Daytona 500, even though he knew it might ultimately cost him on the track. The selflessness was typical of the affable Parsons, who later would go on to make a name for himself during a broadcasting career that lasted long after his driving career ended. His story is one of the best NASCAR ever has had, and deserves being told in detail again.

Parsons was a native, appropriately enough, of Parsonsville, North Carolina. When Benny was a child, work in North Carolina Appalachia was difficult to find, and Harold Parsons, Benny's father, eventually left the area along with wife Hazel to find employment in Detroit. It was a move that would later pay off for Benny's racing career, but as a boy it saddened him. He told his parents that he did not want to move and they agreed to let him stay behind in the care of Julia Parsons, his great-grandmother.

They lived in a clapboard house built in 1890. There was no electricity or running water—or at least no conventional running water. When he was nine, Benny climbed the hill behind the house and dug a ditch that allowed him to at least run a gravity-fed water line into the home. "We dug a trench and built a reservoir and we did have some running water then. But there was no pump, so there were no toilet facilities. We had an outhouse," he said.

The young Parsons intensely admired his great-grandmother, and he kept busy raising chickens and pigs. He also farmed an acre of land and tended to a cow that provided much-needed milk. If coffee, sugar, or salt were required, Benny would trade eggs for those "luxuries," which is what he and Julia Parsons considered them.

It was a spartan existence, but it was all Parsons knew. And he remained happy, coming to believe in later years that those hardships helped shape his character. "It was the way life was for me at the time," he said years later. "I didn't know any different. You know, I guess in a perfect world it would have been different for me. But it's not a perfect world. I may have turned out better off because of it."

Benny's parents made certain that he knew they had not abandoned him, staying in touch by telephone and letters. Shortly after he completed the gravity-fed water line into the house in the summer of 1950, Benny and his great-grandmother excitedly left for Detroit to visit Benny's parents. That opened young Benny's eyes to a whole new world, one that included electricity, televisions, indoor plumbing, bathrooms, and cars.

Especially cars.

Harold Parsons had a love for cars and racing that he quickly passed on to Benny. Occasionally he would come home and take Benny to Hickory Motor Speedway or to the track in North Wilkesboro to see a race. Benny looked forward to it every time and soon grew to love automobiles just as much as his father did. Soon they were attending races together in Michigan as well.

"When I was in sixth grade, we started going to Detroit and spending the summers there," Parsons said. "We went to the races every Friday night up there. It was a quarter-mile dirt track—a quarter-mile, oil-soaked dirt track. They'd start the feature three abreast—three abreast on a quarter-mile track! When they made it through the first corner, I was crushed. I just knew I was going to see a bunch of wrecks."

Benny Parsons liked racing, but that was not all he enjoyed. His father bought him a battery-powered radio that he could listen to even after he returned to North Carolina in the fall to a house with no electricity. So each fall he left the modern luxuries of Detroit behind and returned to the home in Parsonsville, where kerosene lighting and outhouses were ways of life. With his beloved radio now with him, however, he could take some of his new world with him back to his old home in the hills of North Carolina. Because of the radio and the sporting events he could pick up on it, he became a Notre Dame football fan during the fall and a Boston Red Sox fan—or at least a Ted Williams fan—during the summer.

"In football season, you were listening to the radio and you wanted to be the quarterback for Notre Dame. In baseball season, you wanted to be another Ted Williams," Parsons said. "I never got into basketball, but I'd listen to football and baseball on the radio and you'd envision yourself playing those sports."

Like many young folks his age at the time, he did not know what he wanted to do after high school. He tried college, but lasted only one semester at North Carolina State in nearby Raleigh.

"I just wasted my daddy's money," he said. "But at least I realized I was wasting my daddy's money."

So he traveled to Detroit and took a job for Chevrolet, working in one of their factories.

"I worked five weeks and got laid off," he said.

By then Benny's father was reasonably well established in the Detroit area, owning a gas station and a taxicab service that included "fifteen or twenty cabs," according to Benny. He went to work for his father over the next eighteen months, learning as much as he could about his father's business. Chevrolet called Benny back to work, and he returned to the plant for a while but left again for good when his father asked him to come work for him full-time.

"I went to work as a mechanic, changing oil and changing tires," Parsons said. "I did whatever it took as far as the mechanical aspects of keeping those cabs running. I did also have my cab driver's license because I had to road test those cars. On holidays, when drivers were hard to find, my dad and I would both get out and drive and try to service the customers. But my primary job was being a mechanic."

It would prove to be great experience, and it steered Parsons in the direction of his life's calling. One day in the May 1960, Benny was working at his father's gas station when two men stopped by with a race car on the back of a truck.

"It was a 1960 Ford. Being from North Carolina and having read the *Winston-Salem Journal* all the time and being that much of a fan, I was like, 'Wow, a race car!' I knew what it was and it impressed me, where it wouldn't have impressed a lot of guys. They had just stopped to use the bathroom and they knew of my dad."

Parsons was curious about the two men, and struck up a conversation with them after they were done using the station's bathroom.

"Where are you guys headed?" Benny asked.

"Anderson, Indiana," they replied.

Then the two men looked at each other. They could tell the young man was fascinated by their race car.

"Do you want to go?" one of them asked Benny.

Parsons, nineteen at the time, definitely wanted to go. He went back into the station and told his father, and left right then and there. Over the next couple of years, he learned little by little about the racing business while traveling to various events with the two men, Wayne Bennett and Dick Gold.

"It was totally by chance. I happened to be there when that truck and car stopped by the gas station, only because those guys had to go to the bathroom," Parsons said. "They were just two guys who lived there in Detroit and loved to race. One was a driver and the other helped him out financially and mechanically. I started going to the races with them. I didn't drink [alcohol], but most of the guys who hung around did, so I became the truck driver.

I didn't know anything about auto racing, but I would roll a tire and hand them a wrench and all this other stuff. I'd do what I could."

Parsons worked for Bennett and Gold for more than two years before he seriously considered the idea of driving. In the winter of 1963, Gold stopped by the gas station again (Parsons continued to work at the gas station when they weren't out at races, which they were frequently but not anything like 365 days a year) and asked a simple question that would ultimately change the young man's life.

"Did you ever think about driving a race car?" Gold asked.

"Yeah, I guess I've thought about it from time to time," Parsons replied.

"Well, I had to buy this old race car from another fella," Gold added. "It needs some fixing up, but if you want to try it, I'd be willing to let you drive it."

"What did you pay for it?" Benny asked.

"Fifty dollars," came Gold's reply.

Parsons agreed to take a look at the car and consider driving it. They went to Gold's house, where he had the car pulled into an old wooden garage. "When he swung the door open, it was completely dark. But I looked closer and saw the car. My first thought was, 'If he paid fifty dollars for this piece of junk, he got cheated.'"

Still, Parsons was intrigued. It was a 1954 Ford with roll bars in it, and when Gold attempted to start it, the engine, somewhat surprisingly, coughed to life. Parsons's driving career was about to commence.

"We went to the junkyard and got some sheet metal to hang on there and painted it," Parsons said. "Wayne Bennett helped me set the car up to go around the corners. They let me put a tow bar behind the truck and haul my car, so it was a sweet deal. Their car was a yellow 98, so I made mine a yellow 98, too."

Soon Parsons was winning races. And at the end of the year, Dick Gold pulled him aside again and mentioned how great the other yellow No. 98 car was—the one that Gold had been driving at the half-mile track while Parsons was cutting his teeth in the piece of remodeled junk on the quarter-mile track where he used to watch races with his father.

"Why don't we sell you the good car? We're thinking of either quitting or building a new car," Gold suggested.

"How much?" Parsons asked.

"We think we can let you have it for fifteen hundred dollars."

This was no fifty-dollar investment: $1,500 was a whole lot of money in 1963, especially to Benny Parsons, who had come from such a modest background. But Benny wanted that race car. He went to his father and asked for some financial assistance, and Harold Parsons agreed to help Benny acquire the car.

"My dad helped me and I got together the money and went racing. We won like the first four races I was in," Benny said. "That was on the half-mile dirt track in Detroit. I also went to a three-eighth-mile asphalt track up north of Flint, at Dixie Speedway at a place called Birch Run. I won a couple more races up there and some on other half-mile dirt tracks. That's what got everyone's attention."

•   •   •

Getting the newer car had made Parsons understand more than ever that being competitive in racing depended on having the right equipment. It was the same then as it had always been and always would be; the drivers with the best backing were going to be the most successful, as long as they were careful with the equipment that they had been provided.

One day in 1964, Parsons and a friend were working on Parsons's race car when they got the grand idea that they would go see Jacques Passino, then the head of Ford Motor Company's racing program. Parsons wanted to try to convince Passino that Ford should sponsor his ride.

"He's a big shot. Worldwide," Parsons said. "And here we are, dressed in our boots with grease under our fingernails. But we got in to see him."

Once inside Passino's spacious office in Detroit, Parsons got right to the point. He wanted Passino to sponsor his ride on the ARCA circuit in the Michigan area. It was no small request, nor an inexpensive one.

"Listen, I can drive one of these cars you guys are making," Parsons said. "But I'm never going to get a chance unless I can get some money so I can go out and compete."

Passino thought it over. He was impressed with the persistence and spunk being displayed by Parsons. "I'll think about it. Call me in a couple of weeks," he said.

Parsons wasn't sure what to think. "He probably thought we were crazy. I don't know. But maybe the fact that we marched in there and said, 'Give me some help' was all it took," he told his friend.

Again, all Parsons was seeking was assistance in running the local ARCA circuit. But Ford had something else altogether in mind. The officials at the motor company didn't even wait for Parsons to call them back, calling him instead a few days later and stunning him with an offer.

"What would you say if we told you we had a Holman-Moody car ready for you? We want you to run a Grand National race at the track in Asheville, North Carolina. What do you say?" they said.

Parsons was confused. But he felt he couldn't say no, even if he had his reservations about the opportunity.

"I didn't feel like I could compete with those guys down south," he said. 'If I had had any sense, I would have said, 'No, because I'm not ready to run on a half-mile pavement track.'"

It was while sitting in his fancy Holman-Moody car on the starting grid at Asheville-Weaverville Speedway, nervous and sweating as he waited for the race to start, that he had his first encounter with the famous Richard Petty. He had heard of the great Petty, of course, and respected the family name greatly, as did all stock car drivers of the day. The start of the race was not far away when Petty strolled up to Parsons's car and stuck his hand out.

"Hi, I'm Richard Petty. Who are you?" Petty asked as the two shook hands.

Parsons had been around racing long enough to know how cutthroat the competition could be at most places, and he was stunned by Petty's small but friendly gesture. It also helped put him at ease.

"I was twenty-two years old at the time—a nobody," Parsons said. "You would have thought that Richard Petty had better things to do than to walk around before a race and introduce himself to a nobody like me. I never forgot that he took the time to do that. Since then, I've always been a Richard Petty fan."

Petty, on the other hand, thought nothing of it. He considered it simply the right thing to do. "It was a deal where you could do it because there weren't that many people around back then," he said later. "I'd go around and talk to all the owners, all the drivers, all the crews. That was just me. Everybody didn't do it, but some others did. I just liked that. That was my personality. It's an unwritten rule of how you're supposed to conduct yourself with the media and the fans."

And even fellow competitors, which Parsons was that day.

"It builds on itself and has helped make the sport popular," Petty reasoned.

Meeting Petty and sitting behind the wheel in a Holman-Moody car with a mandate from the Ford Motor Company made Parsons feel like he had hit the big time. "Oh, man, this is a big deal! I mean, I'm a factory driver now," he told himself as the race began on August 4, 1964.

What Parsons didn't know was that Ford had gotten together with John Holman of Holman-Moody and said that it would back one new team—and one new team only. They wanted Holman to test out two drivers in that particular race: Parsons and another young driver named Cale Yarborough. While the more experienced Yarborough went on to do well and even led several laps, Parsons spun out twice and looked very much like a nervous rookie with limited experience running on asphalt. It wasn't until later that he learned he had flunked his tryout.

Undaunted, upon his return to Detroit he went to see Passino again. "Hey, I know I didn't do so good in that Holman-Moody car. I know I don't deserve that ride. But I still need some help from you guys to run the ARCA circuit," Parsons pleaded.

Passino wasn't very compassionate, explaining that Ford's only concern, even on less prestigious circuits than the Grand National one, was results. To get Ford's backing, you had to produce. You had to consistently run out front and make the Ford Motor Company look good.

"You go out and get your stuff together, and after you lead ten ARCA races, call me back. Until then, forget it," Passino told Parsons.

Despite having had a small and even bitter taste of it, Parsons was determined now to get back to racing's highest level where he could rub elbows, or at least shake hands with, the likes of the great Richard Petty. Some of his friends thought he was crazy. But he and a couple of buddies quickly put together an old car and took it to an ARCA race in Springfield, Ohio.

"The course was about a half-mile and it had rained," Parsons said. "I qualified and sat on the pole and led the first ten laps. Whatever happened to that car after that, I don't know. But it was like, 'Okay, one down and nine to go.'"

Parsons kept his foot on the gas pedal. He led the ten races required to earn that phone call back to Passino and eventually gained Ford's backing for his ARCA races. He was content enough with that for a while, although he still yearned for another shot at the big time. His next chance came in December 1967 when he was invited to a party by Ford, where much to his surprise he discovered his name on a list of Ford drivers that included such open-wheel greats and part-time NASCAR drivers as A. J. Foyt, Mario Andretti, and Parnelli Jones.

"I didn't know why I had been invited to the party. I didn't know why my name was on the list," he said.

He soon discovered why. A short while after the party, a Ford official called him up and asked a familiar question. "What would you say if I told you we had a Holman-Moody car ready for you to take to Daytona Beach? You'd have to go down to Charlotte and pick up the car."

Parsons was excited. But before he could answer a resounding yes, there was one more little item the Ford guy had yet to mention. The car had no engine in it. "Oh yeah, you'll have to put the engine together. But when you get there, we'll give you everything you need," he said.

Just like the last time Ford surprised him with a proposition, Parsons felt he was in no position to turn the opportunity down. Despite some reservations, he said yes again and quickly hit the road, driving from Detroit to Charlotte as fast as he could without drawing too much attention from state troopers along the way. He also told himself that he was more experienced as a race car driver and better ready to handle whatever might be thrown at him this time around.

Even so, he was not prepared for what transpired upon his arrival at the Holman-Moody shop in Charlotte.

"So I go down and get this car," he said. "They give me a frame with a body hung on it. No fenders, just a roof and quarter panels. No doors, no fenders, no hoods."

And, of course, no engine per se—just the pieces with which to make one.

"They take everything from the car and throw it in my truck and say, 'Here you go,'" Parsons said.

He wasn't sure what to make of it. Or what to do. He hadn't had such a sinking feeling since the first time Dick Gold had swung open that garage door and shown him his first real ride, although in the back of his mind, he kept reminding himself how that had worked out okay.

"We had never seen a car like that before. I didn't have the first clue on how to fix it up," Parsons said. "So I went back to Detroit, and when I pulled up with it everybody said, 'This is ridiculous. You need to call them up and tell them you can't make it. You can't do it.'"

Parsons considered giving up. But then he realized something that would have another profound impact on his life. "I finally figured it out. This was a test," he said. "This was a test to see how badly I wanted to race. Now, if I want to race, I'll get to Daytona. If I call them up and say, 'Sorry, we can't get this car ready in time. We can't make it,' then I really didn't want to do this that bad. I decided it was something I wanted to do badly enough. So we had twenty-one days or something like that to build an engine and get this car ready to go."

Harold Parsons gave Benny the time off from the gas station and cab business that the younger Parsons needed. Benny scoured the city's junkyards for additional parts and spent endless nights for three weeks in a two-car wooden garage behind a friend's house, putting the car together. He was determined to make it to the race in Daytona.

"How do you test someone? You back them up to the wall and give them an impossible task and say, 'Do it.' That's what they did to me. It was an impossible task," Parsons said. "I was working at the gas station, I had a two-year-old child; we had nobody that worked full-time on the car. Everybody had another job.

"That was how badly I wanted it at the time. It turned out the impossible just took a little more determination, but we got it done."

He took his makeshift car to Daytona and sat on the pole for that ARCA race, running at more than 180 miles per hour. He also unknowingly started a little self-promotion campaign when he was asked to list his occupation on the driver application sheet upon his arrival there. He wrote down "taxi cab business" and forgot about it until later.

At the time, he had other concerns. "I get to Daytona and find out you have to have a flameproof uniform to drive," he said. "The only uniform I had ever had was a T-shirt and a pair of white pants. At the time, all the people that handled gas also had to have flameproof clothing. So they had a big black kettle—a huge kettle, like when your grandmother boiled clothing. They boiled water in it and put this chemical in there that rendered clothing flameproof."

Parsons took one look at the kettle of witch's brew and knew what he had to do: he dispatched a crew member to the nearest JCPenney department store to buy a pair of white coveralls. When the fellow returned a little while later with the goods, Parsons took a close look at it. The "uniform" looked a little large, but that was okay.

"We put it in the kettle, rendered it flameproof—and that was my uniform."

There was one problem. It looked horrible.

"I was about a [size] forty-two at the time and this outfit was a forty-eight. It was all the guy could find at JCPenney. I had to roll the sleeves up. It was kind of baggy, and it looked even worse after we dipped it in that kettle."

Parsons didn't care. He was running at the famed Daytona International Speedway, and it so happened that he ran well in the race. In fact, he thought he won it.

"I was running third and on the last turn beat the guy I thought was leading to the line and I thought I had won my first race at Daytona," Parsons said. "I mean, I thought I had won my first race at Daytona! I got back around to try to find where Victory Lane was because I had no idea."

When a NASCAR official approached, Parsons thought the guy was about to congratulate him and give him those much-needed directions to Victory Lane. Instead, the official shook his head and asked, "What are you doing?"

"I want to know where Victory Lane is because I just won this race!" an ebullient Parsons replied.

"You didn't win anything. You were a lap down."

Parsons was stunned. "How can that be?" he asked.

"When the caution flag came out during the race, you went into the pits. You pitted before the pace car picked up the field. You were lapped in the pits because you pitted too soon," the official explained.

Parsons was disappointed, but he knew the official probably was right. He was used to running shorter races on dirt tracks where you didn't even have to pit.

"I had never made a pit stop in my life, so maybe I did pit too soon. I have no idea," said Parsons in only a slight exaggeration. "But I always thought my uniform had something to do with it. It looked terrible. No way they wanted someone wearing something like that getting his picture taken in Victory Lane. I set ARCA back about fifty years."

He set his own driving career on fast forward at the same time. He was credited with third place, and for the first time in his life the press came looking for him to find out just who he was. That is when the legend of Parsons being an ex–cab driver was born and took full flight. In truth, he had mostly worked on his father's cabs as a mechanic, driving the taxis only on holidays or other rare occasions when the regular drivers couldn't or wouldn't work.

"People writing stories on that race said to themselves, 'Benny Parsons finished third. Who is he?' They went to my application for the race, and where it said 'occupation' I had put down 'taxi cab business.' They were like, 'Oh, he's a cab driver. What a great story.' That's how it all got started. But I never actually told anyone I was a cab driver," Parsons said.

Nonetheless, the good finish and extra publicity helped his standing with Ford. And once he started getting some support from Ford toward the end of the 1960s, he became more competitive. Still, he always felt he was short on money. Ford could provide certain parts and equipment, but racing was an expensive proposition and he was committed to doing well at it.

He constantly worked on his race car to try to make it better—sometimes to his detriment. Once he worked on it so long in Detroit that he suddenly realized he had left himself very little time to get to the track in Dayton, Ohio, to qualify for a race. It was a straight shot down Interstate 75, but he would have to hump it.

"We left Detroit at like eight o'clock in the morning to go to Daytona to race," he said. "There was no way we were going to make it, but we've got to. I needed the money. I needed to run well."

He and his crew members were driving a truck that was pulling the race car behind. They weren't far into the trip when calamity struck.

"At the last traffic light on our way out of Detroit, we broke a brake line in the truck," Parsons said. "The truck had a race engine in it. We didn't stop. We ran down I-75 as fast as we could go with no brakes. I can't believe the things that people did to go to the racetrack back then. You can't believe the things I've done."

Despite the herculean effort, Parsons still arrived in Daytona too late to participate in qualifying. "We had to start at the rear of the field, and then we busted a rear tire and it was a disaster," he said.

•   •   •

When Ford decided to back off in its racing program in 1970, Parsons was despondent. He was making maybe $10,000 a year racing in features that usually paid $400 to win. What little he made always went back into the race car. Without Ford's help, he wouldn't be able to keep on racing.

"Now I'm in a panic because I'm out of business. I'm not racing for a living, and I survived [in racing] off what the race car made," Parsons said. "If I cleaned house and won a feature and a heat in the dash [events at a short track], I couldn't have made much more than five hundred dollars. So I'm making no money, but I was doing exactly what I wanted to do. What I thought was that I was building for the future.

"As it later turned out, I was. But at that time, I thought it was over. I thought I was out of business. Ford had been giving me engines and gears and I wasn't paying for it. That's what I lived on."

Parsons was frantic. One of his contacts at Ford reached him and give him the lowdown. "You can take the equipment you have and race with it, but I won't be able to supply you with any more parts. You can keep the stuff you've got, but this well is drying up. You'd better find a new one to dip into," the Ford man told Parsons.

"And just where am I going to find something like that?" Benny asked.

"Listen, Benny, what you need to do is hook up with L. G. DeWitt."

"Who?"

"L. G. DeWitt. He's a guy who's got a car down south. He might be able to take you on and help you out. He might be looking for some driving help right about now."

On the way back from Daytona to Detroit at the time, Parsons and his wife already had planned to stop in North Wilkesboro, North Carolina, to visit with family. DeWitt's operation was located nearby, and Parsons decided to look him up. DeWitt had a car that he owned and operated on the Grand National circuit.

"I hear you might be looking for a driver," Parsons said to DeWitt.

"Well, we have a driver. It's Buddy Young. Right now he's injured. He crashed at Riverside [in California], but we think he's going to be okay to keep racing. Thanks anyway for asking," DeWitt replied.

Parsons figured he had played his hand and that was that. He returned to North Wilkesboro. He was in his uncle's barber shop when Junior Johnson's brother Fred called on the telephone, asking for him.

"They're looking for you down at DeWitt's place. They want you to drive that car," Fred Johnson said.

Parsons quickly dialed up DeWitt's shop. "I thought you didn't need me. I thought Buddy was going to be okay to race."

"He couldn't get a doctor's release. We want you to drive the car."

Parsons went straight back to DeWitt's shop, where they adjusted the seat to fit his frame. Then they were off to race, first at Richmond and then at Rockingham. This time Parsons didn't feel out of place on the bigger tracks nor intimidated by some of the other drivers. He was ready for the big time. The weekend after Rockingham, DeWitt came to him and told Parsons that he wanted him to drive the car full-time.

"I went home to Detroit and packed up the bags and came back to North Carolina," said Parsons, who soon was living in his home state full-time again.

He was making $150 per week driving the car, plus expenses. He also got 10 percent of whatever the car earned in each race—far less than the 40 percent most other drivers earned. But Benny Parsons could not have been happier. Shortly after thinking he was on his way out of racing, he was instead racing at the sport's highest level and showing that he could compete with the best.

His dogged determination really paid off three years later when, in 1973, he won the points championship. He followed that up with a Daytona 500 win for DeWitt in 1975, when he won after starting in the thirty-second position.

*   *   *

By 1979, Parsons was driving for another well-known owner in M. C. Anderson, and for the Daytona 500 he was in a No. 27 Oldsmobile sponsored by Griffin Marine. It had been a good week for Parsons, who qualified fifth and was excited about having the camera mounted inside his car, even though he knew he was risking something in performance over the long haul by agreeing to take on the extra weight that none of the other drivers wanted.

As he took the lead on Lap 50, he led Earnhardt, Tighe Scott, and Dick Brooks to the line as some of the earlier leaders fought for position behind them. Of the top cars, only Earnhardt's did not carry the name and/or logo of a sponsoring company, making it seem strangely out of place. All of the cars had one thing in common: they were hustling to get somewhere in a hurry, and they were running closely together again at high speeds, making it seem another wreck was inevitable.

On-air, Squier said it was like they were "covering a city block a second, in rush-hour traffic."

Jostling for position even farther back from the front were, among many others, the cars of drivers Bruce Hill and Gary Balough. Driving the No. 50 Oldsmobile sponsored by Newport & Associates and owned by Walter Ballard, Hill attempted to maintain his position as they headed into treacherous Turn 4. Suddenly he and the No. 87 Oldsmobile of Balough touched, setting off a chain reaction on Lap 55 that sent former Daytona 500 winner David Pearson spinning off into the infield.

When Pearson's famous No. 21 Mercury sponsored by Purolator and owned by the Wood brothers finally came to rest in the soggy, wet grass, the car was destroyed. There was extensive damage to both the front and the rear.

His day was done.

Seven cars in all were involved in the wild accident, including two that were still stuck motionless on the track—one up against the outside wall on the frontstretch just beyond Turn 4 where the melee had broken loose. Despite their eighteen cameras placed around the track, which they had figured to be enough because that's what it took to do a Super Bowl, it took several minutes for CBS to figure out just which cars were put out of action.

Announcer David Hobbs speculated—wrongly, as it turned out—that one of the mangled cars disabled on the track might be that of contender A. J. Foyt. Squier lamented that so many cars "costing $35,000 to $65,000 apiece were now out of it."

Parsons, carrying the nineteenth camera CBS employed, continued to lead the Great American Race through Lap 59, but suddenly there was someone else lurking close by. It was none other than Richard Petty, who was beginning to think he might just have what he needed to win this race after all.

One thing Petty knew for sure. At least he'd no longer have to worry about Pearson, which was a major relief.

"Along in those years, he was king of the hill on those superspeedways," Petty said. "If you wanted to win the race, you usually were going to have to beat him."

With Pearson out of the race, Petty nodded to himself and got crew chief Dale Inman on the radio. Like so many other times, they almost simultaneously said what the other was already thinking—so much so that years later neither could remember who said it first.

Noting that Pearson had wrecked out of the event, they told each other, "Okay, that's one less we've got to worry about."

The first Daytona 500, in 1959, gets under way. Lee Petty went on to win, but not without a healthy dose of controversy.

Bill France Sr. (left) handed over the reins to son Bill France Jr. in January 1972, but he stayed involved behind the scenes when it came to helping secure live, wire-to-wire national television coverage of the 1979 Daytona 500.

In this picture, taken less than a year after the 1979 race, Richard Petty (left) shares a light moment in the garage area with the young Kyle Petty.

Pole winner Buddy Baker in car No. 28 and Donnie Allison (No. 1) lead the field to the green flag at the start of the race.

Richard Petty's pit crew works feverishly to change four tires and pack in two cans of fuel during this midrace stop.

Driver A. J. Foyt (left) celebrates his victory in the 1972 Daytona 500 with car owner and crew chief Leonard Wood.

Bobby Allison (center) enjoys the victor's spoils after capturing the 1978 Daytona 500. Wife Judy is at Bobby's immediate left, and legendary car owner Bud Moore looks on from Bobby's far right. Bobby had hoped to repeat his win in 1979, but an early accident took him out of contention.

After becoming a racing champion in his own right, Ned Jarrett (left) became a pioneer in the art of broadcasting. Here, he interviews newcomer Dale Earnhardt prior to the 1979 event.

Long before he made the black No. 3 car famous, Dale Earnhardt drove
this yellow-and-blue No. 2 machine for owner Rod Osterlund, making his
Daytona 500 debut in it in 1979.

Proof that they weren't always enemies and, in fact, were usually very
friendly, this picture of Donnie Allison (left) and Cale Yarborough was
taken prior to the running of the 1979 race.

Cale Yarborough (second from the left) and Donnie Allison exchange heated words before The Fight escalates.

Cale Yarborough attempts to kick Bobby Allison after the elder Allison brother jumped out of his car to defend himself. Allison later joked, "I made sure I kept my helmet on."

Cale Yarborough prepares to use his helmet against the Allison brothers as Bobby tries to tackle him and Donnie surges forward in the background and a fireman moves in to break up the melee.

Richard Petty's pit crew piles on after winning the 1979 Daytona 500. Announcer Ken Squier gushed that the No. 43 car it instantly became "a race car turned school bus" as millions watched on television.

An exhausted but ecstatic Richard Petty hoists the winning trophy after capturing the 1979 Daytona 500 in dramatic and unlikely fashion, breaking a forty-five-race winless streak.

8

Second Cousins . . . Sometimes

etty's focus as he worked his way into the lead for the first time of the day was on the task at hand, but watching Pearson climb out of his wrecked Mercury in the infield touched off a memory Petty knew he could never shake, one that was as much a part of his storied legacy as a driver as anything else he had ever done, or hadn't done. It took him back to three years earlier when he and Pearson were the primary players in staging a race for the ages in the 1976 Daytona 500. That, too, was an important race in NASCAR history, for the excitement generated by that fantastic finish finally convinced many important television executives that this might just be a sport they could sell to willing advertisers on a much larger scale.

The '76 race was embroiled in more than its share of controversy before the green flag dropped, signifying the beginning of the race. In qualifying, A. J. Foyt and Darrell Waltrip laid down blistering laps that appeared to earn them spots on the front row for the 500—plus a $5,000 bonus for Foyt, who was the quickest with a lap of 187.477 miles per hour. But in the cases of both drivers, their second qualifying lap was more than two miles per hour slower than their first, and quickest. That caught the attention of Bill Gazaway, NASCAR's technical director. He said he had "reason to be suspicious" and ordered crew chiefs Hoss Ellington and Mario Rossi to let him take a postqualifying peek under the hoods of their cars.

At first the crew chiefs balked, which was in itself even more suspicious. Gazaway also said he wanted to take a closer look at the cars of drivers Dave Marcis and Bruce Hill, who had been the 1975 Rookie of the Year. The crew chief for Marcis was the legendary Harry Hyde, who said he had no objections.

"They can cut my car in half if they want to," Hyde said. "We've got nothing to hide."

For nearly seven hours, NASCAR officials poked and prodded and studied their findings on the four cars. At some point during these proceedings, they also called in their attorney to assist in drawing up a prepared written statement announcing their decisions.

Their stunning final verdict: the qualifying times of Foyt, Waltrip, Marcis, and Hill, who had qualified ninth-fastest with a lap speed of 180.513 miles per hour, were all "disallowed." Per the NASCAR attorney's stipulation, Gazaway, in making the announcement, was very careful never to use the words "cheating" or "disqualified."

Gazaway did go on to say that the cars of Foyt, Waltrip, and Hill "were set up for use of fuel pressure assists which are not allowed." In layman's terms, the cars in question had been found to be using fuel lines that likely had contained nitrous oxide, more commonly known as laughing gas. Nitrous oxide was known to be used by those looking to gain an edge in qualifying because it could provide quick, sudden, and quite significant bursts of horsepower.

Marcis was found guilty of something else Hyde hadn't figured on NASCAR officials ruling a violation. The statement said his qualifying time would also be disallowed because his car was equipped with a "moveable air deflector device in front of the radiator, which is against the rules." Again, in layman's terms, Hyde appeared to have attempted to gain an edge in downforce by illegally tampering with the radiator on Marcis's car.

He denied it, of course, and was furious when he realized that Marcis would be sitting on the pole if the times of Foyt and Waltrip were disallowed and the lap times of Marcis were upheld. After all, Marcis had laid down two quality laps, taking away all suspicion that he, too, might have used the laughing gas for a quick, illegal burst of additional speed.

"We should be on the pole, fair and square," Hyde insisted.

Ellington did not deny that he had a nitrous oxide bottle hooked up to a fuel line in Foyt's car. But he tried to play dumb when interrogated by Gazaway. "Golly, I forgot about that. I put it in there three years ago at Trenton and it's been there ever since," he told the NASCAR official.

Gazaway and other NASCAR officials were not amused. Neither was Foyt. The NASCAR interloper from open-wheel racing was livid. He claimed he didn't know anything about the inner workings of the Ellington car. "I just drive it, dammit!" he said while protesting to anyone who would listen—and to Bill France Jr. in particular.

Young Bill was still relatively new as NASCAR president, having replaced Big Bill France only four years earlier. Folks who wondered how Big Bill would have handled the controversy soon found out when Bill Sr. was called into the garage area to deal with Foyt, who was getting more irate by the minute. Big Bill had earlier enlisted the help of his longtime friend and noted bigot, Alabama governor George Wallace, to serve as grand marshal of the race, and made it clear that he wanted order restored before his esteemed guest arrived in Daytona Beach.

"Governor Wallace told me to make sure all these sonsa-bitches are legal by the time he gets here, and I'm gonna do just that. Right now," the elder France snapped.

Sports Illustrated later reported that it took him about ten minutes. Then Big Bill "emerged from behind closed doors with his arm around the neck of a suddenly compliant Foyt, who was saying, "Yessir . . . yessir . . . yessir."

Waltrip, meanwhile, said he would accept NASCAR's penalty. But he didn't go quietly into the night. Before leaving the track, he commented about how cheating was a way of life in NASCAR. In their official statement, NASCAR had been careful never to use the word; Waltrip had no such reservations.

"In Grand National racing, there are a lot of things you have to do to keep up with the competition. It's common knowledge that cheating in one form or another is part of it," Waltrip said.

"If you don't cheat, you look like an idiot. If you do it and you don't get caught, you look like a hero. If you do it and get caught, you look like a dope. Put me in the category where I belong."

Hyde, on the other hand, was still ranting about not deserving to be grouped with the others. "I don't know why Billy France did this to me," he said. "The way the publicity went, people all across the country think we were using the [nitrous oxide] bottle like the others. I'm branded nationally as a cheater and all we were doing was what they said was okay."

All the penalties stood and all the sonsabitches were in line by the time Governor Wallace arrived to perform his prerace duties. But the pole was inherited by Ramo Stott, a full-time bean farmer and part-time driver from Keokuk, Iowa, who had in the previous eight seasons entered only twenty-nine races, registering a handful of top ten finishes.

The offenders from the first qualifying run were permitted to run in the twin 125-mile qualifying races, which were won, appropriately enough, by Waltrip and Marcis, respectively.

A subsequent headline in *National Speed Sport News* confirmed Hyde's fear about being lumped in with the others. It read simply, "Two Cheaters Win 125-mile Qualifiers."

●   ●   ●

Dale Inman, Richard Petty's longtime crew chief and second cousin, always preferred to be known as an "innovator." No one knew the King better than Inman, though he rarely, if ever, called Petty that. Certainly no one in racing had known Petty longer.

"Well, you know, I guess we're second cousins. His mother and my mother were first cousins. And I always tell people we're cousins sometimes, but not all of the time," Inman said.

It was his standard reply when someone asked about his unique relationship with Petty. They didn't carry the same last name, but they might as well have. And as long as Petty wasn't doing something that irritated the sometimes irascible Inman, laying claim to being the King's second cousin was fine with the crew chief.

Of course, they hadn't always been crew chief and driver, although sometimes, by the mid-1970s, it sure seemed like that. Before they became the best stock car racing tandem of all time, they were kids together.

"We kind of just grew up together. As kids we used to race bicycles. Kids today get cars when they get their license," Inman said. "We got our licenses, too, but you had the family car, and other than that you had to ride bicycles."

They did more than ride their bicycles. They also raced 'em.

"We had a racetrack running out through the woods," Inman said. "We'd build up a little bank of dirt and wet it down like we'd seen at the real racetrack and stuff like that. We'd run over each other, do the whole ball of wax. We were half-grown, in our late teens, when we were racin' bicycles through the woods."

But while they couldn't yet drive an automobile, they were beginning to learn the racing business from Richard's father, Lee. "Before we could play or go swimming or play football or go do whatever we had to do, we had to have Lee's race car ready. We got started doing that," Inman said.

Soon they were driving at least whenever they could get their family cars, which nearly led to big trouble one night that might have clipped the King's reign as stock car driving royalty before it ever had a chance to blossom.

"We played football together, we raced on the highway together. I'm not proud of that, but that's the way it was back in those days. It went on back then," Inman said. "It would be late at night. Oh, Lord, me and him were racing from Randleman [North Carolina, back to Level Cross] one time and it would have liked to have gotten both of us. But we didn't hit nothin'. He spun out a couple times.

"We was comin' home. He lived in the house right there by Lee's race shop. I lived about three-quarters of a mile away. When the soda shop closed up, it was just ideal that we would race home. Somebody stopped in front of us that night. [Richard] had to spin out to miss both of us. But we both got through it without tearing anything up, including ourselves. There were some other close calls like that, but that's the one I remember most."

As they got a little older, Lee Petty started giving Richard and Dale more responsibilities. One of them included towing Lee's race car to events all over the Southeast and sometimes even farther away.

"We would be towing the car up and down the road, towing it all around," Inman said in 2007. "Before we had trailers, we would just hook it up to the family car and tow it to the racetrack. We talk about it today and we're like, 'How in the world did we do it?' Because the highways weren't as good back then as they are today. There weren't as many guardrails.

"Of course Lee fixed it up pretty good for us to tow with, because it had good towbars and we had the steering hooked to the race car. When we'd turn the wheel, it had cables hooked to it so it would turn a little with us, too. We had brakes on the race car, too, and we would run fast. We would run over a hundred miles an hour while pulling the race car."

One time in 1958, Lee Petty was scheduled to run a Grand National race in Trenton, New Jersey. He was leading in the points standings at the time, which was a big deal to him. Driver Jack Smith was second in points. The Grand National race the following week was scheduled for the track in Riverside, California—about as far away from Trenton, New Jersey, as it could possibly be. Lee Petty didn't like the logistics of trying to get a race car from Trenton to Riverside, or even from Level Cross to Riverside. It would be expensive and time-consuming and one major hassle.

So Lee approached Smith with an offer. "If neither one of us go to Riverside, it ain't gonna hurt nobody in points. Nobody else is going to catch us," the elder Petty told Smith.

"Sorry, Lee. I'm going. I'm gonna run Riverside, too," Smith replied.

It forced Lee Petty into his backup plan. Then circumstances forced him to go to the backup plan of his backup plan, which is sometimes how it went in those days.

"Jack said he was going, so Lee got a car ready," Inman said. "Maurice [Petty, Richard's brother, and later his renowned engine builder] and Richard were going to drive the race car to Riverside—not tow it or pull it by truck but just drive it.

"I think Red Myler and myself and Lee were going to Trenton. We were going to tow our car there. I think we had a trailer, or maybe we just towed it on the ground. But we were out in the front yard playing football [beforehand] and Richard hurt his shoulder. I still don't know whether he was faking it or not, but then I had to take his place and go to Riverside. Me and Maurice drove the car to Riverside.

"I often think, 'How in the world did Lee let two kids—and we were older then, but by definition we were still kids—drive that car across the country? He turned me and Maurice loose to go across the country, and I had hardly ever been out of Randolph County. I had only been out of state to a race or two.'"

Lee might have been thinking the same thing to himself not long after dispatching the pair down the road.

"Well, that's a good story right there. He fixed us a speedometer. We had a chassis dyno [measuring the engine's power] and he fixed us a speedometer—1,500 rpms meant fifty miles an hour, or fifty-five," Inman recalled.

Then Lee called the youngsters together and gave them clear and specific instructions. "I just rebuilt the motor now, and put a change of oil in here, so be careful with it," he said. "Drive it to Shreveport [Louisiana] and don't run it over sixty miles an hour. When you get to Shreveport, go into a service station, borrow the lift and change the oil, and then you can run it maybe sixty-five or seventy."

Maurice Petty and Dale Inman listened intently and nodded their heads. "Yessir," they replied in unison.

The next afternoon, the pair embarked on their mission. They took off down the road to Asheboro and picked up Route 49 to Charlotte. Meanwhile, back in Level Cross, Lee Petty had scheduled a meeting with some men who were driving up from Charlotte. When they arrived at the Petty Enterprises shop, they began to make small talk with Lee.

"Did y'all come up 49?" Lee asked them.

"Yessir, we did," came their reply.

"Well, you might have met my boys on their way to California."

The men exchanged glances with one another. "Oh, so that's what that was. They were runnin' so damn fast, we couldn't tell what that was," they said of the Petty race car they had seen running wide open on a public road.

Maurice and Dale didn't slow down then or anytime soon thereafter. "We ran across the desert at probably 115 or 120 miles an hour," Inman said. "It had no windows. It had a windshield and back glass, and we put plastic in the quarter windows. We had two headlights, but didn't have a dimmer switch. They were just stuck in there. We had one taillight—no turn signal, no brake lights, no windshield wipers, no side windows. We crawled in and out through the doors."

They attracted attention wherever they went. It often was the unwanted attention brought on by the whining of a siren from a police car siren trying to catch them from behind.

"Maurice got stopped six times and I got stopped once," Inman said. "We never did get a ticket. They just wanted to know what the hell it was we were driving. Of course, we were speeding a lot of the time. But those were different times. That's just the way it was back then."

•   •   •

Ramo Stott, the bean farmer from Iowa, did not lead the 1976 Daytona 500 for long. By the time ABC-TV Sports geared up for what it billed as its third consecutive "live presentation of the conclusion of the Daytona 500," it was a duel for the ages between two giants: Richard Petty and David Pearson.

Pearson, nicknamed "the Silver Fox," was not only handsome with a winning smile but possessed movie-star good looks. He also happened to be an incredibly talented driver, and by 1976 had quite the lengthy and impressive résumé to back up that claim. He won fifteen of forty-two Grand National starts in 1966 and won his first points championship, finishing first, second, or third in twenty-five of those starts and in the top ten in eight others.

Two years later, driving for the Holman-Moody operation, he won the first of back-to-back points championships, and the numbers were even more incredible: in 1968, he placed in the top ten in thirty-eight of forty-eight starts, won sixteen races, and finished second in twelve others; in 1969, the year most of the top drivers refused to run at Talladega, he won eleven races, finished second eighteen times, and third on nine occasions. He also combined to win twenty-six poles in the two remarkable seasons.

By then, Pearson had come a long way from his modest beginnings in Spartanburg, South Carolina. The first car he ever purchased was a 1938 Ford. It was such a wreck that his mother, Lennie, took one look at it and immediately offered him thirty dollars just to remove it from the family premises. No dummy, Pearson took the money and obliged. Then he took the cash from selling the junker to buy a 1940 Ford that at least looked a little better. But he had to hide it from his mother so she wouldn't make him sell that one, too.

He hid the car and worked on it at Mack's, a local Spartanburg hangout for aspiring drivers and mechanics. He made a roll bar out of a discarded bed frame and fixed it up as best he could, and then went racing at local dirt tracks. Right away, he knew he wanted more.

He got his chance to race at NASCAR's highest level in 1960, after friends had founded the David Pearson Fan Club on a local radio station and begged the public to donate money toward his cause. Pearson was trying to raise enough money to purchase an old race car from NASCAR regular Jack Smith, the driver who once had turned down Lee Petty's offer to avoid the long racing commute from Trenton to Riverside. Despite his friends' best efforts, in the end Pearson still needed to borrow $2,000 from his father, Eura, to complete the transaction.

Running only selected races because of the tight budget of his independent one-car operation in 1960, Pearson still managed to capture Rookie of the Year honors. That landed him a ride the next season with Ray Fox Sr., a respected owner who put him in a Pontiac and told him that good times lay ahead. Pearson wasn't so sure yet. Just to be on the safe side and make certain he'd always have some money coming in, young David also kept a job with a heating and roofing company in Spartanburg.

But Fox was right. He knew driving talent when he saw it, and recognized that Pearson had an abundance of it. Rides with legendary car owners Cotton Owens (with whom he won the 1966 championship) and Holman-Moody followed, along with impressive wins at the big speedways in Charlotte, Daytona, Atlanta, and Richmond. David Pearson was at last doing what he wanted to do, and excelling at it.

"Pearson was a product of a textile mill environment," said Humpy Wheeler, who took over as general manager of Charlotte Motor Speedway in 1976 but had watched Pearson drive for years. "He was very quiet and reserved, very pragmatic, never had much to say.

"You never saw Pearson in a race—particularly at a superspeedway—until the end. The last ten percent, he'd show up. Where was he the rest of the time? He was buried back there in eighth or ninth or tenth, just waiting."

His best was yet to come as the 1970s beckoned. After a brief down period at the start of the new decade, when Pearson wanted to back off a full-time schedule and soon found himself out of the mix at the declining Holman-Moody operation, he hooked up with the Wood brothers out of Stuart, Virginia. It proved to be a perfect fit.

The legendary A. J. Foyt had been driving for the Wood brothers, but Glen Wood, who headed the operation, wanted to select which races the team would run in. He and Foyt had trouble agreeing on which events to enter. To Glen Wood it was simple, and his philosophy fit with Pearson's. "We run only certain events, but they're always the biggest events. We run the ones that pay the most money," Glen told Pearson.

"I like the sound of that," replied Pearson, who earlier in his career also had been nicknamed "Little David" and "Giant Killer" because of his wins in the big races such as the World 600 in Charlotte, the Firecracker 250 in Daytona, and the Dixie 400 in Atlanta.

Pearson knew it was a solid ride. After years of being with the best and then bouncing around with little success in 1970 and 1971, when he couldn't find steady backing, he felt a solid ride was exactly what he needed. He also liked the idea of running only the biggest races.

On April 16, 1972, Pearson made his first start for Wood Brothers Racing at the Winston Cup Rebel 400 at Darlington Raceway in Darlington, South Carolina—Cale Yarborough's old home track. Richard Petty was strong in his 1972 Plymouth that day, but Pearson held him off in his No. 21 '71 Mercury, capturing the first-place prize of $16,850. It wasn't the first time the two had dueled; they'd gone at it twice in 1967 at the same track, first in the Rebel 400 and then at the Southern 500, with Petty finishing first and Pearson second each time. But this time it was different. And this time, it signaled the beginning of a period that would define arguably the greatest driver rivalry in the history of the sport.

•   •   •

With the ABC coverage finally up and running, the final twenty-two laps of the 1976 Daytona 500 went a long way toward defining the Petty-Pearson rivalry. The one big race that had eluded Pearson his entire career was the Daytona 500, and this appeared to be his day to rectify that—if he could hold off Petty. Meanwhile, ABC coordinating producer Dennis Lewin was engaged in a conversation with

Roone Arledge, a higher-ranking producer who was on-site at the network's headquarters in Innsbruck, Austria, where the Winter Olympics were in full swing and for which ABC was providing comprehensive coverage.

"How's it going? Is the race going to run over into our Olympics coverage?" Arledge asked.

"No," Lewin replied. "Everything is fine."

Arledge said he was glad to hear it. What was left unsaid was that no one felt it would be justified for even the finish of a Daytona 500 to cut into coverage time of an Olympics.

A few minutes later, it all changed.

Years later, Lewin would tell author Mike Hembree, "Everything was going along as expected. Then—wham!—so much for that."

Pearson held the lead until Petty shot past him to take over with thirteen laps to go. The pair then rode in nose-to-tail formation for the next twelve laps, with everyone knowing Pearson would make his move at some point very soon.

This was the era of the slingshot pass on the superspeedways—the day of unrestricted engines and bulky body styles that made the simple aerodynamics of the signature move irresistible to the trailing car and virtually impossible to fend off by the lead one. But then, of course, it was all a matter of timing. The process could be almost immediately reversed, and therefore the trailing car, if in second place on the last lap of a race, did not want to make a move too soon. The bulky lead car would create such a tremendous wash of air that once the second-place car pulled out into it, the trailer literally shot past the helpless front-runner.

Among those left wondering when Pearson would make his move was Eddie Wood, Glen's son. He was on the radio with Pearson, serving as the spotter for the Wood brothers' team high above Daytona International Speedway. He watched in tense silence as the cars took the white flag signaling one lap to go.

"They go into [Turn] 1, he didn't say anything," Eddie said of Pearson.

As they went through Turn 2 and came off of it, the radio crackled.

"I'm gonna try it here," Pearson said.

Wood strained his neck to see what was happening. "They head for [Turn] 3, and we can't see anything. We're watching the crowd, and we know he's doin' something because of the way they're reacting," he said.

On the backstretch of the final lap, Pearson executed a classic slingshot pass to perfection and got his Mercury around Petty. He vaulted into the lead.

"I got him!" Pearson shouted into the radio. Eddie Wood almost allowed himself a little smile, but he knew the race was not yet over.

Then Pearson made a slight but seemingly costly mistake. Once in the lead, he drifted high in the third turn, and Petty took advantage to duck under the No. 21 machine.

"He's under me!" Pearson said.

Any hint of a smile disappeared from Eddie Wood's face.

Pearson and Petty then came barreling into Turn 4 in a door-to-door battle.

Through Turn 4, Petty actually had pulled back ahead by half a car length. But as they exited the final turn, this time it was Petty who drifted a little high. In the next instant, the two cars slapped each other. They wobbled. Then Pearson went careening nose first into the outside wall, clipping Petty's bumper and sending the No. 43 car spinning in the process. Both cars spun wildly out of control.

Pearson's voice boomed over the radio again. "The bitch hit me!" he exclaimed.

Petty's No. 43 Dodge fishtailed for two hundred yards or more down the frontstretch and then turned head-on into the wall as well. It finally ground to a halt in the field grass, fewer than one hundred yards short of the finish line. Pearson bounced first into the path of driver Joe Frasson before spinning to a stop facing the wrong way at the entrance to pit road.

Even as he was spinning out of control, Pearson remained calm behind the wheel of his Mercury. He had the amazing presence of mind to ram in the clutch and rev his engine even as he hit the wall and spun, hoping to keep the car running no matter what was going to happen next. Petty made the serious error of ignoring his clutch as his car bounced off the wall and slid to rest in the grassy infield less than a football field short of the finish line and his sixth Daytona 500 victory. As a result, his engine died. He desperately set about trying to restart it, to no avail.

Pearson came back on the radio. To Eddie Wood, he sounded remarkably calm.

"Where's Richard?" Pearson asked.

Silence. Eddie Wood, who had been marveling at Pearson's ability to control his emotions, now needed to do the same and gather himself.

"Where's Richard?" Pearson repeated.

Finally, Eddie forced himself to locate Petty's car, which now was stopped and didn't appear to be going anywhere. In fact, all of the King's men, which included Inman and Maurice Petty and even Richard's son, young Kyle Petty, were running to the wounded car's aid and beginning a futile and misguided attempt to push it across the finish line.

"It wouldn't start because the fan was in the radiator, and wouldn't let the motor turn over to start," Inman said.

"He's stopped! Keep on comin'," Wood told Pearson.

"I'm comin'," Pearson replied.

And he did.

"He kept on coming, right on by him," Wood said. "Right to the finish line."

Pearson inched past Petty and across the line doing an estimated twenty miles per hour. He had won his first Daytona 500, collecting a $50,000 check for doing so in the process.

Petty's crew illegally pushed his listless Dodge across the finish line. It didn't count. But since no one else was on the lead lap at the time and he had completed 199 laps in the 200-lap race, Petty still claimed second place. Maurice Petty, Richard's younger brother and engine man, led a charge on Pearson's car as it crawled down pit road heading for Victory Lane.

"He's all up in David's window," said Eddie, wondering for a long time after what the two men were saying to each other.

"It was really simple," Pearson later explained. "He asked me what happened and I told him. The bitch hit me. Word for word."

Petty's crew seemed to be looking for a fight until Richard climbed out of his car and calmed them down. "If you want to blame somebody, blame me," he told them. "It was my fault."

But Petty never said anything directly to Pearson. Neither man figured he had to.

"He knew what happened," Pearson said. "He was probably faster than me that day. If he hadn't come up into me, he would have won the race. He was that much faster than me. What happened, he was trying to block me more than anything. But he got into me. And, of course, both of us wrecked. I was lucky and kept my car going."

Petty would be haunted by the blown opportunity for many years to come. "After all I've done in my career, the race I'll be remembered most for—and the one I'll remember most—is the one I lost," he said.

Television executives, like others who had watched the spectacle unfold, were ecstatic about the future possibilities of this sport that obviously could be packed with the rare combination of raw emotion and ragged, on-the-edge-of-your-seat excitement. The 1976 Daytona 500 proved the France family's point that it was an event that could hold a nation's attention, arguably for much longer than a few dozen laps at the end. Or at least that was what the France family would contend until finally getting CBS to agree to televise it live from wire to wire in 1979.

"That finish was just another chip to throw out on the table that had a role in moving the sport along," Bill France Jr. later said. "It was one of the better finishes."

It was good enough that ABC's coverage of the Olympics had to wait, by the way. "We stayed with the race and ran over several minutes into the Olympics' time," Lewin said.

The news reports of the race were certainly encouraging as well, giving France Jr. even more ammo as he attempted to score more live TV time for NASCAR. Writer Bob Moore of the *Charlotte Observer* newspaper called it the "most dramatic finish in NASCAR history." Another reporter, Fred Seeley of the *Jacksonville Times-Union*, wrote that "what was supposed to be a great race on asphalt ended with a wild finish on dirt like a half-mile bull ring." Tim Carlson of the *Daytona Beach News-Journal* added, "It was magnificent, heart-stopping and just a shade ridiculous."

But auto racing writer Frank Blunk of the *New York Times* perhaps summed it up best: "What can they do to top that?" he asked in his column.

It took another three years, until 1979, to discover the answer.

•   •   •

Strangely, what had happened in the Daytona 500 one year before the 1976 melee ended up playing a role in what happened in 1979. In the 1975 running of the 500, it had appeared that Pearson was going to break through in the big race. But then Petty gave an assist to Benny Parsons in a history-changing move that helped Parsons win instead.

Wrecks and mechanical failures had taken most of those who figured to be top contenders out of the '75 race, and Parsons found himself running more than five seconds behind the leader, Pearson, with just ten laps remaining. Petty was way off the pace, eight laps down after earlier displaying flashes of possibly having the car to beat, according to Inman. A series of unscheduled green-flag pit stops changed that in a hurry, but it was what they had to do to keep the car running.

"We were down there and we had the Dodge Charger," Inman said. "And just a few laps into the race—I remember this very distinctly—but Richard said to me, 'Can't nobody run with me today.' We were heads and shoulders above everybody. But then we busted a [cylinder] head and we were leaking water. And when it would get so hot, we would have to come in and put water in. With about twelve or fifteen laps to go, we came in and put water in for the last time. We would run for a while and then it would get hot again."

The Petty car was fast when it had water in it. Richard flew out of the pits and went right by Parsons, even though Parsons was running second. That was when Inman got on the radio.

"Back up and get Benny," he ordered Richard.

Petty slowed down and picked Parsons up, leading him around the track. The two started drafting together, gaining steadily on the leader Pearson.

"Pearson had got together with Cale [Yarborough] and had picked his pace up some, too. But Richard and Benny were faster together than they were," Inman said.

With three laps to go, Pearson's lead was sliced to just 2.1 seconds. Then the Silver Fox found himself trapped between the lapped cars of Yarborough and Richie Panch. As Pearson attempted to get around them, he and Yarborough tapped fenders, sending Pearson spinning off into the infield grass. Parsons drove into the lead with help from Petty and beat runner-up Bobby Allison by more than a lap.

It was an assist that Parsons never forgot. Four years later, when Petty arrived in Daytona for the '79 race, he was still struggling to figure out the Oldsmobile he had switched to midway through the 1978 season when he and Inman finally grew fed up with trying to make the Dodge Magnum competitive. Parsons watched as Petty struggled early on in practices at Daytona.

"We were unfamiliar with the coil springs," Inman said.

Parsons noticed and decided to share some information with the men who had helped him win his Daytona 500 four years earlier. He told his crew chief, David Ifft, to give Inman help with setting up Petty's car. They even shared parts.

"Take them springs down there to Dale before Richard kills himself," Parsons told his crew chief.

"It was a big, big help," Inman admitted.

The assistance offered by Parsons was bearing dividends for the Petty car by Lap 60 of the 1979 Daytona 500, when Richard surged into the lead and held it through Lap 69. On Lap 65, though, Petty was passed by Donnie Allison, who got one of his laps back.

Then Dale Earnhardt, the rookie who just wouldn't go away, snatched the lead away for one lap—followed by a bevy of drivers who swapped the lead back and fourth for the next thirty laps. Petty would regain it for a lap or two, followed by Neil Bonnett and Parsons again. Then Lennie Pond led a single lap, Geoff Bodine led five sandwiched around another three-lap parade led by Parsons. Finally, Parsons settled into the lead on Lap 86 and stayed there for a while with viewers getting the in-car camera view as he surged in and out of the lead before getting there for the extended period.

"You were with him as he takes the lead again!" Squier told the television viewers during one in-car camera shot, which because of the limited technology was always the same: a straight-ahead view out the front of Parsons's windshield.

On the CBS telecast, interviews with Big Bill France and actor Ben Gazarra, who was attending his first NASCAR event, were interspersed around live action and a short feature about David Pearson's unique trophy room on his sprawling spread in Spartanburg, South Carolina, where he not only had his own private airport attached and a five-acre lake where he could go fishing but had also purchased what previously was a country general store and converted it into his own personal trophy room. As with the earlier feature on Bobby Allison that ran shortly after a wreck appeared to end Allison's chances on this day, it appeared the television producers jammed in the feature on Pearson because they had it in the can and knew it was now or never to run it after his accident. It was, nonetheless, interesting and helped the viewers at home pleasantly pass the time as the racetrack was cleaned up and the caution period played out.

Despite being the size of a small house, Pearson's converted "general store" wasn't big enough to hold all of the racing trophies won through the years by the Silver Fox. He told Squier that the building held only about two-thirds of the prizes he had claimed.

But he wouldn't be adding to his stockpile on this day. Ned Jarrett finally caught up to him in the garage area after the wreck that had ended his day on Lap 55.

"I was more or less taking it easy, trying to feel things out because I thought the track was still a little wet, especially after Donnie and Bobby [Allison] got into it earlier," Pearson told Jarrett. "I got hit a couple of times out there, but I don't know by who."

Jarrett commented that Pearson, who was smiling and very calm, didn't seem all that upset about it. "There ain't no need to cry about it. It's done over with," Pearson replied.

In his interview with CBS reporter Mary Ann Bunch under a huge CBS Sports banner in a VIP suite above the start-finish line at Daytona International Speedway, Big Bill France downplayed the earlier close call with the weather. "In no way has our weather been as bad as it's been up north," he said.

He was right about that. Doug Rice and millions of other Americans were snowbound, trying to stay warm and beginning to take an even greater interest in how this race day was going to end up. Rice grimaced, however, when English announcer David Hobbs took note of Darrell Waltrip stopping in the pits and said, "They're lifting the hood, the bonnet, on Darrell's car. It sounded rough when he went by last time."

Americans didn't call the hood of a car a "bonnet."

Parsons, meanwhile, made a quick and routine stop in the pits to take on four new Goodyear tires and fill up on gas. During the stop, which took all of 48.66 seconds, Parsons actually gestured toward pit reporter Brock Yates and inquired about how the in-car camera was working out.

"He saw me standing here and gestured as to how the camera was operating," Yates said. "And I gave him a big thumbs-up and told him things were working just fine. He gave me back a big smile. He's very pleased he is contributing to our show as well as leading the race."

He wasn't the only one smiling. The television executives were smiling as well, and so were Big Bill France, Bill France Jr., and other NASCAR brass. This was developing into a fine day indeed.

9

Tougher and Toughest?

P etty's developing fine day not only didn't necessarily start out that way but truthfully was not supposed to occur at all. Richard wasn't supposed to be racing. It was his team's little quasi-secret. Other racing insiders knew at least most of the details, but as Petty himself would say years later, "We didn't put it up on the Internet or anything. Of course they didn't have the Internet back then. You've got to figure, the coverage of what goes on now is so much more than the coverage we used to have."

Never one to carefully watch what he ate or take the best care of himself away from the track—despite the urgings of Inman to do a better job of it—Petty wasn't far removed from a hospital bed when he got behind the wheel of his famous STP-sponsored No. 43 Oldsmobile for the 1979 Daytona 500. In fact, his doctor in Greensboro, North Carolina, had urged anyone who would listen (and even Petty and a few others who flat-out wouldn't) to have the driver skip both the season-opening race at Riverside and the 500. Petty's doctor insisted that the King was in no condition to attempt driving a race car at high speeds for hours at a time. In fact, his doctor suggested that he take three months off from racing.

"They took out about half my stomach the winter before. It was ulcers. They split me open and threw about half of it away," Petty said. "My doctor in Greensboro called the doctor down there [in Daytona] and said, 'Don't let him in that race car.'"

Petty wouldn't even consider taking three weeks, let alone three months, off from the job he loved. "I didn't think anything about it. I'm a big believer in mind over matter, so I didn't even let my mind go there," he said. "You know what I mean? That was last week when we did that, so I didn't even go down that road.

"You had a job to do and you wanted to do it. So you didn't pay much attention to your mother or your daddy or the doctors when you're set on doing something. It might not have been the best thing in the world for me, but I didn't look at the downside. I was looking at the upside, as far as getting in the car and doing my thing."

Inman didn't want his second cousin doing his thing at first in 1979. He tried to get someone else lined up to drive at least the season opener in Riverside. Lee Petty and Maurice Petty agreed with Inman, and tried to talk Richard into letting another driver handle that race so he would have more time to recover. "But he wouldn't hear of it. He didn't even want to talk about it," Inman said.

Mercifully, Petty ran only fourteen laps at Riverside before retiring because of engine failure. He finished thirty-second out of the thirty-five cars entered in the race, which didn't appear to bode well for Daytona.

It wasn't the first time Petty had defied doctor's orders to run a race. Three years earlier, in 1976, he also underwent major stomach surgery because of ulcer problems and emerged, with a full beard, from the hospital to go almost straight to Riverside to open the season as usual. Inman was not surprised.

"There were a lot of times where Richard had to have relief. No disrespect to him, but he just never did take care of himself the way he should," Inman said. "He never ate like he should and

[did] the training he should. I fussed at him about it, but he never paid me any attention on it."

On race day, Petty still wasn't feeling too well. But at least the cooler weather would provide some relief inside the car. Some, but not much.

"Even on a cold day, the car was like a heater. It could be forty degrees outside and you'd be sweating inside the car, doing all your physical and mental stuff—plus all your heat coming from sitting on top of that exhaust and stuff like that," Petty said.

Then, in typical homespun Petty fashion, he quickly added, "But that was no big deal."

Privately, Inman was impressed with Richard's dogged approach to the job no matter what the circumstances. Outwardly, he never let it show. And while he might fret over Richard's lack of dedication to a better training and diet regimen, Inman took comfort in the fact that he knew he never would have to question his heart or desire to get behind the wheel and give each and every race all he had.

"God, he was tough. People have no idea. There were times when he was so sick from the flu that he couldn't hardly stand up—and he would not only get in that race car but go out there and win the doggone race," Inman said.

Then, cracking a smile, the second cousin joked, "He may have been lazy, but, man, he was tough."

Simply climbing into the car for the start of the 1979 Daytona 500 proved that. But to Petty, it was no big deal. Or at least it never became one, for which he was eternally grateful. "It was a fortunate deal in that I had no repercussions from it," he said. "In other words, they cut me open and sewed me up and turned me loose. It never hurt after all the pain pills went away. It never bothered me, so I didn't think anything about it. It was just another day in the life of Richard Petty, you know?"

Another day in the life of Richard Petty was getting mighty interesting by Lap 75 of the '79 Daytona 500. As the 200-lap event approached the halfway point, Benny Parsons remained in the lead. But Petty and others were stalking him. A mere three seconds separated the first twenty-four cars in line. Although not all of them were on the lead lap, they were running together in a tight pack.

"Look at this jam session for the lead," Ken Squier told the CBS television viewers. "This is simply incredible racing. No margin for error! And no speed limit!"

Another accident brought out a caution period on Lap 80, after rookie Terry Labonte ran into the back of Neil Bonnett, who then caused Harry Gant (a rookie in theory but a longtime stock car racing veteran) to spin wildly, hit the inside retaining wall, and somehow career across the track without getting pummeled by anyone else. Bobby Allison also got a small piece of the accident, suffering more damage to his already wounded car.

The accident occurred right in front of Mark Aumann and his father, who were sitting in the grandstands on the frontstretch. "Harry Gant ended up wrecking in front of us and the car was sitting sideways," Aumann said. "It was dead stopped and we thought, 'Boy, there is no way they are going to miss him.' It was pretty impressive to see the other cars avoid him at that speed. It happened right in the middle of the pack. That told me a lot about the talent that was out there at that point because you had seen huge wrecks happen there in the Sportsman class and the ARCA race. To see them dodge that was impressive."

Meanwhile, Donnie Allison gained his lap back because of the continuing procession of cautions, and Cale Yarborough moved into position behind Parsons, poised to draft off him until he could gain one of his laps back as well. The victims of the earlier wreck on Lap 32 were making up for the lost time at every opportunity, figuring they still had time to get back in the mix up front if they could only get back on the lead lap.

The leaders were all aided by quality pit stops, or at least what passed for them at the time, when a minor error might keep a car in the pits for a full minute or more. Parsons had made his first three stops in a total of 2 minutes, 25.78 seconds, which was considered decent. But the fastest crew belonged to the car of open-wheel invitee A. J. Foyt; they had turned their three stops in 2 minutes, 21.88 seconds.

The race reached its halfway point with Parsons pulling Yarborough around the track in a draft so fast that the twosome was pulling away from the rest of the field. Donnie Allison not only was back on the lead lap despite a gaping hole in the driver's side of his Hawaiian Tropic–sponsored No. 1 Oldsmobile, but he was now running in second, with brother Bobby, two laps off the leader's pace but somehow still fast, helping push him swiftly from behind in the draft that Squier called that "magical, mystical, invisible wake."

Lurking in third, just behind the Allison brothers, was Foyt. Dale Earnhardt was hanging in fourth and Petty rounded out the top five in fifth, prompting Squier to comment, "If Richard Petty is in the top five at the halfway point, you'd better pack up the tools and go home."

•   •   •

In a sport littered with Texas-size egos and characters who seemed carved from the old Wild West, none fit the description of "larger than life" better than Anthony Joseph Foyt Jr. He wasn't a full-time NASCAR driver, of course, having built his reputation on the open-wheel circuit, where he became the first four-time winner of the Indianapolis 500 and competed in a wide variety of events held all around the world.

Foyt was born in 1935 in a poor section of Houston just as the United States was emerging from the Great Depression. His father, Tony Sr., was a mechanic who also had a passion for automobile racing. Money was tight, as it was for most Americans at the time. But Foyt grew up working on his father's midget race car while listening to stories from all of his dad's old race pals who used to drop around. He credited his upbringing with teaching him the value of a dollar and a strong work ethic.

All he ever really wanted to do was race. He dropped out of high school several months before graduation to get a jump on his career, which began at Playland Park in Houston in 1953 and soon had him on the road, traveling to wherever the next USAC midget race took him. To save money on hotel rooms, he often slept in his tow vehicle and washed up in the restrooms of gas stations he stopped at along the way. After one particularly disappointing month of racing in the 1957 Florida Tangerine Tournament, Foyt had to call home and ask his parents to wire him money. He didn't have enough of his own left to get back to Houston.

Along the way, however, Foyt's driving skills impressed enough of the right people. Later in the same year that he found it necessary to call for money to make it back home, he landed his first ride in what later came to be called Indy-style cars. One year after that, in 1958, he competed in his first Indianapolis 500, and three years later he won the famed race for the first time.

That's when Big Bill France started taking notice of him. The Indy race was sanctioned by the FIA (Fédération Internationale de l'Automobile), and members of the prestigious racing organization were not permitted to run in nonsanctioned FIA events, at the risk of losing their right to run in places like Indianapolis Motor Speedway, which were FIA-approved venues. So France applied for and was granted FIA status for Daytona International Speedway.

"If you were a USAC member or NASCAR member or if you were driving Formula One or any other form of racing in the world, an event had to be FIA-sanctioned for any of the clubs to cross over," said Jim Hunter, a longtime journalist who became head of public relations for NASCAR. "And Bill France Sr. was the first to do it at any NASCAR track, knowing that guys like A. J. Foyt and others racing against the regular NASCAR drivers would be a helluva terrific draw. That was sort of the start of something pretty big."

Other NASCAR tracks, no doubt at France's urging, soon followed suit. Then they, too, could invite stars from other series such as Foyt and Mario Andretti to run NASCAR events at their venues.

Foyt thus ran five Grand National races in 1963 and five more in 1964—the same year he won his second Indy 500—before gaining his first stock car victory at the Firecracker 400, the July race held at Daytona. He did it in typical hard-charging Foyt fashion.

"I was an outsider. Paul Goldsmith was down there, and Petty was there, and Bobby Issac, and they were trying to wreck us," Foyt grumbled years later. "I was runnin' pretty decent. But Bobby was leading the race, and they go down the straightaway on the checkered flag lap and they [meaning Goldsmith, Issac, and another driver, as Petty was by then out of the race because of engine problems] kind of lined up across. I said, 'This is a bunch of crap. I'm not going for that.' So when we went into Turn 3, I went across the apron, and I lost it. I didn't hit nothin', but I lost it. I turned sideways.

"I come off of Turn 4 and a friend of mine from Champion spark plugs said it was the first time he ever saw anybody come out of 4 where he was able to read the car number—47—on one side first, and then on the other. But it kept going straight. I don't know how, but I didn't care if I parked all of us because I didn't think what they were doing was fair. Luckily, I made it through."

Foyt always seemed to make it through, no matter how bad an accident or situation might have seemed in the moment. One time during his early days of running NASCAR events, he suffered one of what were many close calls during his racing career.

"We were at Riverside," driver Marvin Panch recalled. "And ol' A. J. was runnin' hard, using up his brakes and everything. I was just sitting back there, watching him, saving my brakes. So finally I got brave and passed him going down the backstretch. We got down to Turn 9 and, well, he doesn't have any brakes. And he took a shortcut down in the infield, and he hit so hard that I could feel his car hitting in my car on the racetrack."

Foyt's car flipped down an embankment before coming to a stop. He broke his back, fractured his ankle, and suffered chest injuries so severe that the track doctor pronounced him dead on the scene. But fellow driver Parnelli Jones, one of Foyt's fiercest rivals yet closest friends, saw movement and quickly worked to revive Foyt. Jones scooped dirt from Foyt's mouth that had been suffocating him.

Years later, Panch and Foyt ran into each other at a Daytona 500 and talked about that day.

"I wanted to thank you, because you could have taken me out," Panch said.

Foyt added of the incident, "That was bad. I went down there because I felt like if I had hit Marvin, I would've killed him. Instead, I damn near killed myself. I didn't plan on it being that bad, to be truthful with you."

Perhaps no one in America was more familiar with damn near killing himself than Foyt by 1979. His first close call had occurred some two decades earlier, when he nearly drowned in Galveston, Texas. After the boat he had been riding in capsized, he clung to a buoy for nearly eight hours before being rescued. Earlier during the trip, the young Foyt, who was celebrating his sixteenth birthday, had put on a lifejacket because he was cold. A friend riding in the boat with him didn't and drowned.

It took Foyt ten weeks to recover from the accident at Riverside that almost did him in. But eighteen months after that harrowing incident, Foyt was involved in another one when his Indy car hit the wall during practice for a race in Milwaukee. As the rear-engine Lotus burst into flames, Foyt became trapped in the cockpit. He suffered second- and third-degree burns before rescue workers could get him out.

In 1968, Foyt proved he didn't even have to be strapped in a race car to endure a close call. He was casually looking at a lion that was on display in the infield at the fairground speedway in DuQuoin, Illinois, when the lion broke away from its stake and lunged at him, taking him down. Foyt escaped but was badly bruised and scratched. He raced later the same day, but only after changing into a different uniform because the lion had inflicted multiple lacerations.

Another incident followed in 1972 at DuQuoin Fairgrounds, where he was competing in a USAC dirt champ race one day after running in the Indy 500. This time Foyt was run over by his own race car after jumping out of it as it caught fire during a refueling stop. He sustained burns, plus a broken leg and ankle.

These close calls only made Foyt more daring at times on the track. He was willing to take chances, to be sure. "You don't know how long you're going to be on this earth, so you'd better make it count while you can," he would tell friends and family.

*   *   *

Foyt never entered more than seven NASCAR races in a season, but he backed up his 1964 win in the Firecracker 400 by winning the same event the following season. And in 1971, he was winning the Daytona 500 when he ran out of gas toward the end, which allowed Petty to pass him for the victory. When he returned the following year, Foyt was determined to finally lay claim to stock car racing's biggest prize, and he did so in dominating fashion to add Daytona 500 champion to his growing list of achievements.

Foyt credited Wood Brothers Racing with giving him the top-notch equipment it took to win, and pretty much left it at that.

Asked later how difficult he found it to come over from his regular gig on the Indy-car side to win the most prestigious race in NASCAR, Foyt shrugged. "The Wood brothers had such a fantastic car, it wasn't really no problem running down here. I think we lapped the field. It was just fantastic, and the car kind of drove itself. I was just there along for the ride. What else can I say? It really was pretty damn easy."

He was slow to win the acceptance of the NASCAR regulars, although they knew he was a highly accomplished driver. By 1972, Foyt had traveled to France and teamed with Dan Gurney to become the first all-American team to capture the 24 Hours of Le Mans championship. Eventually he also won races on two tracks in England, and later competed frequently in the twenty-four-hour race at Daytona.

It was in the early 1970s, though, that Foyt came to know and gain an appreciation for another brash driver—sort of a younger, even louder version of himself. That was Darrell Waltrip, who didn't make many buddies among the traditional crowd when he first rose to the Grand National Winston Cup ranks, either. So Foyt and Waltrip kind of gravitated toward each other, and quickly became fast friends.

"That's quite true. I used to try to get Darrell in trouble all the time, because I was kind of an outlaw down here and he was kind of an outlaw, too. But I enjoyed all these guys. I think they accepted me, especially once I won Ontario with the Wood brothers," Foyt said.

Foyt won at the Ontario Motor Speedway in California twice for Wood Brothers Racing, but that should have been no surprise. The place was shaped like Indianapolis Motor Speedway. His first win there came in 1971 and eventually went a long way toward solidifying his credibility with some of the mainstays of the sport. But not at first.

"I got in trouble with *Sports Illustrated* because I supposedly got out of my car and said, 'Okay, I beat these southern hillbillies; now I'm ready to take on the European fags.' I ran Formula One the following week and I said, 'First of all, I don't talk that way. I've got to run with these guys whenever I can,'" Foyt said.

"So the next time I was able to run with the NASCAR guys, I had to go to Atlanta, Georgia. I said, 'Gang, I ain't never called y'all a bunch of southern hillbillies. I want y'all to understand that, so be a little easy on my ass today.'

"It wound up in court because I told *Sports Illustrated*, 'I would appreciate it if you would retract them statements. I don't talk that way. I might have used a little different words than that, but I didn't say *that*.' But they said, 'We're Time-Life. Go ahead and do whatever you want.'"

So Foyt sued and it ended up in court, not long after he won the 1972 Daytona 500, which landed his picture on the cover of the magazine. He eventually won a judgment against the magazine.

Meanwhile, Foyt's friendship with Waltrip blossomed. Waltrip would go to Foyt for advice about anything and everything to do with racing. "I was young and he was the old veteran," Waltrip said. "I'd go to him because he was sort of an outcast and I always was myself. Birds of the same feather tend to flock together."

One day, Waltrip went to Foyt to discuss a particular and ongoing problem.

"A. J., every time I get behind Buddy Baker, he shakes his fist at me. Every time. I don't know what he's trying to tell me. I don't know what to do about it," Waltrip said.

"Next time," replied Foyt, "about the time he takes that hand off the steering wheel and sticks it up in the air, knock the hell out of him. I guarantee you he won't never shake his fist at you again."

"So I tried it—and it worked!" Waltrip exclaimed many years later.

Foyt might have been good at dispensing valuable advice, but he wasn't always good about receiving it. Waltrip recalled one time at Daytona when Foyt was working with former NASCAR driver and chassis builder Dick Hutcherson. "That's when we laid the spoilers flat," Waltrip said. "You'd have about five degrees of angle in the rear spoiler. A. J. was walking around, looking at everybody's car.

"Finally he comes back and says, 'We don't need no damn spoiler. If everybody is gonna run 'em like that right there, just take the damn thing off the car.'"

Hutcherson stared at the stubborn Foyt. "A. J., you don't wanna to do that. It doesn't do a lot, but it does enough to keep the car on the ground," he said.

Foyt wasn't listening. "I said take the damn thing off!"

Waltrip and several other drivers and crew members were watching the scene develop with growing interest. They knew the spoiler, even laid almost flat, helped keep enough downforce on the car to keep it from flying off the racetrack.

"We're all watching. Everybody started coming through the garage saying, 'A. J. took his spoiler off. A. J took his spoiler off.' We were all like, 'Let's get on the trucks, boys, because this is going to be good.' So we did," Waltrip said. "We all got up on the truck and A. J. hauls butt out of the pits. He comes around and gets on the backstretch, and all the sudden he gets to the third turn and you hear him just about lose it.

"And he comes right back around and right back into the pits. They snapped that flat spoiler right back on."

Foyt had some fun at Waltrip's expense, too. By this point in Foyt's career, he may have been a roughneck from Texas, but he also had been to France to win the 24 Hours of Le Mans and was therefore worldly in other ways, or at least he thought so. One year Waltrip and Foyt and a French driver were competing as a team in the twenty-four-hour race at Daytona.

"We're sitting there and I'd done been around some of these foreigners a couple times, and kind of spoke their language," said Foyt, the man who once nearly initiated a brawl with a French driver who supposedly called him "everything but a white man" behind his back.

The race team was going over protocol with the drivers, telling them what they needed to do if the car malfunctioned—especially if it did so during a night shift. "If the car breaks down, you've got to go out there and fix it. And also, remember you've got the torch in the car," they said.

Waltrip jumped to his feet. "Hold up. I ain't gonna race a damn sports car here with a damn torch in there. I ain't drivin' no car with torches in there. If you think I'm gonna do that, you're crazy!"

Foyt nearly doubled over in laughter. The longer he guffawed, the more Waltrip got confused, and eventually angry.

"What's so funny? What the hell you laughing at?" he asked Foyt.

"They're talkin' about a torch that's a flashlight. They call a flashlight a torch," Foyt finally explained.

Over time, Foyt made other close friends in NASCAR. He respected greatly the driving abilities of Donnie Allison, who crossed over the Indy line to claim Rookie of the Year honors following a fourth-place finish in the 1970 Indianapolis 500; and Cale Yarborough, who competed in four Indy 500s, even though he never finished higher than tenth.

Yarborough loved to needle Foyt, and vice versa. Noticing that both he and Foyt were beginning to get a little thin on the top as they began to advance further into middle age, Yarborough once sent Foyt a hair restoration remedy that a friend had passed on to him.

"I knew A. J. was looking for something, so I sent him some," Yarborough said. "A few days later, he called me. But he didn't really need a telephone 'cause I think I could have heard him from Texas. That stuff had really burned his head up. Needless to say, I didn't have to try it then."

Petty also grew to greatly respect Foyt as a driver and a person. "A. J. didn't run with us that much, and he was real respectful of the Cup drivers," Petty said. "In other words, he didn't try to bully his way through or nothing. He just tried to do it on his ability.

"I think sometimes when he was running sprint cars or Indy cars and he was the king of the hill, he bullied himself around, trying to antagonize people and gain a psychological edge with them. He knew he couldn't do that with us. He didn't even go there with us. He would come in and you would swear he was just one of the good ol' guys. He just sort of went with the flow. I think everyone really enjoyed him coming in and running with us whenever he did."

Petty said he knew never to underestimate Foyt's talent. "He had the ability to do it, no matter what kind of car he was in. . . . He had a gift."

Buddy Baker agreed that Foyt was something special to watch behind the wheel of any type of race car. "You'd have to say he was the most versatile, all-around driver of the day. Just put him in any kind of race car and expect him to be up front and win," Baker said. "In his heyday there was nobody better. I put him in a class like David Pearson and Richard Petty as far as just being able to run whatever. A road course or whatever, he was right there."

So eventually Foyt gained the respect of all the NASCAR regulars. But it was with Waltrip whom Foyt bonded the deepest personally.

"I needed some friends, baby. I was glad to have him here, to tell you the truth. I didn't fit in real well with the crowd that was here then," Waltrip said of the mid-1970s. "I was sort of an outsider, too. I'm from Owensboro, Kentucky. I didn't grow up in the Carolinas; and my dad never raced. So I came in with a lot of things against me.

"The hardest thing for me to get used to was how big the sport was. I was used to running in Nashville, Tennessee. I wasn't a part of that show; I *was* the show. And I came down here and all of a sudden I had to kind of find my niche. They didn't need anybody like me. I didn't talk like them; I didn't act like them; I didn't drive like them; I didn't dress like them. So I really didn't fit in."

Foyt added, "They didn't offer nothin', either."

"No, they didn't want to help me. They were not lookin' to do that," Waltrip said. "They didn't need me. So having people like A. J. and Mario [Andretti] come in and run some races really helped me. Quite honestly, when I was growing up in Kentucky I thought I would be an open-wheeler. I thought I would go to Indy. It wasn't until I fell in love with the stock cars at the fairgrounds in Nashville that I decided this was a much better route for me to take.

"I love guys like A. J. His father-in-law and my father-in-law were really good friends, so we had some good times together. It was good to have him come down here and run with us.

"Also, Indy was bigger than Daytona then; it's not bigger than Daytona now, but it was then. So having those guys come down here, I was in awe of them. They raced in the 24 Hours of Le Mans; they raced all over the world. I went to races as a kid, watching him drive with his red bandana hanging out the back and his red gloves that he was wearing. I thought, 'Man, this guy is cool.' When I grow up, I didn't want to be like Richard Petty or David Pearson. I wanted to be like A. J. Foyt. I'll be damned if I didn't turn out that way."

Hearing this years later, Foyt roared with laughter.

"Yep, nobody likes him. But I've got a friend," he said of Waltrip.

•   •   •

Foyt arrived at the 1979 Daytona 500 confident of a strong finish, based on what had been his latest brush with death. One year earlier, he had been running with the leaders in his Foyt Enterprises

Buick when a blown tire sent Benny Parsons, who had been running in front of him, spinning off into the infield. Foyt hit the brakes and attempted to hand-signal those behind him that there was trouble up ahead, so they could do the same. The warning didn't come quickly enough for Lennie Pond, who couldn't slow fast enough and plowed into Foyt from behind.

Foyt's car darted off the track and embarked on a series of wild barrel rolls. When it finally came to rest, the crowd, including Mark Aumann and his father who had witnessed it unfold right in front of them, seemed to be almost collectively holding its breath. Inside the car, Foyt was unconscious. He was taken to the track infirmary and then rushed to a local hospital, where he was kept overnight for observation even after regaining consciousness.

"I still got a knot on my damn head from that," Foyt lamented some thirty years later. "And I learned something, too. When the yellow comes out, don't wave your damn hand. I got booted in the butt like a football at kickoff. I went for a pretty good ride."

But that was 1978. This was 1979, and Foyt continued to run in or around the top five as the race zipped past its halfway point.

Running seventh at the halfway mark, rookie Geoff Bodine suddenly fell off the pace and began to slow dramatically because of apparent engine problems. It led to the fifth caution flag of the day, but not before Yarborough slipped by the leader Parsons to make up the second of the three laps he had lost earlier. Squier speculated that Parsons might have let Yarborough go by on purpose in a gesture of sportsmanship, but that seemed unlikely given that Yarborough's car remained one of the fastest in the field. If Cale could coax it back onto the lead lap, he still could be a threat to win it. Regardless, Yarborough still had one more lap to make up, as he had fallen three down earlier. So he didn't appear to be a serious threat just yet.

As Parsons prepared to come into the pits on Lap 106, relinquishing the lead for the first time in twenty laps, an ominous puff of smoke appeared at the rear of his machine. "Here he is," announced Brock Yates as Parsons arrived in the pits, "the world's fastest cameraman."

Not for long. Parsons's engine was beginning to run too hot. Crew members stretched a garden hose to it to fill the radiator with water. Parsons dropped to eighth and was blown by on the ensuing restart by Richard Childress, who was running just ahead of Waltrip.

The new leaderboard looked like this:

1. Donnie Allison
2. Dale Earnhardt
3. Grant Adcox
4. Coo Coo Marlin
5. Terry Labonte

Many of the others who had been running up front, such as Petty, darted into the pits during the caution to get four fresh tires and a full twenty-two-gallon tank of 76 racing fuel. On the restart, Earnhardt quickly got all over Donnie Allison's bumper. Soon the resurgent Yarborough was there, too, desperate to get into position to make up his final lost lap and rejoin the other contenders on the lead lap.

One hundred eleven laps were complete. There were eighty-nine left to go.

"Donnie Allison is out front," Squier reported to the television viewers. "Can he stay there in this astonishing Daytona 500?"

There was still a long way to go.

On his bumper was none other than A. J. Foyt. Soon, though, Foyt gave up second place and headed for a much-needed pit stop. As he slowed on pit road and almost came to a stop in his pit stall, however, Hutcherson, acting as his crew chief, came on the radio and yelled, "Go! Go! Go!"

Foyt had the presence of mind to listen and stomp his foot on the gas pedal. Hutcherson told him he had seen a car—Blackie Wangerin's No. 39 Mercury, as it turned out—crash in Turn 3. It was sure to bring out a yellow flag for yet another caution, and Hutcherson didn't want Foyt to get caught on pit road, which would have meant he went a lap down. So he sent him back out onto the track before the caution flag officially flew. It was a heads-up call.

In the pits, Ned Jarrett grabbed Kyle Petty, Richard's eighteen-year-old son, who was preparing a set of tires to be put on the King's No. 43 Oldsmobile. Wearing a red ballcap with STP, of course, stamped on the front of it, the younger Petty kept about his work, mumbled a few almost inaudible answers to Jarrett's questions, and never looked up or into the camera lens.

Jarrett did take the opportunity to show viewers how one of Kyle Petty's jobs was to have lug nuts glued to the wheel ahead of time, and how now members of the pit crew used an air gun to attach them "unlike in the old days when we used a lug wrench."

Petty took on only two tires and topped off his gas tank on his stop, which was performed in a lightning-quick fifteen seconds.

In Donnie Allison's pit stall, it seemed the veteran driver was taking advantage of the latest caution by smoking a cigarette that appeared to dangle from his lips. He remained calm and confident. After leading Laps 108 through 114, he gave up the lead to Earnhardt for one lap while pitting, then quickly gained it back again on Lap 116.

Five laps later, Yarborough passed the younger Allison to get his final lap back. He was now on the lead lap.

One hundred twenty-one laps of the 2.5-mile tri-oval at Daytona International Speedway were complete. Just over three hundred miles had been covered, leaving seventy-nine laps and just under two hundred miles left to go.

10

Grand Masters

The seventh caution flag of the day was brought out when the No. 02 Shoney's Chevrolet of Dave Marcis, the former Rod Osterlund driver who now doubled as his own car owner, spun out and off into the infield. Eleven cars remained on the lead lap at the time, not counting the Yarborough machine that soon would be. The CBS announcers noted that Marcis's now disabled car, which was about to get towed from the scene, had begun its journey to the track at the shop of legendary chassis builder Banjo Matthews, located in the shadows of the Great Smoky Mountains in Buncombe County, North Carolina.

That was the lead-in for an on-air piece about Matthews and his operation, designed once again to fill the air time while the track in Daytona was cleared of debris and readied for racing. Reporter Brock Yates noted that in Buncombe County "there is a lot of hunting and fishing here. They grow some tomatoes and apples. But they also build Grand National stock cars."

Edwin Keith Matthews became known simply as "Banjo" not long after classmates in grade school started calling him "Banjo Eyes" because of the round, thick-lensed spectacles he wore. A stocky, down-to-earth, unassuming man, he was a former driver and former car owner who had at one time employed many of the biggest names in Grand National racing as his driver, including Fireball Roberts, A. J. Foyt, Donnie Allison, Cale Yarborough, and Junior Johnson.

By 1979, Matthews built the standardized chassis and roll bars that were then supplied to all Winston Cup Grand National teams. For a little more, Banjo would build the entire car from the chassis up for race teams. What they did with the $60,000 cars after that was up to them, and many, such as Junior Johnson and Dale Inman, would bend every rule in the book and even break a few if he figured he could get away with it, just to get their cars to go a little faster.

In the pits during the caution brought out by Marcis's misfortune, reporter Ned Jarrett caught up with Roland Wlodyka, crew chief for the upstart but very real 500 contender Dale Earnhardt. As Jarrett interviewed Wlodyka, a former driver who had served the previous season as Marcis's crew chief, they examined a tire that had just been removed from Earnhardt's car. It was obvious that the left side of the rubber had been rubbing against the car's right fender, causing the right front tire to blister and have to be replaced after only thirty laps. Wlodyka insisted it was no problem. Jarrett wasn't convinced.

"It looks like a problem to me. But he knows a lot more about it than I do," Jarrett told the television viewers.

On the restart, eleven cars took off and were quickly running at speeds of nearly two hundred miles per hour just two and a half seconds apart. Hobbs, the veteran of so many different automobile races, was suitably impressed.

"I've never seen so much darting and weaving in any race, anywhere," he said. "The way they keep pulling in and out of the draft is quite staggering. It really is quite heart-stopping."

Squier added, "They're like dancing puppets at two hundred miles an hour as they come down the backstretch."

Richard Petty moved into second place behind Allison, Yarborough jammed in between them. This prompted another cryptic observation from Squier, who called Petty "the grand master" and added, "His car always seems to work better in the latter stages of the race."

Yarborough remained on Donnie Allison's bumper for lap after lap until they had completed 131 circuits around the venue, with 327.5 miles completed. It was actually on the next caution, the eighth of the day after the engine blew in the No. 82 Lasky Construction Oldsmobile of Paul Fess, that Yarborough darted past Donnie Allison and gained his last lap back.

In those days, when the yellow flag came out, drivers raced back to the start-finish line. The order for the restart was set by the order in which they crossed it after the yellow flew, so on this occasion the younger Allison attempted to chase down Yarborough and get in front of him again before they reached the line. Had he been able to accomplish it, that would have kept the dangerous Yarborough one lap down.

Alas, Allison's attempt at a slingshot pass down the frontstretch failed. In the pits, Junior Johnson allowed himself a huge grin. Knowing what it meant, anticipating it in fact, Ned Jarrett was standing by for a quick interview almost as soon as Yarborough made the pass to get back on the lead lap. "If we keep it together, we might have a good shot to win now," Johnson allowed.

Overusing the phrase a bit but nonetheless applying it again to the right man, Squier also referred to Johnson as "the grand master" and reported that Johnson came on the radio to tell Yarborough only one thing: "Go to the front."

*   *   *

When it came to working on cars and getting the most out of them, it seemed no one was better in those days—or any days—than

Junior Johnson. He had been around stock car racing since the very beginning. He had hauled whiskey in fast-running cars on U.S. Highway 421, which originated in the hills and backwoods where home brew was churned out by his father and grandfather in makeshift stills, and wound through places like Ingle Hollow, Yadkinville, and North Wilkesboro before it meandered its way to the big cities of Winston-Salem and Greensboro. There were other well-traveled roads leading to the even bigger city of Charlotte where the stuff was in heavy demand, and Johnson often made daily trips to deliver the goods, sometimes even making more than one trip in a day.

There was, of course, no meandering at all if the revenuers were on your tail. In the early days, whiskey haulers typically would load twenty-four five-gallon jugs of the white lightning, or 120 total gallons of the stuff, into their cars. Each jug was placed in its own individual wooden liner, so that they wouldn't rattle against one another during a trip and make loud noises that could tip off cops, who might be listening and lying in wait on a dark country road. In the 1930s, the stuff would fetch ten dollars per five-gallon jug—meaning one trip would be worth $240. That was a whole lot of money in those days in places where the economy was depressed or virtually nonexistent.

Robert Glenn Johnson Jr., soon known to the world simply as "Junior," was born on June 28, 1931, a native of a tiny little place called Ronda, North Carolina. Like Ingle Hollow and hundreds of tiny communities in backwoods country throughout the Southeast at the time, Ronda never made the state maps. Along with his family and friends, it wasn't long before young Johnson was helping churn out and deliver as much moonshine as possible. They affectionately called it "Wilkes County champagne" and eventually adopted a slogan that stated simply, "Those who refuse it are few."

"Just about everyone in Wilkes County messed with it one way or another," said Willie Clay Call, one of Junior Johnson's closest friends, who figured he ran illegal moonshine for about forty years, from the early 1930s until around 1971. "In the 1930s and forties, there were only three places you could work around where we lived: at the sawmill or at one of two small furniture factories. The chicken farm businesses didn't come until later. And the pay wasn't no good at them places anyway.

"If you wanted to have a little money in your pocket, you had to mess with moonshine. It was a way of life for us. You split the profits with the folks who made it, but the hauler made extra. The hauler always made a little extra."

Johnson was never ashamed of making or running moonshine. He never apologized for where he came from, nor for what he did to carve out a living during his formative years. "It was hard, dangerous and scary work," he said years later. "It was how we made our living back then. That's all. It ain't nothin' to be ashamed of. Makin' moonshine was a hand-me-down trade that was passed down through the generations where I came from."

Junior was the fourth of seven children raised by Robert and Lora Belle Johnson. As he was growing up, Junior saw his father hauled off to jail many times for making and running illegal liquor. The senior Johnson ultimately would spend nearly twenty of his sixty-three years in prison because of it, but he would resume the trade again as soon as he got out, figuring it was all he knew and it was the best way he could make a living in Ronda. Junior admired him greatly.

Robert Johnson never made it past the third grade, but Junior once told a reporter of his father, "He was one of the smartest people I've ever known. . . . He wanted to make sure his family was taken care of and he didn't care if he went to the penitentiary doing it. As a kid, you don't appreciate things like that until you're older. Then you look back and see everything that he did for you."

Thus the Johnsons lived in constant fear of the law. Junior's mother made the best of it. Their house was raided so often that she occasionally offered the visiting revenuers a cup of coffee and perhaps a piece of pie as they took a break from hauling out stashes of illegal liquor.

Despite these dubious circumstances, Robert Johnson managed to teach his children certain values that they wouldn't forget and that often helped them out later in life. Robert was a very generous man, often helping out others. He taught Junior and his siblings to treat others with respect and not to lie or steal.

Young Junior Johnson was put to the test very quickly. After running out of gas once during a midnight whiskey run, he had to siphon fuel from a nearby farmer's tractor. Thinking back to what his father had told him and feeling bad that the farmer would find his tractor's gas tank empty the following morning, Junior left $200 cash on the seat of the tractor. He would need to make an extra run or two to make it up, but he felt good about doing what he was sure was the right thing.

Another of Johnson's close friends was Millard Ashley. The pair attended elementary school together. That is, until Johnson dropped out of school after the eighth grade to spend more time helping out with the family whiskey business. Ashley lasted one more year before he quit school.

"There wasn't no work in Wilkes County," Ashley said. "Runnin' moonshine was just the difference between walkin' around with no money in your pocket or havin' a little somethin' to jingle around in there."

Ashley insisted that many of the stories about running moonshine have been embellished over the years. But then he almost immediately and inevitably would launch into a few good ones himself.

"What people don't realize is that a lot of times you wouldn't run into nobody. There was maybe only one time out of a thousand when you really ran into a serious problem," Ashley said. "Think about it. There wasn't no traffic back then. There weren't no other

cars on the road. We would drive down U.S. 421 to Winston and
see maybe one car most trips, and that was about forty miles. And
if you met anyone on the roads we traveled, you knew it was either
another moonshiner or it was the law. It would be so dark on those
roads. You could see the reflection of headlights in the sky a long
time before you actually saw another car, so you usually had a
pretty good sense of when someone was comin'."

That would give the whiskey runners time to react. They usually had the faster cars, ones that could go nearly 100 miles per
hour in first gear and up to 115 in second. This was no coincidence. They all knew that very few police cars could go more than
95 miles per hour, giving them the edge over the cops. Junior
Johnson and others like him also became experts on figuring out
how to get extra power out of their cars and how to get them to
handle better, inserting special springs and shocks to make them
turn corners more sharply and efficiently.

Many local sheriffs were paid off in advance by the bootleggers
and therefore stayed out of their way. But the ones who weren't
desperately wanted to help the revenuers catch the whiskey
runners—not so much so they could bust them for making the illegal liquor that otherwise went untaxed, but because they stood to
make a bundle if they impounded a bootlegger's souped-up ride.
Sheriffs typically sold such automobiles at auctions and pocketed
half or more of the winning bids for themselves. And they weren't
above selling the cars back to the very folks they had impounded
them from, which would then get the cycle rolling down the backwoods country roads all over again.

"It was a cat-and-mouse game all the time between them and
us," Johnson said.

Others accepted moonshiners for what they were: locals trying to make a living. Ashley remembered making regular runs
through one small town that was fortunate enough to have its own
Krispy Kreme doughnut shop.

"We used to be so regular through there that they let us have doughnuts right out of the oven," Ashley said. "They would be waitin' for us and we would stop and they would just give us those doughnuts every time. You know, if you eat those while they're still hot and you drive too fast, it can make you sick to your stomach."

Despite all of the stories, Ashley continued to insist many years later that driving loads of illegal whiskey through the hills of North Carolina was usually more like making a trip to the local bank than a wild scene from *The Dukes of Hazzard*. "I remember telling someone that it wasn't much more wear and tear on my car than if I drove it regular," he said. "I could make my tires last about as long as they would just drivin' around town. You didn't have to run wide open all the time like some people seem to think. You only had to do it from time to time to try to get away from the law."

Except, of course, for Junior Johnson.

"Junior? Hell, he'd run wide open all the time," said Ashley, shaking his head. "Yeah, he was pretty bad about that. He was always blowing a head gasket or somethin'."

●　　●　　●

Going as fast as he could in an automobile simply was in Junior Johnson's blood. There really was no other way to explain it.

Those who ran moonshine didn't do it for the glamour or because they thought it would lead to a big paycheck in auto racing, for there was none of that back then—at least not at first. They did it as a means of survival; as a way of squeezing out a living in the rough-and-tumble backwoods of Virginia and North Carolina and Georgia. Lots of folks were running illegal liquor in the 1930s, from Kentucky and Tennessee on down through the Carolinas and Georgia and Florida.

When they weren't running from the law in their fast cars filled with illegal booty, they soon began running against one another in a number of loosely organized races in a largely futile attempt to prove who was the fastest. At times they raced in old cow pastures or wherever the rough semblance of an oval track could be carved out in open fields along the countryside. Later more sophisticated "real tracks" with crude wooden grandstands started popping up throughout the Southeast. There was still money to be earned in running moonshine; soon enough there was extra money to be won in the races that were held on the side with increasing frequency in the late thirties and into the 1940s, particularly after World War II.

Junior Johnson ran in his first such race when he was sixteen years old. He had been running moonshine for his father since he was about thirteen when Enoch Staley, president and cofounder of the North Wilkesboro Speedway that was located near Ronda and Ingle Hollow, was promoting a preliminary race to "fill in" between qualifying and the main event at his venue in the late 1940s. The catch: Staley didn't decide he needed such a race to keep the restless fans in their seats until about an hour before he resolved to run it. He dispatched a number of associates to round up local moonshiners and their cars to compete in the impromptu race.

One of them visited the nearby Johnson household. The first person he saw was L. P. Johnson, Junior's older brother. "How 'bout you runnin' in this race of ol' Enoch? You might make some extra money," the visitor said.

"Nah. No thanks," replied L. P. "But maybe I'll let my brother drive my car in it."

"Go get him," Staley's associate said.

Junior Johnson was out plowing corn for his father in a nearby field, trudging along behind a mule. He wasn't wearing any shoes. Years later, he smiled as he related the story to a reporter.

"L. P. yelled from the edge of the cornfield that he wanted me to race his car. So I tied the mule to a fence and went to the house to get my shoes. Then I went back to the track with L. P.," Junior said.

It hadn't taken Staley and his cronies long to assemble enough bootleggers for the race. When Junior and his brother arrived at the track, there already were another twenty to twenty-five cars lined up at the start-finish line.

Johnson laced up his shoes and climbed into his brother's car. Then he put the pedal to the metal and raced well enough to finish second to Gwynn Staley, Enoch's brother, who later would perish in a NASCAR crash on a track in Richmond, Virginia. In Junior's case, though, a racing legend was born.

He would go on to win fifty races as a driver at the Winston Cup Grand National level, along with forty-seven poles. But he never won a points championship—a testament to his hard-driving, relentless, and unapologetic driving style. It might not have always been the smartest, but it sure was exciting.

"Junior would go as hard as he could as long as he could," fellow driver Tim Flock once said. "He would never, ever slow up no matter how far he was ahead. If the car didn't break or crash, you couldn't catch him."

Johnson credited his background with making him the fearless, relentless Cup driver he was. But he seemed to enjoy building and working on cars, finding ways to get them to go faster, more than he did actually driving them in races. "Moonshiners put more time, energy, thought, and love into their cars than any racers ever will," he once said. "Lose on the track and you go home. Lose with a load of whiskey and you go to jail."

Johnson would have known. Although he often boasted that he had never lost a load of whiskey and told stories about how the revenuers had never been able to catch him on one of his moonshine runs, he did end up going to jail for a brief spell. He won five times on the Grand National circuit in 1955, all the while continuing to work in the family moonshine business on the side. He came home from a race during the 1956 season to find his father sick with a bad case of the flu.

"Go into the woods and get a fire started under one of the stills, will you, son?" the father asked.

It was more of an order than a request. Junior did not hesitate to do just as his old man had asked. "Of course I did what he wanted," he later said, emphasizing that it never crossed his mind not to do as his father said, even though he was a grown man himself by then.

Revenuers were waiting for him near the still, deep in the woods. Unbeknownst to him or his father, they had staked out the operation that particular morning and were ready to strike. As they emerged from their hiding places and announced that they were going to arrest him, all Johnson could do was mumble, "You got me."

Johnson served nearly a year in a federal prison in Chillicothe, Ohio, for the crime, missing all but one race of the 1957 season and half of the 1958 season as a result. He returned in 1958 and enjoyed his finest stretch as a driver, beginning a string of eight straight seasons when he won at least one race and registering forty-five of his fifty career wins. But after seven starts in 1966, he decided to retire as a driver. He still loved racing and planned to stay involved, but he no longer wanted to drive. Fifty wins in that capacity had given him all of the thrills he could handle, and he wanted to pursue other challenges.

"I think I enjoyed working on the cars more than I did driving them. I kind of got burned out on the driving," Johnson said. "It just didn't do anything for me after I won so many races. I decided to turn the driving over to someone else."

•   •   •

By 1979, Johnson was well established as a successful crew chief and car owner and had for the moment turned the driving over to one Cale Yarborough. Despite his winning three consecutive championships—in 1976, 1977, and 1978—there were rumblings heading into the 1979 season that Yarborough wanted out of his contract to drive for Johnson. Yarborough had been telling friends and family that he, too, was reaching the burnout stage and that he longed to begin driving a part-time schedule instead. Johnson had no intentions of having his championship team run a part-time schedule or employ a part-time driver.

It wasn't about winning championships; it was about winning races. In Johnson's mind, the latter was far more important than the former and the two were dramatically different. But once in for a season, he wanted to be all-in, all the time.

"I didn't care about a championship," Johnson said. "I just wanted to win races and beat the other guys. It's what your goals are in life. I have seen guys win a championship and never even win a race. Some it's maybe one race. It's not too impressive to get out there and run around and just try to stay in the race to get a good finish and take the points. Not in my mind, anyway.

"We went after them, but we didn't go after them and give up winning races. Most of our drivers won championships by winning a lot of races. If I caught a guy trying to win a championship on the racetrack his ass was in trouble. I want to win every race. If the championship comes, it comes."

They came in unprecedented fashion, back-to-back-to-back, for Yarborough in 1976, 1977, and 1978. Along the way, Johnson's reputation as a master mechanic grew even as he downplayed it then and later. Again, though, his genius lay in keeping it as simple as possible, and of course always keeping an eye out for clever "innovations" that might push the envelope a little.

"The way we set our cars up, most anybody could have taken the cars and done a little bit of a adjusting and drove it," Johnson said. "That was the way we ran our operations. We didn't go build to a specific car for one track or whatever like some people would. We built a car that we knew was capable of running on various tracks and we have the records to back it up, and we just adjusted the driver to that car. It's not no big secret. If it was steering a little too much one way or the other or too quick, we could adjust that out and keep the same chassis underneath of it."

By this point, Junior Johnson was used to getting his way. He had not only won gobs of races and the titles with Yarborough, but had helped almost innocently broker the deal that helped change NASCAR forever. In doing so, he transcended the usual titles of driver, car owner, mechanic, and crew chief and helped himself to a loftier status within the sport's inner circle, in some ways enhancing a legacy that was rivaled only by Big Bill France and Bill France Jr.

Johnson had been around Big Bill since the formative years of NASCAR, and always appreciated the senior France's approach to organizing what had been a loose and largely corrupt band of track owners and race promoters in the early days. In the early 1950s, just as the Southeast was witnessing the dawn of a new national sport, Big Bill was making the rounds trying to get guys like Johnson to come together under the ever-expanding umbrella of his one sanctioning body. Average folks who didn't have much money to spend on entertainment were beginning to embrace stock car racing, and NASCAR was assuming control of who raced where and when and for how much prize money.

What defines a sport after it grabs a foothold in a nation's subconscious are the personalities that drive it. And in this sport, especially in the 1950s, that meant the drivers. Big Bill France was a strong personality in his own right, but even he realized quickly that the drivers were the stars of his show. He just had to keep them in line.

With some, like Johnson, that would not prove too difficult (at least until later years when Johnson constantly would butt heads with Bill Jr. over his need to press for "innovations" on the mechanical side of the business). Junior Johnson remembered the first time Big Bill France talked to him "and a bunch of other moonshiners." He recalled the group being receptive to France right away. All France wanted to do was bring order to what had been mayhem. No one objected to that.

"I knew Bill France from the very first time he ever showed up, talkin' about racin'," Johnson recalled. "He was talkin' to a bunch of bootlegger friends of mine who were older than me. I was young, but I was old enough at the time to remember him talkin' to them about wantin' them to get involved in this racin' organization.

"Back then, each track wanted its own rules. They'd have trouble all the time. In other words, they'd go to a track and run a race, and if someone or another was ruled illegal, the track would decide whether they wanted to throw 'em out or not. France wanted to oversee something that could control all that. He wanted NASCAR to be the sanctioning body that would control what went on. That was his big thing—to get it started, to where it could stay organized.

"I think everybody kindly understood what he was tryin' to do. Most of the drivers and the tracks welcomed that idea. Because a lot of times you would go to a racetrack to run, and the track would put up so much money. But the promoter, if he didn't have a good crowd, he would take off before paying the purse and that kind of stuff. So I think all of the drivers were pretty much in line to like what he was doin'."

Of course, there were many drivers who initially liked the general idea of what France was trying to do, but had a habit of doing their own thing whenever they felt like they could get away with it. Even Johnson readily admitted to that. He was a notorious cheater—he preferred to call himself "an innovator"—who was forever trying to skirt the rules France was soon trying to enforce. And Johnson was as proud of that as he was of his moonshine ancestry.

"If you ain't cheatin', you ain't tryin'," he was fond of saying.

So after retiring as a driver following the 1966 season and becoming a car owner and crew chief all rolled into one, suffice it to say that Johnson and Big Bill France formed, at least for a time, a rather uneasy alliance. There was a level of mutual respect there at all times, to be sure. But that didn't mean the two stubborn, set-in-their-ways men didn't get downright mad at each other from time to time.

That started to change in 1971, when the respect level between the two soared to new heights almost overnight, just before Big Bill stepped aside and handed the NASCAR reins to Bill Jr. There was no bigger business in 1971 in the state of North Carolina than tobacco—not even moonshine, that backwoods industry whose last significant remnants were finally beginning to fade. Most of the sponsors over the first twenty-two years of NASCAR had been, predictably, automotive-related companies: Champion spark plugs; STP, the oil additive that was synonymous with Richard Petty's No. 43 baby blue and Day-Glo red car of the moment; Goodyear and Firestone, the tire companies; Purolator; the Pure Oil Company. And, of course, the automobile manufacturers.

But feuds over the years among the big auto companies and between them and NASCAR's governing body kept driving them in and out of the sport. When a rule went against them, the automakers often responded by quitting the sport; they usually didn't stay away for too long, but sometimes the boycotts lasted for years. When France outlawed the special aerodynamic sedans that had been built specifically for racing, and then announced in 1970 that he would require restrictor plates on cars at the superspeedways, the Detroit Big Three began to shy away from sponsoring cars on NASCAR's Grand National circuit. Plus the automotive industry was being forced by the federal government to spend more and more money on emissions control and safety research, leaving less and less to spend on racing programs.

It was a critical time in NASCAR's history. Just when the sport needed more sponsorship money to pump it up and fuel its growth, it was receiving less. And at the same time, the cost of operating a racing team was skyrocketing, as owners were spending more on parts and fuel. Furthermore, race teams were now building and maintaining many more cars during a season than they had in the past.

Like most car owners, Junior Johnson was feeling the pinch. One evening, he was having dinner with a friend who worked at the Hanes Hosiery Company in Winston-Salem. Hanes had been dabbling in NASCAR, but wasn't ready to plunk down the kind of sponsorship money that would make much of a difference in the long run. Johnson initially had intended to try to talk the company into making a larger investment in his team, but he had been thinking about something else he wanted to run by his business-savvy friend, who knew folks at one of Winston-Salem's other major employers: the R. J. Reynolds Tobacco Company.

Johnson had noticed that the big tobacco companies had just been booted off television by the government, in one of the early salvos of its ongoing antismoking campaign. Now Reynolds surely had a little advertising money left over in its budget that it might be willing to spend, wouldn't it? Why not spend it on a NASCAR Grand National race team?

"I been readin' in the newspapers that R. J. Reynolds is lookin' to spend some of that money the government says they can't spend no more on television advertisin'. Do you think they would be interest in gettin' into racin'?" Johnson asked.

"Well, I do know those guys. Let me make a call about that," his friend replied.

He called Johnson soon thereafter to say that he had arranged for a meeting at Reynolds with Ralph Seagraves, a Reynolds executive and acquaintance of Johnson's who also had grown up in the hills of North Carolina. Seagraves asked Johnson exactly what he was looking for in terms of sponsorship money.

Johnson swallowed hard. He was going to go for it. The newspaper had mentioned that Reynolds had millions to spend. Why not ask for a big chunk of it?

"Oh, I don't know. How about five hundred thousand dollars or six hundred thousand dollars to sponsor my race team? It might even take a little more, like say eight hundred thousand?"

Seagraves smiled. "Look, we just got booted off television. To be quite honest, we're looking to spend a whole lot more than that. We were thinking more along the lines of eight hundred million dollars or nine hundred million dollars."

It always has taken a whole lot to shake up the usually stoic and composed Johnson. But on this occasion, his jaw almost dropped to the floor. He later remembered thinking, "That's some ungodly figure you're willin' to spend." But he kept that thought to himself, quickly pulled himself together, and knew just what he had to do.

"Well, let me put you in touch with Bill France Sr., because he'll have some ideas about helpin' you spend a lot of that, I'm sure," Johnson said.

"That sure would help," Seagraves said. "I know you know Bill pretty well. Could you call him for us?"

"Sure, I'll call him and tell him to call y'all."

Johnson did that as quickly as he could. He told France, "Bill, I met with these people from Reynolds Tobacco Company and was tryin' to get some sponsorship money out of 'em. But Reynolds is interested in doing something a lot bigger than what I had in mind."

After a few more minutes of explanation, France thanked Junior and said he would take it from there.

"He listened and took the call," said Johnson, "and I never really did have anything to do with it after that."

It proved to be a historic moment for NASCAR, forged in large part by the business acumen of a man who grew up working around stills and never made it past the eighth grade in school. The former moonshine runner with little formal education once again showed an uncommon knack for getting important things done, having helped broker a deal that would change the face of his sport.

France would be forever grateful. Reynolds agreed to sponsor the very first Winston 500 at Talladega in May 1971. It was an entertaining and exciting race won by none other than Donnie Allison, who was driving for the Wood brothers at the time. Brother Bobby, driving a Holman-Moody Mercury, finished second; and Buddy Baker, then driving for Petty Enterprises, took third. It was the perfect day to showcase many of stock car racing's top teams and drivers in front of the scrutinizing eyes of a potentially huge new sponsor.

The boys at Reynolds had gotten a taste of big-time stock car racing and they liked it. They wanted to do more. They agreed to sponsor what was to be called the Winston Golden State 400 at Riverside in June 1971. This time, Bobby Allison won in a car he owned himself.

Reynolds had taken the bait and not only swallowed it, but the entire boat as well. The company had a huge advertising budget and very few places where it could legally spend the money. The tobacco industry was becoming an outlaw industry, and its marriage to NASCAR, the outlaw sport, seemed perfect. The two parties desperately needed each other to survive and to thrive in an increasingly politically correct world where neither felt it belonged.

The good folks at R. J. Reynolds talked to Big Bill France about doing more. France suggested that they use the Winston cigarette brand to sponsor the Grand National driving points championship each year, and officials at Reynolds quickly agreed to do it. Thus, the official name of NASCAR's top racing competition was changed to the Winston Cup Grand National championship, and later to the Winston Cup series.

The landscape of the sport had been altered forever, and Junior Johnson had his hands right in the middle of making it happen.

•   •   •

With 141 laps completed in the '79 Daytona 500, Johnson was thrilled to have his full-time driver, three-time defending points champion Cale Yarborough, finally back on the lead lap. As the competitors cycled through their yellow-flag pit stops and lined up again for another restart, rookie Dale Earnhardt was back in the lead, just ahead of Donnie Allison. A. J. Foyt sat in third and Tighe Scott was running fourth.

The return to the front was short-lived for Earnhardt. Allison passed him almost as soon as the green flag was dropped again, and then for several laps the cars settled into mostly single-file racing.

As Lap 153 was completed, Yarborough passed Richard Petty to move into fifth place. Suddenly Cale wasn't only on the lead lap, but was pressing to get all the way to the front. The leaders continued to run in a pack that had them bunched together less than two seconds apart.

Alas, Benny Parsons was not one of them. With his crew chief, David Ifft, lamenting "a cracked head or something" in Parsons's engine, his chances of winning disappeared and he began to spend time in the pits during green-flag runs, hood up, quickly falling behind by several laps. Almost in the blink of an eye, he went from running for the lead to four laps down.

"It's over for him," Squier noted sadly on-air. It was, of course, over then for the in-car camera—which had nonetheless given viewers a pretty good first ride. No one would ever know for sure if the added extra weight in Parsons's car had anything at all to do with the wear on his engine that eventually took him out of contention.

Ned Jarrett said nearly thirty years later that he was not surprised it was Parsons who unselfishly stepped forward to volunteer for the in-car assignment, even though he didn't think it was an easy sell at first. "He realized what it could do for the sport and he was interested in innovation," Jarrett said. "So I think the approach was he was talked into it. The weight was up high and it could definitely affect the qualities of the race car and the handling. I thought when they had the in-car camera that it just couldn't work. First of all I was thinking, 'Are they going to have a cable back there? How are they going to get the picture back?'

"I don't remember how they did it. I guess they used a helicopter like they do now [to bounce a wireless signal off of a receiver]. I have no idea. But it was fascinating to me that they could do that. That is one of things that I am very proud of—that I could get in on the ground floor and see the way the technology is today and see how it has come along as opposed to back then and see how it all has changed. It's really amazing to see how far it has come."

It also was amazing to see how far Cale Yarborough had come after being three laps down just thirty-five circuits into the 1979 race. With 160 laps completed, the true contenders were beginning to separate themselves from the earlier pretenders. The top five looked like this:

1. Donnie Allison
2. Dale Earnhardt
3. A. J. Foyt
4. Tighe Scott
5. Cale Yarborough

Richard Petty lurked in sixth, just ahead of Darrell Waltrip in seventh.

Suddenly, with just 100 miles to go, it all changed for Earnhardt. He pitted alone during a green-flag run; most of the leaders hadn't pitted under green all day, with there having been plenty of cautions to take care of their needs without risking the loss of valuable track position. His pit stop, though fairly quick at 18.4 seconds, was out of sequence and left him a lap down after he had been running with the leaders all day long.

Lou LaRosa, the engine builder for Earnhardt's car that day, later related what happened to author Peter Golenbock in the book *The Last Lap*. "They called him in early for gas, and he lost the draft. He got pissed," LaRosa said. "He dumped the clutch, revved it to 9,000 rpms, and broke a valve spring when he left the pits. It was a lack of experience, plus being pissed and hot."

It was Daytona, taking its toll again on a driver who had yet to learn all of the nuances and patience of surviving, and thriving, during a 500-mile race there. Earnhardt would go on to continue in the race, but his car was never the same, and he realized with chagrin that he would now be lucky to finish the race at all.

11

Breaking Away

Nine cars were running seven-tenths of a second apart, with eight vying for the lead, as Lap 161 came off the board. It was quickly becoming apparent, with only thirty-nine laps left to go, that the fastest two cars on the track belonged to Donnie Allison and Cale Yarborough. Although both had languished behind for part of the day—Yarborough longer than Allison—because of their mishap that also involved Bobby Allison on Lap 32, it appeared to be clear sailing for them now.

Announcer Ken Squier noted that Donnie was "holding on like a heavyweight champion in the latter rounds of a world championship fight."

And Bobby was in the mix, too. Although still a couple of laps down, Bobby was pushing brother Donnie from behind in the draft, literally riding almost right on Donnie's bumper. He was still there as Yarborough moved into second place four laps later, on Lap 165. The older Allison brother was the odd man out in a group of six cars, with the others all running on the lead lap. The leaderboard looked like this:

1. Donnie Allison
2. Cale Yarborough

3. A. J. Foyt
4. Tighe Scott
5. Richard Petty

With eighty miles left to go, there had been thirteen different race leaders and twenty-nine lead changes. Suddenly, six laps later, Tighe Scott finally began falling off the pace. On Lap 172, Foyt inherited the lead when Donnie and Bobby Allison made what figured to be their final pit stops of the afternoon. Donnie took on twenty-two gallons of fuel and right-side tires only and was in and out in an amazing 12.3 seconds.

Interviewed quickly in the pits, Foyt's crew chief, Dick Hutcherson, sounded optimistic. "He's been keeping his nose clean. Hopefully we'll get a shot at it at the end," he said.

The end was not far away. With 171 laps complete, there were only seventy-five miles left to go.

Richard Petty made his final fuel stop, urged on by Inman to keep plugging away. If Petty could only get up to third or even second, there was always the chance that Allison or Yarborough, who seemed to have the cars that were the class of the field, might make some kind of mistake or encounter some bad luck.

On Lap 174, Yarborough passed Foyt and led but only for one lap before having to make his final stop for fuel, too. His stop, also for twenty-two gallons of fuel and right-side tires only, was completed in 13.9 seconds.

Foyt led Lap 175, then gave up the lead to Darrell Waltrip for two laps. Yes, Waltrip, his engine still sputtering much of the time, was surprisingly still in the mix. He jumped to the front after the green-flag stops thanks to a great call by his crew chief, Buddy Parrott, who took on fuel only and got Waltrip out of the pits even faster than the likes of Allison, Yarborough, and Petty. Waltrip's stop was timed at nine seconds flat.

As much as Waltrip's sudden appearance in the lead may have been a surprise, given his earlier engine troubles, Waltrip was shocked at seeing the likes of Tighe Scott and Earnhardt run near the front so much on the day. And earlier he had found a new and much-needed friend in the No. 67 Dodge being driven by Buddy Arrington, who was running decently despite having fallen three laps off the lead because of troubles early in the race.

"You would be running along, and you would just be like, 'Who are all these guys?' I'll never forget," Waltrip said. "But Buddy Arrington helped me. I couldn't keep up with guys. I could hang with them for a little while, but after a while they would lose me because I just didn't have full power.

"But Buddy Arrington and I were running exactly the same speed. So I tucked in behind him. He was driving one of Petty's old Dodges that he had gotten, and it would run pretty good. And I tucked in behind him and drafted him.

"Then when we came down to the last stop—everyone had to make one more stop—Richard took two tires or maybe four. Some of the other guys all took tires. We didn't take any tires. Buddy Parrott, he just calculated how much gas we needed to get to the end, knowing that if we could get up with those guys, we would be able to hang with 'em, but that we wouldn't be able to outrun 'em."

Arrington helped Waltrip to avoid getting buried farther back earlier, and Parrott's call in the pits helped carry Waltrip to a better place, which was right in between Petty, now running third, and Foyt, running fifth. Waltrip was starting to think to himself that a fourth-place finish in the Daytona 500—especially in a car that wasn't fully powered—wouldn't be all that bad.

"Sure enough, we come down and dump half a can of gas or whatever it was into the car and we take off. And here comes Cale and Donnie by, and I can't hang with them. They're way too fast.

But here come Richard and A. J. by, and I was able to force my way in between them. And I was in the perfect spot. I was drafting Richard and A. J. was behind me, pushing me. So not having full power then didn't really hurt me that much.

"That's how I ended up being able to hang with them. It was just a great call in the pits, and luck that I was able to blend in between those two guys. Their cars were handling terrible, which was perfect for me because I could run my car wide open. I couldn't run fast, and they were handling bad. So they would push me down the straightaway, and I would hang with them in the corners."

Waltrip could hang on to the lead for only two laps before Donnie Allison resumed his now-familiar place in the top spot. With 178 laps complete, and Yarborough now tucked in right behind the younger Allison, their two cars were clocked at 195 miles per hour.

Announcer David Hobbs noted that Yarborough, "the master tactician, is right where he wants to be."

Squier added, "It's going to be a land rush to decide the Daytona 500, in what could be one of the most amazing finishes we've ever seen."

•   •   •

Parrott's clutch call underscored the importance of having cool heads in the pits. The crew chiefs of the day were not as publicly celebrated then as they would come to be years later, but no one had to tell the drivers of their importance. They were responsible for figuring out everything that was going on in the race and how it might affect their driver. They formulated strategy on when to pit and what to do once they were in the pits, whether it be taking on two or four tires and fuel, or, as Parrott had done on his final stop with Waltrip, fuel only toward the end. They sometimes had to play part psychic and part psychoanalyst with their drivers.

And this was only during the race. Much of their work—indeed, perhaps their most important work—was done prior to the race. It was the job of the crew chief to find hidden ways to make the car go faster, yet they could not in any way sacrifice durability, especially in a 500-mile race.

If Johnson, who also served as jack man on Yarborough's car, was considered the best, Dale Inman wasn't far behind, and vice versa. More importantly, Richard Petty would not trade Inman for anyone. They had a chemistry that went beyond the normal driver–crew chief boundaries, and they knew it.

"We grew up together, went to school together, dated together, played ball together. Then, when he came out of the service—he always had hung around the racin', hung around with us and went to the races and piddled around—so when he came out of the service, he went to work for us," Petty said.

"The deal was that we grew up together, so we understood each other. In other words, if you talk to him and ask him a question, he'd tell you the same answer I would tell you. It was just like one person in two bodies. That's how close we were as far as our thinking, our strategies, our whole deal. There couldn't have been a better combination than me and him."

In later years, the King scoffed at one writer's suggestion that Ray Evernham may have been the greatest crew chief of all time. Evernham made his mark as Jeff Gordon's crew chief at Hendrick Motorsports in the early 1990s and later founded Evernham Motorsports (now Gillett Evernham Motorsports).

"How do you put Evernham in front of, well, first, Len Wood or Junior Johnson? There ain't no way. He ain't even in that class, okay?" Petty said. "I'm not trying to disparage Ray. But if you told me to look at all these guys—the Dale Inmans, Bud Moores, Junior Johnsons, and Leonard Woods—he ain't even on the same page of what they had to accomplish. Because they accomplished all that they did with their ingenuity—not a bunch of engineers' ingenuity—and then taking that and putting it together and making it work. They were the engineers. They done the building and they done it all—the strategy of the racin' and the whole deal."

It was a different time, too. There were no computer monitors or television screens in the pits with which to monitor a race. Oftentimes a crew chief had to go on instinct when he couldn't see what was happening on other parts of a track, especially one as big as the 2.5-mile tri-oval at Daytona International Speedway.

"I tell all the guys now, 'It ain't always been this easy now,'" said Inman in 2007, even as he continued to go to races and work as a consultant for Petty Enterprises after "retiring" nearly a decade earlier.

Inman said the dramatic differences between the early days of racing and thirty years later hit him when he and Richard were paying a bill at a Cracker Barrel restaurant following breakfast one recent morning. "There was a book we bought at the Cracker Barrel where they had a picture of me, Richard, and Maurice pitting at Martinsville for Lee with no shirts on," said Inman, laughing at the memory. "I'll say those days were different."

In the 1979 Daytona 500, A. J. Foyt's crew wore red-and-white-checkered short-sleeved shirts. Pit reporters Brock Yates and Ned Jarrett walked around in jeans and light sweaters. By the turn of the century, everyone that close to the action on pit road would be required to wear long-sleeved, buttoned-up fireproof suits, and crewmen going over the wall had to wear those plus protective helmets.

In the middle of all of it every Sunday was the crew chief, trying to figure everything out. There were lots of good ones, but Richard would take second cousin Dale over any of them. "He was able to take us to seven championships. I won one hundred ninety-eight races with him, I guess. And then he went on with Terry [Labonte] and won some more races and another championship [for Hendrick Motorsports]. So he's been a crew chief for eight championships. When you talk about [all-time] crew chiefs, everyone else is fighting for second. He's so far ahead."

If he couldn't have had Inman as his crew chief, though, there was little doubt that Petty probably would have chosen Johnson next. It was because of Johnson's taciturn approach and Yarborough's dogged determination that Petty was not surprised when the No. 11 car surged toward the front late in the '79 race, despite having been three laps down earlier.

Of Johnson, Petty said, "He's low-key even though he's not low-key, if that makes any sense. Junior had a good sense of what the circumstances were. He raced, so he understood racing. And he understood the competition. And he knew what he had and what he needed to beat that competition with.

"Here's a guy who is a crew chief, but he's also out jacking the car and still thinking about, 'How's our tires looking? How's our fuel mileage?' Without computers or anything like that, he knew they could run this far on tires without slowing down. He had all that stuff figured out all the time. He was the total package. He was *the* package. He was the one who made Cale look good; he was the one who [later] made Darrell [Waltrip] look good. Because it was his show. He just had someone doing the driving for him, and he had good enough drivers that he could always get the best out of what he had. But first he always made sure he gave them the best to work with."

Petty said that Inman possessed different strengths as a crew chief. "Dale's strong suit was in understanding the car. He was not a mechanic. He didn't invent things or change a lot of stuff. He knew what he had and worked with it," Petty said. "Junior come up with a whole bunch of new ideas—whether it was a new way of cheatin' or whatever it might be. Dale was pretty good at that, but not as far as the mechanical part of it. He was so good with people. He was able to get everything out of a person, plus more—out of the crew, out of the guys who worked on the car.

"And he touched every part of the car. He might have some-body doing a front end or a rear end, but he was always right there checking on it when they were through. Junior was the one who engineered all this stuff.

"We had a couple of boys here who would come up with ideas. And we tried everything. They would be like, what if we did this or what if we did that? Dale was always real open-minded to trying stuff. He understood the car, the mechanisms of the car: what it could do and what it couldn't do. But his strong suit was people, being able to handle people."

•　　•　　•

Junior Johnson knew how to handle his people, too. Pete Wright, who worked under him for many years, fairly quickly found out it was like joining a family when he first came to Johnson's race team as a jack man. It wasn't only Junior who treated crew members like kin but also Junior's first and longtime wife, Flossie [whom he later divorced]. The Johnsons' home was on a hill overlooking the shop.

"Floss and Junior didn't have any kids, so we were their kids," Wright said. "You didn't go to the bank. If you wanted a new car, or to buy your wife something for Christmas or her birthday, you didn't go to the bank or use your credit card. You went to see Flossie, and she would help you. I mean, I wish I had a dollar for every meal I went up there and ate while I worked there for eight years. . . . I remember times when me and some people would go off to eat and come back, and she'd pull us in. She'd call the shop wanting to know why we didn't come up to the house and eat."

There were many nights when Wright would look up the hill toward the Johnson house and see Junior staring down from a window up above. "Junior stood up there in that house and looked down there on the shop," Wright said. "He could see in the shops from the house, see the lights on. You knew he wasn't up there talking about you or anything like that. He was up there appreciating what you were doing. He would come down and say, 'You need anything? Need me to go to the store and get you anything?'

"If you worked all night, you didn't even think about going home until you went up to the big house and ate breakfast with Floss. That was just their way of showing their appreciation. I was there a good month before I really started feeling a part of the family; but I had known Junior, or at least known of him, ever since I was a kid because of his moonshine days. I had family that made moonshine, and moonshiners stuck together back then."

Darrell Waltrip, who later drove for Johnson, would insist that Johnson's impact on the sport cannot truly be measured because so much of his influence was felt primarily by the guys in the shops who subsequently went on to achieve their own measure of fame and success in NASCAR's garages.

"Drivers come and go, but so many mechanics have gone through Junior's doors, so many guys that have done so much in this sport . . . engine builders and car builders and crew chiefs . . . I can't even think of all of them," Waltrip said. "That's what we called the University of Ronda, and when you left there you had one of the best educations in racing that you could ever hope to get.

"Junior was an innovator. He never technically cheated or broke any rules because everything he did, no rules had been made pertaining to that particular [car modification] at that time. So Junior is more responsible than anybody else for language in the rule book. Because he would lay awake at night, studying, thinking, 'Okay, it says this but it don't say that.' Then he would always have a little bit of an edge on everybody."

The edge wouldn't last long, as Junior himself was willing to admit. Soon one of his guys would move on to another shop, taking little shop secrets along with him. Then someone else would catch on to whatever Johnson had tried, and they, too, would try it. Pretty soon after that, everyone in the garage would be doing it—but by then Junior would have long been on to his next "innovation."

It was a never-ending cycle, and most of the time the other crew chiefs and car owners were playing catch-up when it came to keeping pace with Junior Johnson. The notion suggested by Waltrip that Johnson didn't "technically cheat" was absurd to even Johnson himself. He brazenly admitted to it time and again, making no apologies. "We all cheated. There's no question about it. We all cheated at one time or another," he said.

Johnson's constant pushing of the envelope, ironically, played a role in the development of the NASCAR rule book, and enforcement thereof, that later would be blamed for not allowing crew chiefs to be creative enough in preparing their cars for battle. Johnson admitted that the inspection process in recent years would have made it difficult for him to race back in the 1970s.

"Oh, if they had done to us back in the days what they do now, or found stuff we was all doing, none of us could have raced," Johnson said in 2007. "We went to the race with ten things wrong, and we knew it. If they found one, we could run the other nine. That is the way it was.

"There were so many things going on in the sport back in those days. If you found something that worked that nobody else knew about yet, it was a big advantage to people. It was awesome. You could offset the cars, move the motors back. Just do everything. Nobody knew anything about it until, say, one of my guys quit and went to work for somebody else and said, 'Hey, we need to do what Junior is doing.' That is how it all gets scattered around."

It wasn't always done on the up-and-up, which eventually contributed to shattering the family atmosphere that had always permeated any shop Johnson ran. "They would sell secrets for money and that kind of stuff. A lot of the mechanics and stuff are the problems in a lot of our races. When they move, they have some reason for moving. They will take the ideas and go with it and the next person you see them at the race with is one of your competitors. That ain't right," he said.

Still, Johnson was able to keep some secrets to himself for an incredibly long time. Not long after Waltrip began driving for him (Waltrip replaced Yarborough when Yarborough finally was able to fulfill his desire to run a part-time schedule), Junior grabbed his new driver after qualifying for a race at Bristol Motor Speedway in the hills of Tennessee one afternoon.

"Let's go for a drive," Johnson suggested.

Waltrip agreed, but then began to have second thoughts about accepting the invitation as the pair drove on for a couple of hours through many twists and turns on mountain roads.

"Where in the heck are we going?" Waltrip asked.

"You'll see," Johnson answered.

Finally, they arrived at what appeared to be a small farm-house. Johnson pulled up to a barn in the back, and they went in to meet with a very old and businesslike man.

"This is Jim Hyder. He makes the best camshafts in the business. Nobody can make 'em like he can. I won't get mine from nobody else," Johnson told Waltrip.

A little later, Waltrip pulled Johnson aside. "Where did you find him? We're in the middle of nowhere here," he asked.

"He's a very smart person," Johnson said of Hyder. "He worked for General Motors for twenty-five years. Then he moved back down to Elizabeth [Tennessee] and lived up in the mountains. You want to find somebody that has the knowledge and he's got it to himself and you work with him. It's just a secret."

If Johnson got caught doing something illegal to his car, his usual reaction was to accept whatever fines and penalties

NASCAR would hand out with as little fanfare as possible. His idea was that it was better to accept the punishment and move on down the road.

"You are better off to eat a little crow sometimes than you are to stir a bucket of shit and let everybody smell it," he explained as only he could.

As a crew chief, Johnson could be demanding. He feuded with drivers at times, including Bobby Allison. But then Bobby Allison feuded with lots of folks, especially early in his career. He and Junior bitterly parted ways after a brief union in 1972, and Junior was known to hold a grudge.

One day years later, Allison endured a very difficult day at Riverside. He kept running off the track and getting flat tires, eventually suffering through a total of six on the day. As soon as the race was over, reporters rushed to ask Allison why he thought he had gotten all of the flat tires.

"Well, you know, I believe Junior hired one of them Wilkes County sharpshooters to sit up in Turn 6 and shoot my tires out," he deadpanned.

One of the writers went back to Johnson to report what Allison had said. "Shows how smart he is. I wouldn't a been shootin' at his tires," Johnson replied.

Despite the success as a team, Johnson and Yarborough had moments where they clashed, too. In July 1977, after finishing second in a race at Talladega, Yarborough lamented that he "had the sorriest Chevrolet" in the event. "If I had won, I'd be in court Monday for stealing," he added.

Informed of Yarborough's comments, Johnson's response was clipped and left no room for misinterpretation on Yarborough's part. "We're in the middle of some engine problems right now and we're also in the middle of the championship battle. If Cale starts running his mouth, he'll be looking for another car. We don't have to listen to a bunch of lip from him."

Plus it was obvious that Johnson was trying everything he could. Prior to that very race, their car was one of five that was found by NASCAR to have illegal and oversized fuel tanks on pole day. Each was fined $200.

At heart, Johnson was a master motivator, as Waltrip came to discover rather quickly after replacing Yarborough as Junior's driver. Johnson's mere hiring of Waltrip was a stroke of genius. He knew Waltrip and Yarborough had not always gotten along.

Late in the 1977 season, even as Yarborough was putting the wraps on his second consecutive points championship, Waltrip was throwing verbal jabs Cale's way. After winning the 400-lap event at North Wilkesboro Speedway in October of 1977, Waltrip said it wasn't that big of a deal. "I'd have to say this was about a one-and-a-half or two on the Cale Scale. I think his problem could be his years. I know I'm finding out I can't do the same things I could ten years ago."

At the time, Yarborough was thirty-eight years old. Waltrip was thirty. Neither could ever run quite fast enough for Junior Johnson.

"The thing you have to realize about Junior Johnson is that you can be lapping the field, you can be runnin' a second ahead of everybody else, and you still weren't going hard enough for him," Waltrip said. "He would come on the radio and call me 'Cale.' He knew I hated that. He'd have that stopwatch out and if he thought you might be slowing down even just a little bit, he'd come on the radio and say, 'Cale, you ain't layin' down on me, are you?'

"I'd be like, 'Cale? My name ain't Cale!' And that stopwatch would immediately go the other way. I'd pick up two- or three-tenths. That's all the motivation I needed, and he knew it. He did that to me quite a lot, especially after I first started driving for him."

Johnson never forgot his roots. Indeed, he never strayed far from them, continuing to live near where he grew up and used to run moonshine long after he made it big in racing. One day in the late 1970s, his old friend Enoch Staley, who once made the call that lured Junior out from behind the mule in the Johnson family cornfield, called to tell him that he wanted to erect a wooden grandstand in Junior's honor at his North Wilkesboro track. Johnson welcomed the honor, but was apprehensive when he learned that Staley's plan was to christen the Junior Johnson Grandstand with a half-gallon jug of Wilkes County champagne.

"I don't want nothin' to do with any of that stuff right now. It caused me enough trouble when I was a young feller," Johnson told Staley.

"Don't worry, Junior. I promise you won't even have to touch the stuff," Staley replied.

When Johnson arrived at the small ceremony a few days later, he found the jar of moonshine tied by a long cord to the very top of the new grandstand. Junior grabbed the middle of the cord, pulled back and let it smash into a railing, where it shattered into hundreds of pieces. "He was right. I never had to touch it. But the smell from that stuff was pretty bad," Johnson later said.

Johnson had his doubts when Bill France Jr. took over as the head of NASCAR in 1972, too. It was right about the time Big Bill had cut the deal with the R. J. Reynolds Tobacco Company that opened the doors to a lucrative new era. Johnson and many others questioned if Bill Jr. could fill his father's large shoes. By 1979, they had their answer, and the shrewd negotiations led by Bill Jr. to get the Daytona 500 televised live from start to finish were merely more evidence.

"I like Bill France. I think he's a great person," Johnson said many years later, just before France Jr. passed away in 2007. "I had fights with him. I won a few and lost a few. That is not personal. You have to stand up for what you believe. He did the same thing to me and I did the same thing to him. When it was all over with we shook hands and went on down the road.

"I think he's the best of all the promoters—in any sport. When they announced he was going to take over NASCAR, I was kind of looking for another job because I didn't think he could pull it off. But I was wrong. I was dead wrong. He did a better job than his father did, and he succeeded in every aspect of it."

While they got along well on a personal level, that wasn't always the case professionally. "As a competitor, sometimes I felt like he was trying to hold me back to keep the competitors all equal. I didn't like that because I worked for what I got and I wanted to keep it. He didn't want me to ask him about that all the time and I understand why," Johnson said.

"One thing he did well was he was smart enough to bring in the type of people who could really promote the sport to a whole new level. Television was a big part of that. Once he got a hold of it, he expanded that thing so greatly that it was so awesome at the end of his day. . . . He didn't have a weakness. He occasionally did something I thought was stupid, but he didn't have a weakness. He never, ever done anything that was devastating to the sport. He might have done something you didn't like or you thought was wrong, but it was not devastating to the sport."

•   •   •

Junior Johnson wasn't the only one in racing savvy enough to cut favorable business deals that belied his seemingly simple country upbringing. Perhaps no one had been further ahead of the game when it came to procuring lucrative sponsors than Petty Enterprises, but by 1979 even their long-term relationship with STP was beginning to become at least a little strained.

It was a relationship that dated back to 1972. Andy Granatelli was the CEO of STP, and largely responsible for the aggressive promotion of the oil additive and gasoline treatment products the company sold. Granatelli also was quite full of himself, once penning an autobiography titled *They Call Me Mr. 500*, even though his career as an open-wheel driver was cut short very early in his life by a horrendous crash. Despite many years of trying as a car owner, Granatelli fielded a winning car in the Indianapolis 500 only once—in 1969 when driver Mario Andretti finally won it for him.

Granatelli had been speaking directly with Richard Petty about cementing a sponsorship relationship between Petty Enterprises and STP just prior to the 1972 season. He called and asked Petty to come to Chicago to meet with him. Inman and Maurice Petty, Richard's brother and engine builder, also went along.

"I was in the [STP] office in Chicago; we were on our way to Riverside for the season opener in '72," Inman said. "The truck had gone on to California with no sponsor."

Richard briefed Inman and Maurice on the way to the Windy City. "I've talked to Granatelli. I don't think anything is going to happen, but we'll go back and see."

Inman noticed very quickly that Richard had misread the situation once they arrived at Granatelli's office. "As soon as we walked into his office—and it was during a terrible snowstorm—it was a known fact that he was going to make it work. It was just a matter of working out some of the details," Inman said.

Granatelli had always made a point of having his Indy pit crew members wear garish coveralls with the STP logo plastered on seemingly every square inch of available space. One of the "details" was that he wanted the Petty crew members to do the same. Maurice balked. "I ain't wearin' those coveralls with STP written all over it," he said.

There were some other sticking points. "One of the things he offered us was that he wouldn't let but seven sponsors on the car. You know, contingency people," Inman said. "He said, 'I'm paying for the [primary] sponsorship. I'm not giving the others a free ride.' And we said, 'Well, we've got to have Goodyear and a few others.' But I think he limited it to seven."

Eventually, though, all of the minor details were worked out. And so was the big one. "They paid us $250,000 for a full season. Man, that was great. That was like manna fallin' from the sky," Richard Petty said.

Richard did hold firm on one point. Granatelli said, "I'll give you $50,000 more if you paint it solid Day-Glo [sort of a combination of red and pink] and you win the championship. The Day-Glo will really make you—and us as your sponsor—stand out."

"No, I don't think so. We're going to stay with some Petty blue," Richard replied.

Inman smiled at the memory. "So we did and of course we won the championship that year. . . . So we overcame the Day-Glo, but we didn't get the extra $50,000."

As they were wrapping up the negotiations, Granatelli threw his arm around Richard Petty's shoulders. "You stick with me and someday you'll be as famous as I am," he told the future King.

•   •   •

Heading to Daytona earlier in that month of February 1979, Kyle Petty sensed a familiar air of confidence around his father's racing operation. Or maybe it was a mixture of confidence and a bit of desperation. Coming off the winless 1978 season, Petty Enterprises had yet to officially sign their annual sponsorship agreement with STP, and, well, times did not appear to be what they used to be around the Petty shop in Level Cross.

"This is not an arrogant statement," Kyle Petty insisted. "But when we were young until the mid-seventies, until I was fifteen, sixteen years old, I never thought about going to Daytona and Richard Petty not winning the race. You know what I mean? You just never thought about it. You prepared all winter long and you figured you were going down there and would win the race. That's just the way it was."

Although Dale Inman and Richard both would insist that beginning a season in those days without an officially signed agreement with STP was not unusual and that signing it was a mere formality, the fact is that Kyle remembers it was a little different heading into 1979.

"In '79, we were out of money. And if you go back and look at the pictures on the car, you'll notice there's not a huge STP on the hood of that car. And also on the quarterpanels there's a company called Southern Pride, which is a local car-wash company. That was on the side of that car, because we had to find financing elsewhere," Kyle said.

The STP logo remained on the Petty uniforms and hats they wore during the race, as well as on the rear quarterpanels on the sides of the car. But the usual, larger logo was indeed conspicuously missing from the hood of the No. 43 machine for the Daytona 500. Inman recalls that there had been a change in leadership at STP, and also that the rising costs of the sport appeared to be outgrowing the company that had done so much for Petty Enterprises. He noticed that the new company officials who had come to introduce themselves, see what racing was all about, and hopefully negotiate the latest annual sponsorship deal hadn't even stayed for the start of the 500, citing bad weather and bolting back home to Chicago.

"We were coming off '78, which was a terrible year," Kyle Petty added. "We started with the Dodge and switched to a Chevy. We were doing all this stuff. We built a couple of cars and went to test, and ended up coming back and throwing a body on an Oldsmobile and building an Oldsmobile to take down there.

"I think my father at that point in time really wanted to go back to Chrysler. We built a Dodge Mirada and went to test in '79, and it just wouldn't go anywhere. So we went back and built the

Oldsmobile. And we didn't have a lot of employees; we had to lay some guys off and some guys had quit because we were running a little lean. . . . There were really only three or four guys who hung the body on the car and worked on the car to get the car done in time. And I was going to school. So I would go to school and come up and work. Man, we worked a lot of hours to get that thing put together. And Dale and all those guys worked a lot of hours to get it done."

Drivers back in those days frequently jumped from one manufacturer to another, oftentimes in the middle of a season. Richard Petty was no exception. Although he was then and always would be mostly identified as a Chrysler man, at one point he had tried driving a Ford and then, of course, he made the somewhat reluctant switch to Chevys midway through the fruitless 1978 season.

There was a feeling back at the shop that the team simply needed to do whatever it took to get back on the winning track. There was a sense that the good folks at STP in the Chicago home office had the same feeling, and it was all intertwined. Winning doesn't just breed winning; in NASCAR it breeds sponsorship money, the lifeblood of any Winston Cup operation.

"We just needed it for cash flow. . . . Seventy-eight had been such a bad year. Starting the year with one brand and switching to another," Kyle Petty said. "It's a funny deal. Guys switch manufacturers and sponsors all the time now, like they change uniforms and change [their cars'] paint colors. You come to the track one week and it's Marathon and come back the next and it's Wells Fargo and it's no big deal.

"In the mid-seventies, for Richard Petty to switch anything, that was highly unusual. He already had switched to Ford and that was huge, man. I remember hate mail coming to the house when I was nine years old, when he switched to Ford. You would have thought it was the end of Dodge as we had known it.

"For him to all of a sudden say, 'Okay, we throw the towel in on this. Dodge is going nowhere,' it was a real big deal. And Dodge was having some hard times financially, too. It was just different. It was a lot different time in the sport and a lot different of a time for us."

It was a mad scramble just to get the Oldsmobile ready to go to the season opener at Riverside, where the ailing Richard had struggled to complete fourteen laps before the engine faltered. Times were not necessarily looking up for the most storied racing program in NASCAR history.

"Then we went to Daytona, and it was like the Week That Was. Everything just began to fall into place," Kyle said. "We won the ARCA race, my grandfather won a golf tournament. I mean, there were just goofy things that happened all week long. It was just strange."

It was beginning to feel like old times, when Richard Petty so often appeared to have a date with destiny in Daytona. But as the laps wound down in the '79 Daytona 500, he at first seemed to be losing ground. On Lap 186, A. J. Foyt passed Waltrip for fourth and then got by the King for third.

Donnie Allison and Cale Yarborough were still out in front, and they were getting away. Aiding each other in a two-car draft that arguably was being manned by the two fastest machines entered in the race, they were pulling away from the next pack—that of Foyt, Petty, and Waltrip—by more than one second per lap.

"We were in our own race for third," Richard said. "We weren't even in that other race."

The real race was between Allison and Yarborough. It clearly was their Daytona 500 to lose. Only a catastrophe could prevent one of them from winning.

12

The Last Lap

As A. J. Foyt passed Richard Petty and Darrell Waltrip to move into third place on Lap 186, the trio still trailed leaders Donnie Allison and Cale Yarborough by fifteen seconds. On the television broadcast, they cut to Ned Jarrett in the pits. He was standing by with Junior Johnson, and asked the legendary car owner, crew chief, and living icon of racing what his driver intended to do.

For the moment, Yarborough didn't intend to do anything more than continue to ride right on Allison's bumper for the next several laps, Johnson replied. Then he would make his move. It was, Johnson stressed, going to be up to Yarborough to decide when and how.

"Well, I think Cale will stay there probably until the last lap," Johnson told Jarrett, and by extension all of the viewers at home. "Then he'll try to get Donnie either on the backstretch or coming off the fourth turn. It's just hard to say. He knows pretty much where he can set him up and get by him. And that's where he'll try it. If everything goes like he's planned, he just might make it."

Up in the broadcast booth, announcer David Hobbs grinned. "Donnie Allison must be one nervous man right now, just wondering what's going on in the beady brain of ol' Cale Yarborough," he said.

Lap after lap as the race wound down, Yarborough stayed right on the younger Allison's bumper. Hobbs noted that Cale had to dance in and out of the draft on occasion to make sure cool air got to his engine. At this point, engine trouble was the last thing Yarborough wanted to encounter.

Back in the pits, reporter Brock Yates caught up with Hoss Ellington, Donnie Allison's car owner and crew chief. "We just heard from Junior Johnson that Cale Yarborough will probably wait until the last lap to make his move. What will Donnie do to counteract that?" Yates asked.

Ellington, looking like a nervous man indeed, replied, "I don't know. I kind of figured Cale would do this. . . . We probably would have kept him some laps down earlier in the race if we had known the truth. A while back when he was three laps down, some of 'em said he was five [down]. So we miscounted a bit. I'm sure it's going to come down to the wire on this last lap. And, you know, I just hope we can hold him back. I really do."

For viewers watching in their snowbound homes along the East Coast, this was riveting television. Interviewing some of the main combatants in the unfolding drama as it played out was a spectacle of sport that could not be attempted during telecasts of most sports of the day, and added to it greatly.

Lap 190 went off the board. Ten laps remained. The lead for Allison was up to eighteen seconds over the second group of three cars that included Foyt, Petty, and Waltrip.

Speaking of Yarborough's plan to wait until the last lap to attempt a slingshot pass for the lead and the win, announcer Ken Squier turned to Hobbs and added that the race was going to come down to "perhaps one roll of the dice. You're going to have to be absolutely right or it's second place. No one remembers second place, David."

Hobbs agreed. "They certainly don't."

●   ●   ●

Hobbs went on to note that one of the reasons Foyt and Petty were now falling farther behind the leaders was Waltrip. He said that they were having to pull Waltrip along because Waltrip's engine appeared to be at less than full strength and perhaps was "going sour." Inside his car, Waltrip knew he had been fighting it all day. He also thought he knew why. He blamed it on all of the slow riding around during the many cautions of the day, including the long one at the beginning of the race while officials were waiting for the track to dry out.

By this time, with only ten laps left to go, Waltrip's run as the "rabbit" to test the track just before the start of the race seemed literally light-years earlier. Waltrip reflected on his eventful day, which had included unexpectedly having to battle some scrappy newcomers like Dale Earnhardt.

"The track had just been resurfaced before the race. So the track had tons of grip; the cars were handling great. Earlier on people like Bruce Hill, the little guy from up north who was driving Harry Hyde's car [Tighe Scott], Dale Earnhardt, they were up front fighting for the lead, doing things they had never done before. And there were crashes galore because there were so many people running good and there were so many people running up front, people you weren't used to seeing up front, that there were crashes every time you turned around," Waltrip said.

"Well, every time there was a crash, we'd go into the pits. They would open the hood and we would change spark plugs, we changed plug wires. . . . I mean, we worked on that car all day long and couldn't fix it—because, unbeknownst to us, all that slow riding around there we had worn the lobe off the camshaft. So it would run, but it would only half run."

They had reported during the telecast that he was running on seven cylinders, which Richard Petty never did believe. "That's what he said. But he was running as good as I was, and I was running on all eight. Darrell was keeping up in the draft, that's for sure. We wasn't outrunning him down the straightaways," Petty said.

"I'm not saying that his car didn't perform exactly the way it should have. It might have been running on seven and a half [cylinders] or seven and three-quarters. But he wasn't runnin' on seven, you know what I mean?"

That assessment proved to be pretty accurate, by Waltrip's own later admission. "It was probably more like seven and a half. We had worn that lobe down. In the beginning, we must not have had that camshaft oiled up right or something, and all that circling around there at slow speeds had worn that lobe in the camshaft down. So it wasn't like it wouldn't run at all; it just was not running like it should."

In the grandstands along the frontstretch, fans such as Mark Aumann and his father had no idea what was going on with Waltrip. "They didn't have pit reporters to the depth they have now and the information wasn't available to fans who were at the race, anyway. We were basically watching cars go around in a circle," Aumann said.

Despite whatever the extent of his engine troubles were, Waltrip remained in the mix as the laps continued to tick off. Allison continued to lead, with Yarborough in hot pursuit. Much of America waited to see what would happen next. With 191 laps completed, Squier described it as "an event that has dwarfed any previous Daytona 500."

Then CBS went to a commercial. Hey, it was live TV, but they still had to pay the bills.

•   •   •

When they returned from commercial, only six laps remained and Allison's lead over the second group of cars had grown to twenty-two seconds. Yarborough had been right on Allison's tail for twenty laps, waiting for the right moment to attempt his pass.

With four laps to go, Allison briefly pulled ahead by four car lengths. But the increased lead was short-lived as Yarborough gulped some clean air for his engine and then quickly closed the gap again to best take advantage of the draft. Meanwhile, Petty passed Foyt to reclaim third place. Waltrip lingered for the moment in fifth, right behind Foyt.

With two to go, the lapped car of Buddy Arrington, which earlier had aided Waltrip in helping keep up with the leaders, lurked in front of Allison and Yarborough. A well-timed and somewhat prophetic prerace interview with Donnie Allison popped into one small corner of the television screen as the action continued to unfold.

"If it comes to the last lap and a run for the checkered flag, I'm gonna do it on the backstretch—because I just don't think we have enough room from the fourth turn to the finish line to beat anybody," Allison had told CBS prior to the race. "The cars are too equal for that. You'd have to do it on the backstretch."

Squier was quick to add his own insight to the interview. "Donnie Allison . . . sounds to me like he has to throw the block, and it has to be absolutely perfectly timed or he's going to be the also-ran."

Hobbs added, "It has to be perfectly timed, and he's got to use what remaining traffic is out there to his advantage. And there really isn't much traffic out there."

Arrington still loomed ahead for the leaders but caused only a brief few seconds of anxiety. They quickly passed him without incident.

"One hundred thousand people on their feet, watching these two cars . . . looking for any signs of distress from either automobile as they lap Buddy Arrington in the tri-oval," Squier told the viewers. "Cale stays right there, just staring down in that rearview mirror of Donnie Allison. Two laps to go to decide the most incredible Daytona 500 in history.

"A shallow lead for Donnie Allison. Cale stays there, moves in again."

About this time, Yarborough came on his in-car radio and made a surprising comment to Junior Johnson. He suddenly was worried about Bobby Allison helping out his younger brother.

"I'm worried about Bobby holding me up. He's going to help Donnie win this race, and keep me from doing it," Yarborough told Johnson.

Johnson was perplexed. Again, there were no televisions for him to check to see where Bobby was on the track. But by his calculations, Bobby was nowhere near the leaders at the time. Bobby was not going to be a factor in how they ultimately finished no matter what happened, no matter what he might have wanted to help Donnie do.

Johnson double-checked and confirmed to himself that this was going to be the case. His driver was needlessly worrying about something that could distract him down the stretch.

"Cale, Bobby isn't even close to y'all. He ain't even close. Just set Donnie up to pass him and win this race. Don't get aggravated and stuff," Johnson told Yarborough.

Running behind the leaders, Petty was happy to be back in third. "I was busy trying to outrun Foyt and Darrell," he said. "We wasn't even in that other race. We had a race of our own. We were racing for third just as hard as they were racing for first."

●　　●　　●

Back at his father-in-law's house in Salisbury, North Carolina, Doug Rice hadn't noticed yet if the snow had stopped falling outside. He was too mesmerized by the race unfolding on the television in front of him inside. Thirty years later, he still was able to recall his emotions in the moment. He and his wife were rooting hard for Petty, but it didn't seem the King was going to be able to get it done.

"Waltrip was winning everything back then and we didn't want him to win. Petty had gone almost two years without winning a race so it had been a long dry spell," Rice said.

With about three laps left to go, Rice's wife looked at her husband and winked. "Maybe Donnie and Cale will wreck each other and Richard can win this thing," she said.

Doug chuckled to himself. Much as he wanted it to happen, he didn't believe it would. And he took the comment for what he believed it to be: "sort of [an] elicited remark for my father-in-law, who is a Cale guy."

On the television screen in front of Rice and his family, Squier and Hobbs were touting the virtues of Yarborough. It was becoming obvious that they expected him to be able to execute a slingshot pass on the vulnerable but still leading Allison. It was becoming obvious to everyone, Rice thought. He said later, "That is how you made the pass at Daytona. If you were in second place, you pulled out on the backstretch and you slingshot past him. Sitting there watching, that's what all of us were sure Yarborough was going to do."

In the stands at Daytona, Mark Aumann was spending most of his time as the laps wound down monitoring the progress of his favorite driver, A. J. Foyt. "I was watching him most of the day. Most fans watch their favorite. He was running in the top five with the race running down and there was a large stretch between the first two cars and then the next three of Foyt, Petty, and Waltrip. I don't remember if I used a stopwatch, but there was a good twenty seconds [between them]," he said.

"It was almost a half-lap. Allison and Yarborough would come by us and the other three still weren't high enough to see on the backstretch. You have to be high enough [in the stands] to look over the infield garage and all of that. We still weren't high enough to see the backstretch. You see them in the two corners, but then they would go down in your view and you didn't pick them up again until they came out of [Turn] 3. So when Allison and Yarborough came through the tri-oval and by us, the others were on the backstretch. It stayed that way for lap after lap. You could tell the leaders were trying to set up something."

Aumann had a thought, too, as the laps were winding down. He turned to his father and asked, "What is going to happen if those two guys crash?"

Robert Aumann said nothing. "He kind of gave me that wink deal that fathers are all-knowing. Sort of a grin," the son said.

A couple minutes later, Robert Aumann opened his mouth just long enough to muse, "Just imagine what will happen if Petty wins this race, how crazy this place will get."

Squier and Hobbs and the rest of America were figuring that Yarborough was going to execute the slingshot pass, and that Allison would attempt to block him. But it seemed to most that Allison was a sitting duck in first place. Because of the quirky draft at Daytona, second was the better place to be at that moment—as long as you stayed on the bumper of the first-place machine.

Yarborough was doing exactly that. "I always felt I was going to win the race. I was exactly where I wanted to be," Yarborough said.

It looked that way to the men in the broadcast booth, too. "Cale is reputed to be one of the toughest drivers there are. If the car won't handle, he will manhandle a car into the first place," Squier noted.

To which Hobbs quickly added, "Cale Yarborough is one of the toughest men I've ever met. . . . He never gets fazed."

Hobbs went on to say how much of Yarborough's toughness was mental, and how it gave him an advantage in precisely these kinds of situations on the track. He explained that Yarborough also was a tough man physically, but that the mental aspect of his toughness would permit him to remain calm in this scenario. He said that he expected Yarborough to carefully plot out and execute whatever plan he already had developed in his mind to grab the lead from Allison.

"The white flag is out. One lap to go," Hobbs then noted.

"Stand by for a photo finish," Squier added.

●　　●　　●

The crowd of more than a hundred thousand rose to its feet. Actually, much of the crowd already had been standing for several laps. But those who hadn't been certainly did so now.

The leaders were sitting, but they were, in racing terms, standing on the gas pedals in their cars. So was the group behind them, thinking they were dueling for third.

As Petty passed the start-finish line, Dale Inman clicked his stopwatch. There was good news and bad news. Richard was in third place, with Waltrip and Foyt in hot pursuit. That was the good news.

The bad news was that Donnie Allison and Yarborough, the leaders, were long gone. They had crossed the stripe a full seventeen seconds earlier, according to Inman's trusty stopwatch. Richard was running for third. "If you don't see nobody, you're runnin' for third, bud. Don't let them by you," Inman told Petty over the radio.

Squier set the scene for the television viewers. "Two of the greatest fiddling here, fidgeting with first place, trying to get to the stripe on the last lap, trying to take it home. It's all come down to this."

"Out of Turn 2, Donnie Allison in first. Where will Cale make his move?"

In the stands, Aumann strained to see what was happening. In snowy Salisbury, Doug Rice and his relatives moved ever so closer to the very edges of their seats. Squier was making the call on television, the action unfolding in front of all of them as Yarborough at last made the move they had all been anticipating.

"He comes to the inside. Donnie Allison throws the block. Cale hits him! He slides! Donnie Allison slides! They hit again! They glide through the turn! They're hitting the wall! They're head-on into the wall!

"They slide down into the inside. . . . They are out of it. Who's going to win it?"

Halfway down the backstretch, Yarborough had attempted his slingshot pass. Donnie moved down the track to successfully block him and close off the inside lane. But Yarborough refused to back off, and a series of broadside slams ensued. After repeatedly making contact, Allison drove Yarborough onto the edge of the infield grass and Yarborough began to lose control of his car completely.

In his attempt to recover and get all four wheels back on the track, Yarborough had to make a hard right—directly into Allison. Both cars then shot up the banking, out of control, and slammed into the outside wall before sliding down and coming to rest in the infield.

They would argue for years—even decades—afterward over who was at fault. And they would not be alone.

"I had Donnie set up just like I wanted," Yarborough said thirty years later. "I had the slingshot move ready to make it. We came down to the last lap and down the backstretch. I pulled out to go slingshot by him and he kept moving down and moving down and moving down. I tried to stay away from him. Eventually, he ran me completely off that racetrack into the mud. I lost control of the car. At two hundred miles per hour, they're hard to drive in that mud."

Naturally, Donnie saw it differently—and so did Bobby.

"If I had to do it over, and I know what I know now, I would have done something different," Donnie said in 2007. "But to be perfectly honest, it caught me by surprise. It caught everybody by surprise because how many times in the fifty years they've run the Daytona 500 have you seen the leader and the second-place car wreck coming off of Turn 2? Turn 4, yes. I expected something to happen down there.

"People don't realize and I'm not going to sit here and dwell on it, but I never watched a car behind me in my mirror. For some reason or another, I looked up in that corner of my mirror and saw him going down and I said, 'You are not going to get under me on the back straightaway.' And the rest is history."

Bobby blamed the wreck on Yarborough, too.

"Cale bumped him a little bit coming off of Turn 2 and got him wiggling a little bit and tried to drive under him. And Donnie wouldn't give him the room," Bobby said. "He just crowded him, and Cale went off into the grass but stayed wide open and came out of the grass and really hit Donnie about as hard as he could."

In the pit stall for the No. 11 car, Junior Johnson couldn't believe his driver's chance to win had just disappeared in an instant. He, of course, blamed Donnie for the mishap.

"We had the fastest car. Our car was the dominant car," Johnson said. "Cale was sitting there behind Donnie and he was a good bit faster. We knew Cale was going to win. But Donnie was determined to wreck Cale before he let him win the race, and that's what he did."

Johnson was furious, to say the least. "I don't appreciate anybody wrecking anybody—my cars or someone else's," he said. "I couldn't believe that he was a foolish enough to think he could get by with that with Cale to start with. Plus he was better off in second than he was to get wrecked. That was stupid. It was damn stupid. He took Cale down in the grass and he knew damn well Cale couldn't keep control of his car after he did that. He thought Cale was going to back off and Cale wasn't going to back off because he had the fastest car."

More than three decades after the wreck, Johnson still grimaced and shook his head at the mere mention of it. "It was just so damn stupid. I can't handle stupid, you know?"

●   ●   ●

The view from the stands was stunning. And confusing.

"I don't remember a lot of cars running at that point," Aumann said. "There had been a fairly high attrition rate. There were a lot of cars out, so it was easy to focus on the pack. You knew there were the top two and the three after that. I'm not sure there was anyone else on the lead lap."

There were, in fact, only the five cars of Donnie Allison, Yarborough, Petty, Waltrip, and Foyt on the lead lap as they headed into Lap 200. The first car one lap down was the No. 30 being driven by second-year Cup driver Tighe Scott, who might have been running with the leaders if not for a rookie-type mistake when he overran his pit box on his final stop to lose precious seconds. Scott was followed by Chuck Bown and Dale Earnhardt, the only other drivers piloting cars that were one lap down. Everyone else was two laps down or more, with a total of just twenty machines out of the original starting group of forty-one still making circuits on the famed 2.5-mile tri-oval.

"The fans were standing when the two leaders came by," Aumann remembered. "I was watching what was happening in the pack racing for third, because I was trying to keep up with Foyt. I glanced up when they took the white and out of the corner of my eyes . . ."

Out of the corner of his eyes, he realized very quickly that something was amiss as Allison and Yarborough tangled. Their wreck began on the other side of the track and, again, there were no television monitors or anything else—not even a scanner handy—to aid those in attendance as they tried to sort out what was happening in real time.

"When the cars go through the turns they take different grooves, but they are aimed where they are parallel to the race-track. They are always running in a line," Aumann said. "At that instant the cars were side by side, but they were at a funny angle. And suddenly you realized they are going up toward the upper wall. You see tire smoke. Then you see two cars bang the wall and skitter back down the racetrack sideways.

"Right away you could tell one was the Hawaiian Tropic car [of Donnie Allison], right? That was a very recognizable car. It was bright red with a big No. 1 on the top of it and you could tell it was that car. And you knew it had to be Yarborough, too, because they were running side by side.

"And now all of a sudden, everything was changed. I don't know if anybody in the stands recognized it that quickly, but you could sort of hear this murmur go through the crowd as Petty goes by, followed by Waltrip and Foyt. You could almost tell instantly, even without the public-address announcer, that people realized that one of those three cars is going to win the race if they don't wreck each other."

In snowy Salisbury, Doug Rice's father-in-law, Ben Mitchell, rubbed his chin as he watched on television. A Cale Yarborough man, he wasn't too happy about what had just happened. "Well," he told his son-in-law after a brief few seconds of stoic silence, "I kind of figured that was going to go on. Cale was up there tan-gling with Donnie Allison. Something was bound to happen."

Rice had other thoughts on his mind. "What was agonizing is that it seemed like forever because CBS had a little trouble, if I remember, following the wreck and then finding the guys behind them who were now racing for the win. They got mesmerized by the wreck for a little bit and they're yelling about that—and my wife and I are like, 'Where's Richard?'

"It wasn't until Turn 3 or maybe 4 where they finally picked up the race coming back to the flag. And they had to be forgiven because they didn't have a blueprint for this. They were following the leaders and the leaders crashed. They stayed with them. But this was in the day when you raced back to the checkered. We're like, 'Find the cars!'"

•　　•　　•

Inside the cars still moving around the track, a revelation was coming over Richard Petty as he came around Turn 2 on Lap 200.

"The big deal was we came off the corner and the lights came on, and I think Foyt hesitated. Me and Darrell knew we had to get back [to the start-finish line]. We was racin' for third. Foyt didn't run with us that much, and I think maybe he hesitated just an instant before he realized what was going on," Petty said.

"We knew there was a caution, but we looked down the frontstretch and the backstretch and through the corners—and there was nobody on the racetrack. So we didn't know if they had wrecked off of [Turn] 4 or what, but we knew we were going to be runnin' wide open when we got there.

"The deal was that the cars had gotten down on the inside and the smoke had all cleared, and we didn't see nothin' until we started into the third corner. And then sort of out of the corner of your eye, you were like, 'Oooo, there's number one and two down there.'"

That meant they were racing to become number one now.

"But we didn't race any harder," Petty insisted. "We didn't change our philosophy from when we were racing for third and fourth. We raced just as hard going for first and second as we had when we were going for third and fourth. We were just trying to win that particular race."

It hit Waltrip at about the same time as it did Petty what the implications were of the smoking wreckage that had become the cars of Donnie Allison and Cale Yarborough.

"When we come down to get the white flag, heck, the white flag had been out for a long time by the time we get it," Waltrip said. "When Donnie and Cale went by the start-finish line [to begin the final lap], I guess Richard and A. J. and I were probably in the third or fourth turn. And we come off and get the white flag, and I'm thrilled. I'm gonna run third or fourth in the Daytona 500 in a car that should have been in the garage. I'm pretty darned happy.

"We go down into Turn 1, and the caution lights come on. Well, initially, when caution lights come on, anytime that happens, no matter when it is, the first thing you think about doing is lifting. Because there must have been a wreck somewhere.

"Richard lifted just a little, and so did A. J., who was right behind me. Which was good for me, because that tightened our little three-car draft up right there. We go down the back, and as we go down there, we start seeing smoke and stuff down in the third turn. But this is the Daytona 500, and we're going back for the checkered because, you know, you raced back. We get down there in the third and fourth turn, and I'm hanging on to the back of Richard, just wanting to finish fourth. I mean, I'm just tickled to death.

"Then we look off into the dirt, and there lay Donnie and Cale, their cars all wadded up. Well, I'm sure Richard was like I was—and probably A. J., too. We're all looking down there with our mouths hanging open, thinking, 'My gosh! Those guys wrecked!'

"Then you start off Turn 4 and suddenly you're like, 'Holy cow! We're fightin' for a win here! We've got a shot at winnin' this thing!'"

•   •   •

By running wide open, Petty and Waltrip were taking chances going through the final two turns. They weren't sure what was up ahead at first.

"We didn't have no idea," Petty said. "We didn't know if the wreck was behind us, or if somebody had just blowed up, or what had caused the caution. We could have gone tearing into the corner, and if it had been full of oil we wouldn't have known it. We were just busting our butt to do the best we could, to get the best finish we could."

Once they realized what the real deal was, it was on. But Petty had the better car, and still possessed all of the guile that had allowed him to win five previous Daytona 500 extravaganzas.

"He tried to pull out coming off [the] fourth turn," Petty said of Waltrip. "He tried to get by me to the inside. But I kept him down there. I had him on the flat.

"But you never know for sure that you've got a win until you get to that stripe. All I had to do was run out of gas or have my car skip a beat, and you're back there behind again."

Waltrip added, "I couldn't pass Richard. I tried to duck out from behind him right at the last second and go down on the apron, and maybe scare him a little bit. But I knew I couldn't pass him."

Rice watched on television as Aumann watched from the grandstands. Even though he had been rooting all day for Foyt, Aumann knew how popular a win for Richard Petty would be. If he had forgotten, the throng in attendance was about to remind him.

"As soon as the crowd realized that Richard had taken the lead, it got quiet enough to where we could have heard the P.A. announcer, and then the place just erupted," he said. "There was this huge, huge roar from the crowd. I immediately thought back to what Dad had said just a few minutes before: 'Just imagine what will happen if Petty wins this race, how crazy this place will get.'"

But the race wasn't yet over.

"Now everyone in our section is wondering: Is Waltrip going to spin him out? Does he have anything for him? What is happening? They broke out low into Turns 3 and 4 and Petty still had him by a significant amount," Aumann said. "It looked like for a minute Waltrip might get a run on him. But by the time they flashed by us, I was thinking he has got this in the bag and I don't think Waltrip has got a move on him."

Kyle Petty and Dale Inman stood on the pit wall, straining to see what exactly was happening . . . wondering . . . hoping.

"It's hard for people to believe. But especially with those buildings back then, those overhangs on pit road, everybody just stood on pit wall," Kyle said. "That was before the invention of insurance—when they made you get off the wall. You would just stand on the pit wall lap after lap after lap, man.

"When it came down to the end, we're standing on pit road and the fans start screaming. Inman's clocking people. You're standing on pit road and the fans are screaming. So we all jump up on the pit wall, because all you can see is them coming right there, just straight off the end of pit road. The other two cars don't come around, so you know something's up . . . and then you just gotta wait. And it's an agonizing ten or fifteen seconds, because you don't know what order they're going to come back around in. When he came back around on the inside, when he came into sight there, you knew you had won the race. That was a pretty ecstatic moment for a whole lot of people right there. You hated it for those other guys, but it was good for us."

Squier had the call in the booth. "They're coming around to the finish, between A. J. Foyt and Richard Petty. . . . The leaders are still up in Turns 3 and 4. Coming down, Richard Petty is now pulling out in front. Darrell Waltrip is in second. A. J. Foyt is in third.

"Here they come. Waltrip trying to slingshot. Petty is out in front at the line . . . Waltrip . . . Petty wins it!"

Rice said, "[The television cameras] finally found the new leaders, and right there is Waltrip and you just knew somehow or another he will get around the King. But he didn't. If you think back—Waltrip, Petty, and A. J. Foyt—that is pretty illustrious company racing at the end. To have it end like it, it was just perfect."

The Petty crew was going crazy, jumping up and down. Kyle Petty was right in the middle of it. "Of all of 'em he won at Daytona . . . as a family, as a child, as his son, and then as a crew member, when he won in '79, that was huge for me," Kyle said in 2007. "When I look at everything I've been around in racing, him winning in '79 has remained one of the two most satisfying wins I've ever been a part of [the other was when his son Adam won his ARCA debut at Charlotte many years later], because that was one of the first times I was ever really a part of building a race car from the ground up, and he drove it and won with it. I mean, it was amazing. All we had gone through, we were about out of money and everything else, and then you get to the 500 and you come down to the end of the day and think you're running for third, and all of a sudden you end up winning the race. I think that was more of a gift than anything."

If it helped prop up a sagging Petty Enterprises, it was a gift to the entire sport. Everyone seemed genuinely happy for them, and the STP folks were making immediate plans to get their huge logo back on the hood of Richard's car by the next week's race at Rockingham. "But it was too late then," Kyle joked. "All the pictures in Victory Lane at Daytona were already taken without it on there."

Waltrip pulled up alongside Petty to congratulate him as they made their way around on a cool-down lap. "Man, I was so excited," Waltrip said. "I had run second in the Daytona 500 in a car, like I said, that should have been in the garage. Had it been running like it should, I probably never would have finished second. I probably would have been in a wreck.

"So I was jumping up and down. I was cheering. I pulled up beside of Richard, and Richard thought I was excited because he'd won. For years, he always thought I was really excited about him winning. I wasn't excited about that at all. I was excited about running second."

Petty laughed at the memory and added, "I think I was as thrilled winning that race as any I had won. Out of the blue, there's a wreck and they give you the race. Winning the Daytona 500 anytime is a big, big deal. But that was overshadowed by the way this one happened. It wasn't a deal where you had it made and all you had to do was make the laps.

"They talk about the finishes to races being anticlimactic. Not this one. It was climactic in a whole bunch of ways right up to the finish. It was just thrown on you all at one time. It was like, 'You just won this race! Wow!'

"And Darrell, I thought he was going to come out of the car. We went down through Turns 1 and 2, and coming off 2 he pulled up beside me and was jumping up and down—with seat belts on—throwing his hands up, and just jumping up and down. I'll bet you he wasn't any happier when he actually won the race than he was to run second that day. He was thrilled to death with it. I think he was even more excited about running second than I was about winning the race."

The crowd outside Petty's car continued to roar as the accolades began to rain down on the No. 43 Oldsmobile. "Richard Petty has won his sixth Daytona 500, and this crowd is going absolutely mad," Hobbs told television viewers.

Squier commended Petty and commented that he was coming off a season when he had been "driving most of the year with a battered and broken body," and noted that in the Victory Lane, "son Kyle is waiting for his father."

Then a shot of the Petty car with more than a dozen Petty employees sitting on it, all over the place, flashed across the television screen. Richard was rolling into Victory Lane with his car looking like a World War II tank packed with weary infantrymen catching a ride.

"And here it comes: a $60,000 car becoming a twenty-two-passenger school bus, to bring his crew to Victory Lane. Richard Petty, the great master, has just recorded his—" And then Squier stopped before completing the sentence.

"And there is a fight between Donnie Allison and Cale Yarborough," Squier shouted as the cameras swung ever so briefly to action in the infield, near the site where the cars of the two had skidded to their final resting places.

"A couple of hard men . . ." Hobbs offered, noting that the No. 15 car of Bobby Allison also was parked at the scene.

●   ●   ●

The fight—or The Fight, as it would come to be known—actually was between Yarborough and Bobby Allison. It was brief, and truthfully not much of it was caught by the television cameras. But thanks to some terrific still snapshots of it, The Fight would live in infamy and grow in legend in the coming years.

Again, the accounts of The Fight depend on who is telling the story. From Bobby's perspective, Cale started it . . . well, Bobby's temper didn't help matters, either, by his own admission.

"When Richard went by and saw the two cars down there, there was no fracas yet. Donnie was just getting out of his car, and I think Cale was still sitting in his. The two cars were probably seventy-five or a hundred feet apart," Bobby said.

"I went by all that mess and I saw Donnie climbing out of his car, and I knew he wasn't hurt bad. I felt bad for him because I knew he had been leading the race. I went on around and got the checkered flag, which is my job—to finish the race. And then I came back by and I yelled out, 'Donnie, do you want a ride back to the garage area?'"

By all accounts, Donnie waved Bobby off and told him to go on. But Yarborough, infuriated by what had happened and looking for someone—anyone going by the last name of Allison—to blame, started in on Bobby with a verbal assault.

"Cale started hollerin' that the wreck was my fault, and I think I probably questioned his ancestry, which did not calm him down any," Bobby said. "He ran toward me, got about fifteen feet from my car, and yelled at me some more. And I think I was dumb enough to question his ancestry a little bit further. He lunged at me and hit me in the face with his helmet. And it hurt. He cut my lip and bloodied my nose. Blood ran down into my lap."

Looking at the blood dripping from his nose and lip, Bobby Allison made a decision that would forever earn him a place in NASCAR history.

"I've got to get out of the car and address this right now, or run from him for the rest of my life," he said to himself.

The decision to get out and fight was easy. There really was no question in his mind that it had to be done.

"Well, none of us wanted to run from each other—ever. We were out there doing our deal, but we were proud of what we had done and we also had that cockiness that it takes to be a competitor in any competitive arena," Bobby said. "So I got out to the car and, like I've said many, many times over the years, the guy started beating on my fist with his nose. That's my story and I'm still sticking to it."

Yarborough came out of The Fight looking like the big loser. Not only had he lost a race he and most others figured he should have won, but the perception was that Bobby Allison had gotten the better of him after he struck the initial blow with his helmet. That also was perceived by some as a cheap shot or sucker punch, further damaging Yarborough's hard-earned reputation as one of the toughest drivers on the Winston Cup circuit.

Through the years, Yarborough would label these perceptions as false and blame them on the photographs—none of them all that flattering—of him attempting to do battle with the two

Allison brothers. Donnie was in on the fringe of the fight, but eventually joined in ever so briefly before it was all broken up by some firemen and track officials who had arrived on the scene.

"That was the most unfair fight there ever was, two Allisons against one Yarborough," Cale said.

But that statement was not meant the way many initially took it.

"I thought it was unfair on their side, not my side," he proudly explained.

So Yarborough had the advantage, even though it was one against two? "Yeah, yeah," Cale insisted with a chuckle thirty years later.

Yarborough, the man who once wrestled snakes and bears and other wild animals with his bare hands, also claimed that the television cameras and still shots by photographers ended up telling a misleading tale.

"Well, the cameras didn't catch it all," Yarborough insisted. "They've got pictures of me on the ground. The way I got on the ground was one of the firemen grabbed me by my leg. He was trying to separate us. The fireman was the one that pulled me to the ground, not an Allison."

The fact is, Allison admits, the fight lasted "about 3.2 seconds" and really wasn't much of a fight.

"No," admitted Yarborough, "but it made for good TV, and people are still talking about it."

•   •   •

Meanwhile, the race was finally over. Richard Petty was declared the winner, followed by Waltrip and A. J. Foyt. They were the only three drivers to complete all 200 laps. Donnie Allison was credited with fourth and Yarborough fifth despite their crash, as they had completed 199 laps and most of the 200th before expiring. No one else completed more than 199 even.

The top ten ended up also including the surprising Tighe Scott in sixth, Chuck Brown in seventh, the promising rookie Dale Earnhardt in eighth, veteran Coo Coo Marlin in ninth, and Frank Warren in tenth. Bobby Allison finished eleventh, three laps down and one spot ahead of Buddy Arrington. Richard Childress completed 188 laps but was still running at the end, and that was good enough to put him in seventeenth place, sandwiched between another rookie in Terry Labonte, who finished sixteenth, and the selfless former 500 champion Benny Parsons, whose decision to place the wieldy in-car camera in his No. 27 Oldsmobile may have cost him dearly. Parsons ended up eighteenth after completing only 183 laps, but at least that was considerably more than the likes of David Pearson, who crashed out after only 53 and finished thirty-seventh, and hard-luck pole sitter Buddy Baker, who completed only 38 and finished next-to-last in fortieth place.

In Victory Lane, the CBS broadcast was about to come to a close as Brock Yates prepared to interview the race winner.

"It's absolutely pandemonium down here, Ken," Yates told Squier and all of the viewers. "It looks like there are about three hundred people in a Petty uniform. I don't know where they all came from. Richard is still in the car, having a glass of milk. He obviously is just so happy, ecstatic."

Richard accepted a kiss from his wife, Linda, as he climbed out of the car. Then and only then did he turn to face Yates and the millions of viewers who had stayed with the race on television.

"Richard, could you believe it? You've been in a lot of races. Has there ever been a weirder finish than this one?"

"Well, I'll tell you: I've lost some this close; but this is the first time I can remember in a long time that I've won one this close. I tell you, it's just unbelievable. We come down here last week and Kyle won, and then we come down here and luck up and win this one."

"What's your doctor going to say?"

"I ain't worried about the doctor. But I'm feelin' good no matter what he says."

Yates closed by asking if the King ever really thought he had a chance to break his forty-five-race winless streak on this day.

"Well, I tell you what, I had a real good feeling as we run down pit road that we had a super good chance today," Petty replied. "We run all day and we were really close to everything, and we kept getting through all the mistakes [others] were making. So I thought, 'Maybe this is the day.'

"But then when Donnie and them got out in front right there at the last, I thought, 'Well, if I can salvage a third, it's gonna be a good day.' Then when I saw the caution flag come out coming out of the third corner, or the second corner, my heart just went right through [my chest]."

The King was not alone. As Yates threw it back to Squier upstairs for a closing word, the iconic announcer said simply, "A hundred thousand people cannot believe what they have just seen."

It was far more than merely the hundred thousand in attendance at the racetrack. The telecast drew record numbers, paving the way for a new era of television in NASCAR. That, in turn, fueled phenomenal growth for the sport throughout the 1980s and 1990s.

The day that had begun so uncertainly, under dark skies, ended in a way that no one could have envisioned. All of the stars aligned just so, the biggest star of all ended up winning the race, and The Fight illustrated that these were hard, tough men who believed passionately in what they were doing.

"People were mesmerized and glued to the television set because from about Macon, Georgia, to Bangor, Maine, the whole East Coast was in the middle of the biggest snowstorm anyone had seen in years," Waltrip said. "So no one could leave their homes. They were stuck—in front of their TVs, watching this incredible Daytona 500.

"And a lot of the other sporting events that had been scheduled for that day had gotten canceled. So the only thing happening that afternoon on television was the Daytona 500."

Yarborough added, "Eighty percent of the country was snowed in that day. Everybody was watching TV. Some of the sports fans that watch ballgames had never watched a race before. But they didn't have anything else to do, so they did. When the race was over and the fight broke out and all the excitement was going on, instead of turning over and going to sleep on the couch they were up in the middle of the floor jumping up and down whooping and hollering. It helped our sport tremendously."

Petty said he did not become aware that there had been a postrace fight in the infield until he went upstairs to the press box to do his postvictory interview with the media.

"I didn't know that there was really a fight, per se, until we went up to the press box; and they kept showing the last lap and Cale and Bobby hitting each other, and the shoving and fistfighting when it was over with. I didn't know and I was too excited to ask about it, because it didn't make no difference to us," he said.

"We had won the race. We had won the Daytona 500. That was all that mattered."

Well, it wasn't quite all that mattered. As Petty gave his postrace interviews, the Allison brothers and Yarborough licked their respective wounds, and the fans in attendance began to make their way to their cars, the television folks from CBS began to pack their equipment away. They knew they would be coming back the following year, and for a long time after that. They sensed that they had just been part of something unique, something lasting.

Ned Jarrett took one last look around Daytona International Speedway before putting away his microphone.

"I think things were done as good as they could be done," he said. "The ending, I had a feeling that was going to make a lot of news. It was at least a few days before it totally sunk in. But even right after it was over with, I felt that it was something special. I was proud to have been part of it. I think everyone involved was. We had a sense that we had maybe just helped make a little piece of history."

Epilogue

Richard Petty was too busy celebrating after the race to notice much about The Fight, but he did put it in perspective pretty well many years later.

Asked if he knows of any other fight that has gotten more mileage than the brief one between Bobby and Cale, the King chuckled and replied, "Not in the racing world. It was just pushin' and shovin' and a couple of swings. That kind of stuff happened all the time at races back then. Guys would get mad at each other and get into it, but then once they got back to the garage five minutes later, it was over and forgotten and you were on to the next place to race. The big deal was that this one was on TV, and they just kept reshowing it and reshowing it.

"In fact, when the wreck happened, I don't think they really knew who was running third through fifth, or at least they didn't know where we was at on the track. They had a heck of a time at first trying to figure out who was going to be the winner [on television]. And at that time, you've got to figure that they probably only had four or five cameras. Now they've got hundreds of 'em. They've got 'em all up there, and with electronics the way they are now, they can keep up with it and just punch a couple buttons and be right there.

"Back then, they had no idea, I don't think. It happened and they followed the wreck. That was the most important thing that was happening at that moment. But then they were like, 'Well, this is the last lap. We've got to find out who is winning this race. We don't want to miss that!' I think they finally found us coming off the fourth corner."

They found 'em, all right, and pretty quickly under the circumstances. And there were nineteen cameras in place, for the record, if you included the in-car camera in Benny Parsons's car. Petty said that the wreck between Donnie and Cale reminded him of his own famous last-lap wreck at the same event three years earlier, when David Pearson ended up taking the checkered flag after they wrecked each other.

Petty said, "That's what I told Donnie and Cale after they all settled down over the next week or two. I told 'em, 'You all didn't have any class in wreckin'. Me and Pearson wrecked in front of the grandstand where everybody could see us. Y'all wrecked on the backstretch, where nobody could see you.'

"The people in the grandstand had no idea what was going on. The TV seen 'em, though."

Asked how they took his joke, Petty said of Donnie and Cale, "They just snickered and went on down the road."

The King kept on going down the road, and making left turns, in Winston Cup racing until he retired in 1992. He won twelve more races, including four more en route to winning his record seventh [and final] points championship in 1979. He remains one of the greatest ambassadors of the sport as owner of Petty Enterprises, which fields two teams in what is now known as the Sprint Cup series.

•   •   •

Dale Inman continued to be Richard Petty's crew chief until they won another Daytona 500 in 1981 (Petty credited Inman with securing the win on a late call in the pits for fuel only after others had taken on tires and given up track position). Then Inman left

Petty Enterprises to work at Hendrick Motorsports for several years, including in 1984 when he was crew chief for Terry Labonte and helped Labonte win the points championship. That gave Inman one more championship than his second cousin, the King.

Inman finally retired from racing in 1998, and spent much of the next four years of his life helping care for his sister, who had Down syndrome. Now seventy-two, he returned to Petty Enterprises in 2002 as a consultant and still enjoys going to the track every chance he gets, which is almost every weekend. He missed only one race while battling prostate cancer a couple years ago, matching Petty's penchant for displaying unparalleled toughness.

He spends much of his time these days watching his grand-children excel in sports near his home in Randleman, North Carolina, where he still lives close to second cousin Richard.

•   •   •

Cale Yarborough drove full-time only one more season after 1979, leaving the Junior Johnson team after the 1980 campaign. He won a total of eighty-three Cup races and won the Daytona 500 four times—a total that ranks second only to Richard Petty's seven victories. But he never again won another points champion-ship after 1978.

Yarborough resides in Sardis, South Carolina, and owns a car dealership in Florence. But he is semiretired and can be found there only for a few hours at a time a couple days of the week. And he still has moxie. When NASCAR wanted him to attend a reun-ion of former Daytona 500 winners prior to the fiftieth running of the race in 2008, Yarborough said he would under one condition.

"Tell the France family to send one of their planes for me. That's the only way I'm coming," he said.

The plane was dispatched.

•   •   •

Donnie Allison never won another NASCAR race. On May 24, 1981, on Lap 152 of the World 600 at what was then known as Charlotte Motor Speedway, his car slid sideways and slammed into the outside retaining wall, coming to rest right in the path of the oncoming car of driver Dick Brooks. The ensuing collision was violent, and left Donnie with several broken ribs, a bruised right lung, a broken left knee, and a broken right shoulder blade.

Allison never completely recovered and competed in only a few more races before retiring as a driver after starting forty-first and finishing thirty-fifth at Michigan International Speedway in 1988.

He and Cale Yarborough posed for a photo at Rockingham two weeks following the 1979 Daytona 500, when the next Winston Cup event was held. They were smiling and each had one arm thrown around the other's shoulder. Then they went out and wrecked each other again in the ninth lap of the race. Both claimed it had nothing to do with their wreck in Daytona two weeks earlier.

Donnie lives in Salisbury, North Carolina, and enjoys watching his grandson pursue his own budding career as a driver.

•   •   •

Bobby Allison has experienced perhaps more heartbreak in his life than anyone in the history of stock car racing, but somehow continues to keep smiling through the pain.

He was credited with a total of eighty-four races in his career (which kept him in a tie for third all-time with Darrell Waltrip until Allison was mysteriously credited with one more win by NASCAR, lifting Bobby's total to eighty-five and giving him sole possession of third on the all-time list). He won only one championship, in 1983, but he captured the Daytona 500 three times, including at age fifty in 1988 when he ran one-two with his beloved son Davey. He has called that the greatest moment of his life, but he lost all memory of it when he was involved in his own catastrophic racing accident later the same season at Pocono.

His extensive injuries left him in critical condition for weeks afterward and required intensive physical rehabilitation for years, and he still suffers physical problems and memory loss related to it.

Bobby also subsequently lost two sons within less than a year—Clifford, then only twenty-seven years old, in a racing accident at Michigan International Spedway in August 1992, and Davey, when a helicopter he was attempting to land in the infield at Talladega crashed, claiming his life in July 1993. Though it paled greatly in comparison to those incomprehensible losses and his own physical problems, Bobby never quite got over younger brother Donnie's last-lap wreck at the 1979 Daytona 500.

"I really felt bad for him," Bobby said thirty years later. "Cale really was at the height of his execution as a race car driver. He really attacked every racetrack he had ever went to. He just, as far as I'm concerned, went over the line when he wrecked Donnie. And it was heartbreaking for me."

Remarkably, all three men involved in the last-lap wreck and ensuing brawl remain friends to this day—until someone brings up The Wreck or The Fight. Then they start arguing again about whose fault it was.

•   •   •

Darrell Waltrip continued driving until 1999, winning three points championships and finishing his career credited with the aforementioned eighty-four race victories. Only Richard Petty, David Pearson, and Bobby Allison have more.

Upon his retirement, no one in racing was surprised to find that Waltrip made a smooth transition to the broadcast booth.

•   •   •

A. J. Foyt continues to live life large. If he were a cat with nine lives, he would have run out about two lives ago.

In August 2007, at age seventy-two, Foyt was operating a bulldozer on his ranch in Waller, Texas, when a bank of dirt he had been working on gave way. Along with the 35,000-pound bulldozer, Foyt plunged sideways into a lake. For a while, he was trapped in the steel cage that was on the top of the machine, but then he got out and started calling for help.

"As I was calling for help, I saw a water moccasin swim by. I started splashing like hell then," he said.

When paramedics arrived, Foyt refused medical treatment and spent the next four hours supervising the recovery of the bulldozer. For those keeping score at home, that made a total of at least ten close brushes with death for Foyt over the years, including five since the running of the 1979 Daytona 500.

In July 1981, he nearly lost his right arm in an Indy-car crash at Michigan Speedway. He spent the entire autumn painting miles of fencing on his ranch as his self-prescribed therapy for the badly broken arm. Then in July 1983, he crashed his stock car in practice at Daytona but won the Paul Revere 250 sports car race later that same night, only to wake up the next morning unable to get out of bed. He had broken two vertebrae in the crash. And in September 1990, he sailed off the mile-long straightaway at a track in Elkhart Lake, Wisconsin, crashed into a dirt embankment, and suffered severe injuries to both of his legs while missing a huge rock boulder that would have ended his life by about two feet.

Finally, in August 2005, he was attacked by a swarm of Africanized killer bees while clearing land in Hempstead, Texas. He sustained over two hundred bee stings in his head and went into systemic shock but still refused to go to the hospital, at one point reportedly lying under an oak tree and insisting, "Just let me die here."

No way, A. J. Despite your penchant for buttering your steaks and avoiding all vegetables at the dinner table, you're destined to live until at least a hundred.

•   •   •

Junior Johnson eventually registered 139 victories as a car owner, second all-time. He still lives near where he once helped his father make and deliver moonshine all over the South, and in 2007 became a partner with a North Carolina distillery that makes what one writer called "a legal and refined rendition of his old rot gut."

Johnson, now seventy-seven, still makes it to some races and even ponied up to have Midnight Moon, his legal moonshine, sponsor the No. 70 car driven by Jeremy Mayfield in the 2008 Daytona 500.

●   ●   ●

Ned Jarrett continued to work in broadcasting for nearly another two decades, including stints at ESPN and Fox in addition to CBS. He was in the booth to call son Dale's first Cup victory at Michigan in 1991 and openly coached and rooted Dale to victory over Dale Earnhardt in the 1993 Daytona 500.

Embarrassed by his loss of objectivity in the heat of the moment, Gentleman Ned sought Earnhardt out after that race and apologized for pulling against him.

"That's okay," Earnhardt said. "I'm a father, too."

Jarrett continues to live in the same home in Newton, North Carolina, where he has resided for some twenty-five years. Now seventy-six, he plays golf as often as his health permits—sometimes up to five times a week.

●   ●   ●

Buddy Baker returned to Daytona and won the 1980 Daytona 500 with an average speed of 177.602 miles per hour, which remains a record. He is one of only eight drivers in NASCAR history to have won what is considered the career Grand Slam by capturing four of the sport's major races: the Daytona 500, what is now known as the Aaron's 499 at Talladega, what is currently known as the

Coca-Cola 600 at Lowe's Motor Speeway in Charlotte, and the Southern 500 at Darlington. The other seven drivers to accomplish this through 2008 were none other than Richard Petty, David Pearson, Bobby Allison, Darrell Waltrip, Dale Earnhardt, Jeff Gordon, and Jimmie Johnson. Of the eight, only Baker failed to win at least one point championship.

Baker resides in Sherrills Ford, North Carolina, and dispenses advice to current Sprint Cup drivers whenever they ask.

●　　●　　●

Dale Earnhardt went on to become one of the greatest and most successful drivers in NASCAR history, tying none other than Richard Petty for most points championships in a career with seven. He won seventy-six races, including finally taking the Daytona 500 title in 1998 after trying unsuccessfully to win the sport's most prestigious race for nearly twenty years. He passed away in 2001 in an accident toward the end of yet another Daytona 500.

His son Dale Jr. remains one of the most popular drivers in the sport today.

●　　●　　●

Benny Parsons ended up with twenty-one career Cup victories before retiring as a driver following the 1988 season. He did television commentary for NBC and TNT until he passed away from cancer on January 16, 2007. He was a kind and generous man whose death was mourned by many.

●　　●　　●

Kyle Petty has never come close to living up to his father's incomparable legacy as a driver, but he has won a total of eight Cup races. Although he contended for several championships, he never finished higher than fifth in the points standings (which he did twice, the last time in 1993). He continues to drive part-time for Petty Enterprises in what will be his thirtieth season of competition in 2009.

He lost his son, Adam, in a racing accident at New Hampshire in 2000, and devotes much of his time these days to helping run the Victory Junction Gang Camp, which was founded in Adam's honor. The camp, located near the old Petty shop in rural North Carolina (Petty Enterprises moved to a more modern facility in Mooresville, North Carolina, just prior to the 2008 season), benefits terminally and chronically ill children from across the country. A second Victory Junction Gang Camp is in the works for Kansas City, Missouri.

●   ●   ●

Doug Rice went on to become president and general manager of Performance Racing Network, which broadcasts many Sprint Cup races and NASCAR-related racing shows.

Of sitting at his father-in-law's on a snowy February afternoon in Salisbury, North Carolina, and watching the 1979 Daytona 500, Rice said his fondest memory was "to see the King back in Victory Lane. I remember that a lot more than the whole fight. That didn't really register with me as much. Being a Petty fan, with him winning the race, especially the Daytona 500, that was just so cool.

"And this was a day, too, where there weren't any coolers of beer at the house because my father-in-law wouldn't allow that. So we're drinking tea and eating breakfast food. I guess that is why I can remember the race so well."

That and because it was on television, of course.

Bibliography

Center, Bill, and Bob Moore. *NASCAR: 50 Greatest Drivers*. New York: HarperHorizon, 1998.

Fielden, Greg. *Charlotte Motor Speedway*. Osceola, WI: MBI Publishing Company, 2000.

———. *Forty Years of Stock Car Racing: The Modern Era, 1972–1989*. Surfside, SC: Galfield Press, 1990.

Golenbock, Peter. *The Last Lap*. New York: Macmillian, 1998.

———, and Greg Fielden. *The Stock Car Racing Encyclopedia*. New York: Macmillan, 1997.

Hembree, Mike. *NASCAR: The Definitive History of America's Sport*. New York: HarperCollins, 2000.

Howell, Mark D. *From Moonshine to Madison Avenue: A Cultural History of the NASCAR Winston Cup Series*. Bowling Green, OH: BGSU Popular Press, 1997.

Hunter, Don, and Ben White. *American Stock Car Racers*. Osceola, WI: Motorbooks International, 1997.

Menzer, Joe. *The Wildest Ride: A History of NASCAR*. New York: Simon & Schuster, 2001.

Wolfe, Rich. *Remembering Dale Earnhardt: Wonderful Stories Celebrating the Life of Racing's Greatest Driver*. Kannapolis, NC: Rich Wolfe, 2001.

Index

Page numbers in *italics* refer to photographs